Disruptive Transport

With the rise of shared and networked vehicles, autonomous vehicles, and other transportation technologies, technological change is outpacing urban planning and policy. Whether urban planners and policymakers like it or not, these transformations will in turn result in profound changes to streets, land use, and cities. But smarter transportation may not necessarily translate into greater sustainability or equity. There are clear opportunities to shape advances in transportation, and to harness them to reshape cities and improve the socio-economic health of cities and residents. There are opportunities to reduce collisions and improve access to healthcare for those who need it most—particularly high-cost, high-need individuals at the younger and older ends of the age spectrum. There is also potential to connect individuals to jobs and change the way cities organize space and optimize trips.

To date, very little discussion has centered around the job and social implications of this technology. Further, policy dialogue on future transport has lagged—particularly in the arenas of sustainability and social justice. Little work has been done on decision-making in this high uncertainty environment–a deficiency that is concerning given that land use and transportation actions have long and lagging timelines.

This is one of the first books to explore the impact that emerging transport technology is having on cities and their residents, and how policy is needed to shape the cities that we want to have in the future. The book contains a selection of contributions based on the most advanced empirical research, and case studies for how future transport can be harnessed to improve urban sustainability and justice.

William Riggs is an Assistant Professor at the University of San Francisco, USA.

Routledge Equity, Justice and the Sustainable City series

Series editors: Julian Agyeman, Zarina Patel, Abdou Maliq Simone and Stephen Zavestoski

This series positions equity and justice as central elements of the transition toward sustainable cities. The series introduces critical perspectives and new approaches to the practice and theory of urban planning and policy that ask how the world's cities can become 'greener' while becoming more fair, equitable and just.

Routledge Equity Justice and the Sustainable City series addresses sustainable city trends in the global North and South and investigates them for their potential to ensure a transition to urban sustainability that is equitable and just for all. These trends include municipal climate action plans; resource scarcity as tipping points into a vortex of urban dysfunction; inclusive urbanization; "complete streets" as a tool for realizing more "liveable cities"; the use of information and analytics toward the creation of "smart cities."

The series welcomes submissions for high-level cutting edge research books that push thinking about sustainability, cities, justice and equity in new directions by challenging current conceptualizations and developing new ones. The series offers theoretical, methodological, and empirical advances that can be used by professionals and as supplementary reading in courses in urban geography, urban sociology, urban policy, environment and sustainability, development studies, planning, and a wide range of academic disciplines.

Just Green Enough
Urban Development and Environmental Gentrification
Edited by Winifred Curran and Trina Hamilton

Design for Social Diversity, 2nd edition
Emily Talen and Sungduck Lee

Urban Gardening as Politics
Edited by Chiara Tornaghi and Chiara Certomà

Disruptive Transport
Driverless Cars, Transport Innovation and the Sustainable City of Tomorrow
Edited by William Riggs

Disruptive Transport

Driverless Cars, Transport Innovation
and the Sustainable City of Tomorrow

Edited by William Riggs

Routledge
Taylor & Francis Group

LONDON AND NEW YORK

First published 2019
by Routledge
2 Park Square, Milton Park, Abingdon, Oxon OX14 4RN

and by Routledge
52 Vanderbilt Avenue, New York, NY 10017

Routledge is an imprint of the Taylor & Francis Group, an informal business

British Library Cataloguing-in-Publication Data
A catalogue record for this book is available from the British Library

Library of Congress Cataloging-in-Publication Data
A catalog record has been requested for this book

ISBN: 978-1-138-61316-4 (hbk)
ISBN: 978-0-429-46465-2 (ebk)

Typeset in Goudy Oldstyle Std
by Cenveo® Publisher Services

Table of contents

List of figures

List of tables

Notes on contributors

Bruce Appleyard is an Associate Professor of City Planning/Urban Design at San Diego State University where he helps people and agencies make more informed decisions about how we live, work and thrive. He is humanist/futurist at the intersection of transportation, urban design, and behavioral economics, crafting articles, workshops and lectures designed to help people reach their sustainability, livability, and equity objectives by helping them measure and understand the key underlying issues, and then enact solutions to effectively address them.

Will Baumgardner, PE, Principal, directs Arup's Intelligent Mobility Business in the Americas. He has over 20 years of multimodal transportation planning experience on site, campus, corridor, and regional projects. His practice is focused on the implications rapidly emerging urban mobility trends and technologies on the transportation and property markets. He is advising public and private sector clients on the implications of autonomous vehicles, smart mobility, new modes of transportation, shared-use concepts and technology-enabled mobility services. He served as Principal In Charge for *Autonomous Vehicles: A Horizon Initiative Perspective Paper* on behalf of the San Francisco Bay Area Metropolitan Transportation Commission.

Michael R. Boswell, Ph.D., is Department Head & Professor of City & Regional Planning at Cal Poly, San Luis Obispo and is an expert on strategies to reduce greenhouse emissions and increase community resilience to climate change. He is lead author of the book Local Climate Action Planning and most recently advised UN-Habitat on climate planning as a part of COP 21.

Andrea Broaddus is a transportation policy expert focused on managing the demand for travel through behavioral incentives and land use practices. Her current research focuses on the impacts of autonomous and connected vehicles on urban transport systems. She has published articles on road pricing and transit oriented development and has served as a lecturer at UC Berkeley and San Jose State since 2010. She has private sector experience as a researcher on future mobility topics for Robert Bosch LLC, and as a planning practitioner with Nelson/Nygaard Consulting Associates. She has also worked in non-profit advocacy on local and state transportation policy in Madison WI, and federal policy in Washington, D.C. Her research on European transportation policy and practice led to year-long fellowships in Hamburg, Germany and London, England. She holds a Bachelor of Science in Geology from the University of North Carolina at Chapel Hill, Master of Public Policy / Urban Planning from the Harvard Kennedy School and Ph.D. in Transportation Planning from UC Berkeley.

Christa Cassidy is a graduate student working with Arup's Integrated Planning team on issues surrounding the future of mobility, transportation funding, and transportation equity. Previously, she worked as the program manager for The Nature Conservancy's Infrastructure and Land Use team building tools, developing programs, and shaping legislation to integrate conservation and climate change into statewide and regional policies and plans. Christa is a candidate for Master of City Planning at the University of California, Berkeley and holds Bachelors of Science degrees in Urban Planning and Environmental Studies from the University of Utah.

Benjamin Y. Clark is an Associate Professor of Public Administration in the School of Planning, Public Policy and Management at the University of Oregon. He has expertise in local budgeting and finance and has been an Executive Committee member of the Association for Budgeting and Financial Management (ABFM) since 2013. His research examines how technology can be used to improve city management (smart city technology) and how cities need to be planning for future innovations (autonomous vehicles). Prior to his arrival at the University of Oregon in 2016, Clark was an Associate Professor of Public Administration at Cleveland State University and served as the Executive Director of the Great Lakes Environmental Finance Center, an EPA-funded research and technical assistance provider to governments in EPA Region 5. Prior to his career in academia he worked for nearly a decade as a public servant at the local, federal, and international levels.

Greg P. Griffin, Ph.D., researches how people work together with networked tools to improve urban planning, particularly for sustainable transportation and health. He is a doctorate candidate and Eisenhower Transportation Graduate Fellow at the University of Texas at Austin, and researcher with the Texas A&M Transportation Institute, as of this writing. Greg leverages over a decade of experience working as a planner to advance theory and evaluate and improve planning practice. Greg is a member of the American Institute of Certified Planners, and is a lifelong bicyclist.

Michael Johnson is Director of Urban Design at Smithgroup. Michael's ability to understand and distill complex urban challenges spans catalytic landscape architecture and urban design projects in major American cities, innovative campus plans for top urban research universities and Fortune 500 companies, and international large-scale mixed-use development efforts. Michael serves on the Board of the Landscape Architecture Foundation (LAF), where he advances the measurable role that placemaking and urban design can play in fostering healthy cities and supporting landscape and streetscape performance. He holds a Bachelor's degree in Landscape Architecture from Ball State University, and a Master's in Urban Design from the University of Michigan.

Joshua Karlin-Resnick is an expert in parking and transportation demand management who has published writing and research on the future of mobility, parking management, and the evolving use of transportation performance metrics, among other topics. Before joining the San Francisco Giants as transportation manager in 2018, he worked at Nelson\Nygaard, where he led the creation of parking and TDM programs for several major mixed-use developments in the Bay Area, including the Giants' Mission Rock and Santana Row in San Jose. He has also led parking and access studies for cities and universities across the west.

Matthew Kawashima is an Environmental Analyst for the Contra Costa County Public Works Department and a Master of Public Administration Candidate at the University of San Francisco where he also serves as Research Assistant to Professor Riggs in his research on autonomous vehicles. He is passionate about alternative transportation, emerging technologies, and sustainability and how these will shape the built environment. Matt received his B.S. in City & Regional Planning from Cal Poly, San Luis Obispo and in his free time enjoys travel and photography.

Rebecca Lewis, Ph.D., is an Assistant Professor in Planning, Public Policy and Management at the University of Oregon and a Faculty Affiliate at the National Center for Smart Growth Research and Education at the University of Maryland. She serves as the Research Director for the Sustainable Cities Initiative at the University of Oregon. She holds a master of public policy degree from the University of Maryland and a Ph.D. in urban and regional planning and design from the University of Maryland. Dr. Lewis was a 2010 Lincoln Institute of Land Policy C. Lowell Harriss Dissertation Fellow and received 2012 Barclay Gibbs Jones Award for the Best Dissertation in Planning from the American Collegiate Schools of Planning for her dissertation evaluating the efficacy of smart growth in Maryland. Her research has been published in peer-reviewed journals including the Journal of the American Planning Association, State and Local Government Review, and the American Journal of Public Health. Her research broadly focuses on state land use policy, the integration of climate, transportation and land use planning, state and local finance and measuring urban form. Her research has been funded by the National Science Foundation, the National Institute for Transportation and Communities, the Department of Land Conservation and Development and the Lincoln Institute for Land Policy. At the University of Oregon, she teaches courses in growth management, sustainable cities, public budget administration and research methods.

Meg Merritt is a Principal at Nelson\Nygaard and has more than 12 years of experience in managing major projects that bring transit and mobility technology to communities. She began her career in transit and land-use planning and more recently, spent time in the technology startup Ridescout/moovel where she managed the multimodal mobile experience for private mobility companies and transit authorities. Her expertise in traditional transit planning and cutting edge mobility technology makes her a skillful navigator into the future of transportation.

Ronald T. Milam, AICP, PTP, is a Principal with Fehr & Peers actively involved in big data research, VMT analysis, multimodal performance measures, and land use/transportation interactions. In addition to consulting and research, he teaches transportation planning and SB 743 courses for the UC Berkeley Tech Transfer, UC Davis Extension, and UC San Diego Extension programs and served on the TRB Special Committee for Travel Forecasting Resources. Ron has an extensive background in travel demand model development and applications, traffic operations analysis, micro-simulation modeling, and transportation impact studies involving NEPA and CEQA. He has also published papers on a wide variety of transportation planning and traffic engineering topics and received recognition for his work that includes the Institute of Transportation Engineer's (ITE) National Past President's Award and best paper honors at the Transportation Research Board (TRB) Conference on Planning Applications.

Adam Millard-Ball, Ph.D., is an Associate Professor in the Environmental Studies Department at the University of California, Santa Cruz. His research bridges urban planning and environmental economics, and addresses some of the key challenges in transportation, energy and climate change policy. His current work examines global patterns of urban sprawl and car ownership, the effectiveness of local climate planning efforts, and the design of carbon trading programs. Adam also has broad interests in transportation planning and policy, particularly parking management programs to reduce vehicle travel and emissions. Before UC Santa Cruz, he was an assistant professor in the Department of Geography and McGill School of Environment, McGill University. Adam holds a Ph.D. in Environment and Resources from Stanford University, and was formerly a Principal with transportation planning firm Nelson\Nygaard Consulting Associates.

Frank Petrilli is an Associate at ArentFox. He specializes in land use law, entitlement strategy, and environmental compliance under the California

Environmental Quality Act. Frank has worked with clients to obtain entitlements and permits for a variety of complex and controversial developments, including office, mixed-use, residential, industrial, and institutional projects. He has also successfully represented both public entities and private developers in litigation at both the trial court level and on appeal, and has substantial experience with ballot initiatives and referenda related to the land use process. The 2017 edition of Legal 500 ranks Frank as a recommended attorney, noting that clients describe Frank as always able to "find solutions to difficult problems." Frank's practice is focused on the San Francisco Bay Area, where he has represented clients such as Facebook, Bohannon Development Company, and LinkedIn.

William (Billy) Riggs, Ph.D., AICP, LEED AP, is a global expert and thought leader in the areas of future mobility and smart transportation, housing, economics and urban development. He is a professor at the University of San Francisco School of Management, and a consultant and advisor to multiple companies and start-ups on technology, smart mobility and urban development. This follows two decades of experience working as a planner, economist, and engineer. He has been both a fellow with the National Science Foundation fellow and the University of California Transportation Center, is the founder of ReStreet.com (app.restreet.com)—an online tool for democratizing street design. Dr. Riggs sits on the City of Palo Alto's Planning and Transportation Commission and is a member of the Transportation Research Board (TRB) Committee on Transportation Economics and Transportation Research Board's (TRB) Committee on Transportation Economics and the Standing Committee on Policy and Law.

Melissa Ruhl is a Transportation Planner for Arup in San Francisco where she manages autonomous vehicles strategies and policy efforts. Partnering with cities and transit agencies, Melissa helps communities plan for tomorrow while improving quality of life today. She co-authored the *Autonomous Vehicles: A Horizon Initiative Perspective Paper* on behalf of the San Francisco Bay Area Metropolitan Transportation Commission, and she regularly speaks in both the San Francisco Bay Area and nationally on autonomous vehicles and the future of cities. In June 2018, the Northern California American Planning Association granted her the Special Recognition Award – Emerging Planner. Melissa earned a Master of Urban Planning from San Jose State University and a Master of Arts in History from the University of Oregon.

Marc Schlossberg, Ph.D., is Professor of City and Regional Planning and Co-Director of the Sustainable Cities Initiative at the University of Oregon.

Elizabeth Shay, Ph.D., AICP, is an Assistant Professor in the Department of Geography and Planning at Appalachian State University in Boone NC.

Shivani Shukla, Ph.D., is an Assistant Professor and Researcher at the School of Management, University of San Francisco. Her research focuses on dynamic programming, optimization, and game theory applied to transportation, service operations, and security. Her work has led to publications in some of the prominent journals like European Journal of Operational Research, Annals of Operations Research, and Transportation Research Part E. Besides academia, she has industry exposure with multiple years of experience working in the consulting sector and in an industrial research lab based out of Palo Alto.

Deborah Stamm has worked in commercial real estate for over a decade. During that time, she has led commercial and industrial development projects in the Bay Area, Boston and the Pacific Northwest, where her work has ranged from urban redevelopment and to large, new-build suburban projects. She currently serves as a Senior Associate at Trammell Crow Company. Deborah was on the team that delivered California's first Net Zero Energy building and throughout her career she has been active in advancing sustainable design in the real estate industry. She has written and spoken about the intersection of Vehicle Autonomy and Real Estate, and has predicted that New Mobility will radically transform the way we live, where and how we build, and our environmental footprint. She believes that we can and should harness our New Mobility technology to create better cities and a better quality of life for all. Deborah holds an MBA from Stanford Graduate School of Business and a Bachelor of Science in Environmental Science from Brown University. She lives with her husband in Seattle where she enjoys hiking, skiing, surfing and any good excuse to get outdoors.

Jeffrey Tumlin is a Principal at Nelson\Nygaard who has developed downtown, station area, citywide and master plans for cities such as San Francisco, Seattle, Portland OR, Vancouver BC, Santa Monica, Denver, Washington, D.C. Trenton NJ, and Abu Dhabi. He has also led the transportation component of transit-oriented development plans for over 60 station areas and new towns across North America. He is the author of the book, Sustainable Transportation Planning, published by Wiley in 2012.

Louis Yudowitz is currently a graduate student studying Mathematics at the University of Warwick. He received a BSc in Mathematics and Computer Science with a first class honors classification from King's College London in 2018. His research interests include statistics and its applications, as well as areas of analysis. This has recently included projects concerning determinants of elliptic differential operators and microlocal computations of heat trace invariants, as well as analyzing data pertaining to transportation and urban planning.

Stephen Zoepf, Ph.D., is the Executive Director of the Center for Automotive Research at Stanford. He holds a Ph.D., M.Sc. and B.Sc. from MIT and has 15 years of experience in transportation and mobility. Dr. Zoepf led U.S. Department of Transportation efforts to integrate confidential data into national vehicle energy policy modeling, and previously worked as an engineer and product manager at BMW and Ford. He was an ENI Energy Initiative Fellow, a Martin Energy Fellow, and a recipient of the Barry McNutt award from the Transportation Research Board and the Infinite Mile award from MIT. His research has been covered in numerous popular press articles, initiated a Congressional probe, and has been lampooned in The Onion.

Acknowledgements

Thanks to the editors and reviewers and Routledge whose feedback and assistant helped improve work in this book, particularly to Dr. Stephen Zavestoski, who encouraged me to put together the original submission. Also, a huge thanks to the student assistants who helped with some of the review and editing on this project, including: Matthew Kawashima, Therese Perez and Louis Yudowitz. Finally, thank you to the organizing committee of the Autonomous Vehicles and City Symposium (including sponsors Arup, Cal Poly, the Mineta Transportation Institute, and University of San Francisco), colleagues at Urbanism Next, Association of Pacific Rim Universities, 3 Revolutions, and at the University of San Francisco who helped develop and refine many of the concepts that formed the basic construct of this text. I know that I can speak for all of us in saying, that we hope you enjoy it and keep asking big questions about how technology can and should revolutionize the future of our cities.

Part I

The big picture

1 Introduction

William Riggs

A new story emerges daily about disruptive transport—be it ride services, scooters, dockless bikes, or self-driving cars. Such changes can seem overwhelming, particularly with how quickly technology is evolving. The auto industry is rapidly embracing a broader mobility concept (not just making cars) and competing with technology companies to deliver smart and on-demand mobility services as quickly as possible. Government at all levels is working to ease vehicle requirements of the emerging platforms and relax safety standards for vehicles to encourage innovation (McKay 2017) while at the same time being pressured to grapple with new mobility services and an increasing number of things like e-bikes and scooters flooding streets in many cities.

Many societal benefits result from this accelerated vehicle design innovation and evolution in the mobility sector—including the potential for saved lives, due to reduced collisions, and increased productivity while driving (Riggs and Boswell 2016), but there is a flaw in this vehicular focus. It is a dialogue that focuses solely on the vehicle and not on the city around it.

While this may sound simple, our cities are complex organisms that support more than just automobiles. Yet disruptive transportation could dramatically reshape them, for good and for bad. For example, personal transportation devices like e-scooters or Segways could provide cheap mobility to people at the fringes of cities, providing greater access to jobs and housing.

Likewise, technologies like Hyperloop could reshape the cost of long-range travel between cities. There are also exciting possibilities for cities to rethink streets as autonomous vehicles become more prominent. Consider the width, traffic direction, and allocation of road space for vehicles. Might cities optimize space for bicycles and pedestrians in an autonomous future? Does two-way traffic really matter in an algorithmically-driven traffic system?

Alongside these travel shifts, possibilities exist to change how cities support logistics and deliveries. Might cities more aggressively zone deliveries by time, type, and location in the future? There are also opportunities to rethink urban land use and growth, for example, developing parking lots and auto servicing real estate into new uses. Or perhaps we might prioritize housing on former roadway parcels to help address the housing crunch that many of our cities face. We might consider suburban growth or encourage dense downtown.

We might set up standards to ensure transportation accessibility at all socio-economic levels in the autonomous future.

If any of this interests you, then you are in the right place. There are many impacts of new transportation innovations, and this book focuses on those that impact the city and its environs, and how we plan and grow a future for us all that is both sustainable and socially just. We are already seeing increases in driving caused by transportation network companies like Uber and Lyft, and changes to how most of us travel because of mobile phones and e-commerce (Clewlow and Mishra 2017; Clark and Larco 2018). Now is the time for us to start a conversation about these changes and to map out policy for our cities. If not dealt with thoughtfully, disruptive transport could pose a major challenge to the livable, sustainable, and equitable future of cities.

Richard Florida (2017) recently suggested that we may be near the end of the urban century, documenting a revival of suburbanism and alluding to the fear that millennial preferences toward urbanism are overstated. This is a pessimistic view of the future, yet within this pessimism I believe there is some hope.

If our society is really at the apex of the urban century, a century that has brought us a more just and prosperous city, then we need to consider what kind of future we want—and clearly this future involves creative, dynamic, and disruptive transportation. But we need to have dialogue about more than vehicles—and that's the point of this book.

But before we jump to that conversation and an outline of the book, I think it's important to frame some terms and transportation speak that will come up as a part of this book, as well as a key assumption. Let's start with the terms.

Key terms

First and foremost, my authors and I will use the terms new mobility, disruptive mobility, and future mobility synonymously and interchangeably. The goal in using these terms to describe one thing is to provide you, the reader, a little variety but also to be encompassing of many new and emerging forms of transportation. In this book we talk about bikes, scooters, trains, shuttles, cars that drive themselves, and touch on drones. We don't pretend that this encompasses all of the crazy and cool transportation innovations that will arise in the next twenty years, but hopefully, we can have more long-term impact on things like land use, housing, social equity, and the environment by starting a broader discussion about new and disruptive transportation that "jump-starts" action.

Key acronyms

AV:	autonomous vehicle
ART:	autonomous rapid transit
CEQA:	California Environmental Quality Act
LiDAR:	light detection and ranging
MaaS:	mobility-as-a-service
MPO:	metropolitan planning organization

OEM: original equipment manufacturer
RTP: regional transportation plan
TNC: transportation network company

Second, we are all excited about the promise of autonomous vehicles, and we talk a lot about that in this book. We use the term autonomous rather than automated, which is more proper, and self-driving, which is less formal. We abbreviate it AV, but as for the term, it's a bit of hybrid between the formal and informal, yet it has a whole background in itself. Here's an excerpt from a recent American Planning Association report I authored with Jeremy Crute, Tim Chapin, and Lindsay Stevens that provides more information on how autonomous cars work and how they are classified.

What is an automated vehicle?

Automated vehicle technology is an umbrella term that includes a wide variety of features and technologies that enable vehicles to take control of some or all of the major driving functions normally completed by the driver. This includes fully autonomous vehicles that no longer require a human driver to operate them, as well as a range of advanced driver assistance systems (ADAS) that enhance driver safety by taking temporary control of one or more driving functions (speed, lane position, braking, etc.).

An autonomous vehicle no longer requires a human operator to drive. Instead, the vehicle navigates streets safely and efficiently through a complex mix of software and hardware that combines remote sensing, recognition algorithms, network analysis, and "experience" drawn from millions of hours of driving that is shared across AVs. The vehicle's combination of sensors, cameras, light detection and ranging (LiDAR or light radar), high-definition maps, and advanced software creates a digital picture of its surroundings and makes intelligent driving decisions on routing and maneuvering without any input from an operator or information broadcast by infrastructure or other vehicles.

More specifically, just as radar does with radio waves, LiDAR shoots pulses of light and measures how long it takes for the light to return to the sensor to assess how far away an object is. Placing an array of rotating lasers on top of an AV provides a continual 360-degree "point cloud" or picture of the vehicle's surroundings. The vehicle's central computer can then be programmed to recognize specific LiDAR returns as another car, a pedestrian, or even a stop sign. LiDAR systems are typically supplemented by cameras and other sensors to provide redundant detection systems that will not fail to detect objects that LiDAR could miss, particularly in the area immediately surrounding the vehicle. More sophisticated systems add another layer to this by assessing how surrounding vehicles and pedestrians are moving and predicting where they will go next. In the case of a pedestrian crossing the street, the vehicle can predict the pedestrian's movements and begin slowing down before the pedestrian enters the street instead of waiting until the pedestrian is directly in the vehicle's path.

Unfortunately, whether an AV uses LiDAR or cameras or both, it is very difficult for these systems to work properly in inclement weather conditions and poor visibility. Rain and snow refract the laser returns, and cameras struggle to identify objects accurately through precipitation, functionally blinding the AV.

Most of the attention on AVs is centered around fully autonomous vehicles because many of the technology's most significant effects on the transportation system and the built environment will only be viable when fully autonomous vehicles are adopted. However, AV technology includes a range of levels of automation. It is important for planners to be familiar with the full array of AV technology, because many semi-autonomous features and applications are already available today and will likely play a major role in the transition to a fully autonomous world.

In addition to autonomous vehicles, there is a wide range of automated technologies that can operate as standalone features. These range in sophistication and complexity from cruise control to autopilot. To classify these ever-evolving technologies, the National Highway Traffic Safety Administration (NHTSA) and the Society of Automotive Engineers (SAE) International developed a classification system that divides automated technologies into six levels of vehicle automation. These range from 0, where the driver is in complete control of all driving tasks at all times, to 5, where the vehicle is designed to perform all driving tasks without an operator (SAE International 2016).

With Level 1 automation, the driver remains in control of the vehicle, but the technology can assist the driver by controlling one of the vehicle's functions, either its speed or lane position. Level 2 takes this a step further by allowing the vehicle to control two driving functions at the same time. A vehicle with Level 3 automation can take full control of the vehicle for certain parts of a trip, but drivers must be ready to take back control of the vehicle when the vehicle prompts them. The vehicle takes full control of all major driving functions in Level 4. Level 4 vehicles can even drive themselves for the entire trip, but they are only able to do so under specific conditions. Finally, Level 5 automation refers to fully autonomous vehicles that can operate without an operator in all conditions and without the capability for a human to retake control.

Automated driving features that aid the driving process but do not fully control the vehicle (Levels 0, 1, and 2) are generally referred to as advanced driver assistance systems (ADAS). Even though fully autonomous vehicles have received most of the attention and are the focus of this report, ADAS can significantly improve driver safety, thereby improving user mobility.

Assumptions

Now that we covered a couple of key terms I'd like to run by one key assumption—that of the idea of an ecological consciousness. What do I mean by that? I mean that each of the authors in this book likely has a bias toward environmental stewardship in a way that preserves the planet for generations to come. The term ecological consciousness comes from esteemed Jesuit scholar Thomas Merton. In 1968 he wrote to Barbara Hubbard, who was then director of the Center for American Living in New York (Merton 2008). He discussed the advent of the millennial consciousness that was driving innovation like the space race and the emerging digital revolution, and he noted the importance of a balanced "ecological consciousness" in the face of this new technological innovation. He called for a balanced exuberance saying,

> The real thing is about to happen: the new creation, the millennium, the coming of the Kingdom, the withering away of the State, etc. But if you want to entire into the Kingdom there are certain things you have to do. They consist partly in acts which destroy and repudiate the past (metanoia, conversion, revolution, etc.) and partly in acts which open you up to the future.... The ecological consciousness says: look out! In preparing this great event, you run the risk of forgetting something. We are not alone in this thing. We belong to a community of living beings and we owe our fellow members in this community the respect and honor due them... we must not try to prepare the millennium by immolating our living each, by careless and stupid exploitation for short-term commercial, military or technological ends which will be paid for by irreparable loss in living species and natural resources.... Life is sacred... that of plants and animals (as well as that of our) fellow man.

I am pretty confident that all of my co-authors share this love of life, the planet and their fellow humans, and we also believe that there has been very little discussion about the secondary impacts of disruptive transport, that grapples with issues of sustainability and social justice. We hope we can fill that role. So, with that, let's talk about how this book is structured.

Book outline

This book has sixteen chapters divided into three sections: a focus on the big picture (Chapters 1 to 3); then going small and exploring changes at the city scale (Chapters 4 to 9); going big again with ideas for the regional scale (Chapters 10 to 13); and then concluding with a vision for livability and sustainability (Chapters 14 to 16).

The first three chapters deal with the big picture of what is happening and what it means. This includes this introduction, which is followed by Chapter 2. In that chapter, Will Baumgardner, Christa Cassidy, and Melissa Ruhl from Arup talk about the promise of new mobility and what paradigm cities will follow in the disruptive transportation future. They grapple with the potential for urban accessibility gains and the idea of planning for multiple scenarios in an uncertain environment.

This is followed by Chapter 3, in which Ron Milam and I talk about new mobility that balances both promise and peril. The two of us attempt to balance between promise and peril focusing on some of the principle functions of transportation engineering and trip generation. The chapter talks about the essential factors transportation professionals consider in planning for development. It dialogues the way new mobility changes that paradigm and pulls out key principles and considerations that need to be considered in light of new and disruptive transport.

Chapter 4 moves from this broad topic to the city scale. Michael Johnson from Smithgroup works with me to write the kind of land use and design we should be engaged in, in light of disruptive transport. We explore how we might rethink open spaces around cities that are sometimes used to limit urban growth, and we offer insights on what kind of landscapes, urban infrastructure, and land uses planners should be considering in cities.

I then work Marc Schlossberg, Adam Millard-Ball, and Elizabeth Shay on Chapter 5, which focuses on the street itself. The chapter dialogues how a community might envision future streets and allocate the space on the road differently. It also explores programs that might be used to encourage more walking and cycling at the same time as supporting new forms of transportation from TNCs to automated vehicles. It concludes with key lessons for engineers exploring what neighborhood streets might look like in the future.

Chapter 6 with Deborah Stamm stays at the city scale and looks at the real estate implications of new mobility and the ways the technology will impact the space outside the vehicle—the urban environment itself. The chapter evaluates how the land currently dedicated to streets might be reused and how streets can become real estate assets that can be used for societal good, as things like parks, bike lanes, or affordable housing.

In Chapter 7, Ben Clark and Rebecca Lewis, from University of Oregon, focus on budgets at the city scale and how cities can get smart with revenue. This includes things like parking, the transit business, and speeding tickets. This is followed by Chapter 8 in which Josh Karlin-Resnick, Jeff Tumlin, and Meg Merritt talk about global examples of policies to direct new mobility. This includes inventory and curb management, along with best practices to begin planning for autonomous vehicles and prepare for changes in the way transit is delivered. The authors end with suggestions about how policy or programs may need to evolve to address the increasing challenges of technology-enabled transportation in cities large and small around the globe.

Chapter 9 provides a more data-driven and theoretical look at jobs and local economies. My University of San Francisco colleague Shivani Shukla and I look at the potential for increased revenues and the broader impacts on the economy. We grapple with the idea that even as our society becomes more technical, humans play a large role in the sustainability of our cities.

After that we jump back to the big picture on a larger regional scale. In Chapter 10, we hear from Greg Griffin who talks about co-producing mobility and ridesharing. He emphasizes the importance of governments collaborating with and listening to consumers. Chapter 11 then focuses on the electric and shared aspects of future transport. Stephen Zoepf and I focus on how these two factors can work in concert to promote social justice.

In Chapter 12, Frank Petrilli, an attorney from ArentFox, talks about the environmental ramifications of future transport. Not only does he talk about the costs, he explores trends and case studies on how environmental policy has evolved in parallel with changes in housing and transportation, and how they need to evolve further. Michael R. Boswell, Louis Yudowitz, Matt Kawashima, and I then follow this up with a dialogue in Chapter 13 with a focus on the environment and climate change. We talk about emissions and 3 strategies for mobility to transition to an equitable future that is also environmentally sustainable.

Moving to Chapter 14, we begin to conclude with a focus on livability. Bruce Appleyard and I talk about a livability framework for new mobility. This is followed by Chapter 14, in which Andrea Boaddus explores how lessons from the past, demographics and trends from the automaker sector, and consumer preferences might influence the way we think about future travel. Finally, Chapter 16 offers parting thoughts and conclusive directions, in which I offer 3 considerations. Specifically, I challenge planners, policymakers and citizens to do 3 things:

1   Consider that the future of mobility will likely be much different than we anticipate;
2   Recognize that trip data and the user experience are the new currency of travel, not the trip itself;
3   And to consider the social costs of decisions that both support and limit the acceleration of disruptive transportation.

My goal in focusing on these considerations, and with the dialogue in all of these chapters, is to facilitate action. We need citizens, planners, consultants, and policymakers, who can talk with providers of new mobility and help shape the dialogue on future cities. So, as I alluded previously, if you're interested in streets, economics, land use, sustainability, or the equity implications of disruptive transport, this book is for you. If you're interested in conquering the language of future mobility, this book is for you. Whether you are student, policymaker, city planner, elected official, academic or citizen; whether you come from a science or humanities background; my hope, our hope, is that we can provide you a guidebook for action—in shaping the sustainable mobility of tomorrow.

We need to reshape cities, reshape streets, so they are consistent with social, economic, and environmental goals. We need to think beyond the vehicle—plan the kind of cities that we want to see and be the kind of cities we want to be. So, let's get on with it.

References

Clark, B. and N. Larco. 2018. "The Impacts of Autonomous Vehicles and E-Commerce on Local Government Budgeting and Finance." *UrbanismNext*. https://urbanismnext. uoregon.edu/files/2017/07/Impacts-of-AV-Ecommerce-on-Local-Govt-Budget-and-Finance-SCI-08-2017-2n8wgfg.pdf.

Clewlow, R. R. and G. S. Mishra. 2017. "Disruptive Transportation: The Adoption, Utilization, and Impacts of Ride-Hailing in the United States." Research Report UCD-ITS-RR-17-07. Davis, CA: University of California, Davis, Institute of Transportation Studies.   https://itspubs.ucdavis.edu/wp-content/themes/ucdavis/pubs/download_pdf. php?id=2752.

Florida, R. 2017. "The Urban Revival Is Over." *The New York Times*. 2017. https://www. nytimes.com/2017/09/01/opinion/cities-suburbs-housing-crime.html?_r=0.

McKay, T. 2017. "California DMV Ditches Rule to Limit Liability for Self-Driving Car Manufacturers." *Gizmodo*. 2017. https://gizmodo.com/california-dmv-ditches-rule-to-limit-liability-for-self-1820959217.

Merton, T. 2008. *Thomas Merton: A Life in Letters: The Essential Collection*. Harper Collins.

Riggs, W. and M. R. Boswell. 2016. "Thinking Beyond the (Autonomous) Vehicle: The Promise of Saved Lives." https://works.bepress.com/williamriggs/71/.

2 The promise of seamless mobility

Autonomous vehicles and the mobility-as-a-service revolution

Will Baumgardner, Christa Cassidy, and Melissa Ruhl

Introduction

Transportation systems underpin the health of our cities and regions. The physical design and operational performance of the transportation ecosystem have ramifications for nearly all aspects of modern life. Transportation is the lifeblood of cities; from the food we eat to the air we breathe, our most basic needs are impacted by transportation decisions. Historically, each new transportation technology has brought with it added convenience, economic growth, and transformative changes to urban form. In the nineteenth century, railroads reliably connected places over long distances, fueling the growth of cities and propelling the industrial age. In the twentieth century, the private car and the interstate highway system enabled the rapid growth of suburbia and fundamentally changed the character of most of our urban areas.

Today, the country is connected by networks of highways, rail lines, bus routes, ferry services, air travel, bicycle infrastructure, and sidewalks that help people connect with opportunities. Our transportation system has never been more advanced or robust than it is today, and incontrovertibly, it has helped propel the United States to its place of global prominence. We have become accustomed to hypermobility: an affordable car in the driveway ready to go at all times, along with an extensive air transportation network with potential fares for intercity travel. More recently, the advent of real-time traffic information, navigation apps, car- and bike-sharing platforms, as well as on-demand ride-hailing services, such as Uber and Lyft, are early indicators of another transformative revolution in transportation technology: ubiquitous, easily accessible on-demand mobility services.

This chapter explores this coming shift in the mobility landscape and examines the implications of such a shift for transportation networks and urban and regional ecosystems. It begins with an overview of the current transportation status quo. From worsening congestion to aging infrastructure, the need for drastic improvement is stark. Next, the chapter presents a vision for mobility-as-a-service (MaaS), enabled by autonomous vehicle (AV) services, including autonomous high-capacity transit. The chapter concludes with an analysis of the implications of a new mobility system and an action plan for leveraging benefits through leadership.

The state of transportation

Despite many technological advances, the performance of our transportation system is declining. Transportation in the United States is chronically underfunded, and infrastructure across the country is in a state of crisis. For example, the American Institute of Civil Engineers reports there is $836 billion of unmet needs for highway and bridge improvements (American Institute of Civil Engineers 2017). Public transit ridership declined in thirty-one of thirty-five major metropolitan markets between 2016 and 2017 (Siddiqui 2018). Drivers in Los Angeles spend an average of one hundred hours per year stuck in congestion (Cookson 2018). The challenges to our transportation system are multifaceted, and the solutions are increasingly complex. A study done by the Brookings Institute found that inefficiencies in the U.S. transportation system are worth more than $100 billion; this figure captures inefficient pricing, inadequate investments, and increased production costs that are manifested in congestion, delays, budget deficits, as well as excessive time costs and direct monetary costs to users (Winston 2013).

The critical importance of the transportation system means that when it is not performing well, our entire society suffers. An objective look at our urban transportation systems reveals that it is frequently performing poorly by many metrics and is generally trending in the wrong direction to meet the increasing demand for the movement of people and goods. The legacy of past transportation technologies influences our daily lives in the form of various social, economic, and environmental issues.

Thankfully, new transportation solutions are on the way. Autonomous vehicles (AVs) present the most significant change to transportation since Henry Ford first made automobiles accessible to the masses. The last decade has seen a virtually exponential increase in the amount of activity on the development and testing of AV technology. In California alone, the Department of Motor Vehicles has licensed over fifty companies to test AVs on public roads. Autonomous technology will be complemented by advancements in electrification, public and private mobility services, ubiquitous mobile connectivity, improved infrastructure funding, and management strategies, as well as improved user interface. These changes will not only reshape how people and goods are transported, but will also have far-reaching environmental, economic, and social implications.

We are on the cusp of major disruption, bringing the potential to revolutionize transportation with new mobility systems. The resulting opportunities are massive—but so are the risks. We are at a crossroads: We know our transportation future will be built on this new technology, but its implications remain uncertain, making it challenging to adequately plan and prepare. Interestingly, we can see this change coming. As Apple's Tim Cook has said, "The [transportation] industry is at an inflection point for massive change, not just evolutionary change" (*Wall Street Journal* 2015). With foresight, planning, and collaboration we can harness the potential of mobility innovation to revitalize our transportation ecosystem. In an effort to foresee the uncertain, to anticipate the unexpected, this chapter aims to imagine a future that harnesses the incredible promise of new mobility systems as a solution to transportation challenges while recognizing the unprecedented risk they present.

Components of a new mobility system

In a utopian future, mobility is seamless. Instead of users adjusting to systems, systems will adjust to users. No longer will vehicle ownership, and the inefficient use derived from sunk cost, be the dominant form of transportation. Instead, mobility will be a collection of coordinated services. This concept of mobility-as-a-service (MaaS) describes a holistic, dynamic system. MaaS as a concept came to international notice in April 2015 when the Helsinki, Finland government published a press release proposing a new mobility ecosystem by 2025. In this document, Helsinki provided this definition for MaaS:

> The term Mobility as a Service (MaaS) stands for buying mobility services based on consumer needs instead of buying the means of mobility. In the present model the user may either buy means (a car or a bike) or tickets for transport (bus ticket, train ticket, etc.)…With the MaaS concept, the user may buy transport from the place of departure to the destination (Greenfield, 2014).

With an integrated digital platform, users can access high-capacity transit to travel through congested corridors, fixed-route transit to travel between popular destinations, demand-responsive shuttles during low-demand time periods or in low-density areas, passenger vehicles to rapidly access destinations in an emergency, and a suite of bicycles, scooters, and other partially- or fully-human-powered devices to travel within local areas. The mode will fit the trip rather than the trip fitting the mode.

With twentieth-century transportation, travelers were stuck with the mode they originally selected, despite the particular needs of a trip. If a traveler purchased a vehicle, it was likely she would use that vehicle for most trips, since the investment had already been made. Driving her car to work, she would have to drive it home, otherwise the vehicle would be stranded. If a traveler rode his bike somewhere, he would have to ride it back home, otherwise it would likewise be stranded and at risk for theft. Even transit riders who had the luxury of riding the bus or train one way and taking another mode the way back would have to rely on carpooling, taxis, or walking if not transit. With a twenty-first-century MaaS system, travelers can prioritize the greatest need of the moment for each trip: speed, affordability, comfort, sightseeing, etc. If a traveler prioritizes speed when accessing a destination but comfort on the return trip, she can use an integrated MaaS platform to cater her modes to her needs with, for example, a high-capacity transit trip to her destination and a demand-responsive shuttle on her way back. Across all trips the commonality need only be the MaaS integrated digital platform.

Seamless mobility, or MaaS, will require three critical but related components: (1) a wide variety of mobility services, (2) physical and virtual infrastructure, and (3) a management regime to ensure the system is optimized and sustainable. The basic needs inherent in MaaS are no different from the perennial needs of all transportation systems—transportation needs to be safe, affordable, intuitive, flexible to innovation, and able to provide a diversity of options to meet the needs of different types of trips, people, and geographies.

Modal options for right-sizing travel

Most important for a vital MaaS environment is significantly greater choice than today with more variety and flexibility by mode, vehicle size, and price. An open and dynamic marketplace for modal options ensures that innovation is constantly happening and modality is always being improved upon for the end user. Having a robust suite of modal options enables widespread coverage of cities, allowing people to access many different destinations within an area. Additionally, the variety of options ensures a diverse citizenry can achieve all of their needs without a personal vehicle, from the disabled and elderly to families of all sizes. MaaS relies on the presence of many modalities—bus, rail, shuttles, ferry, bikeshare, carshare, scooters, and walking to create vital links to opportunities, from jobs and education to healthcare and recreation. Choice and flexibility empowers the users with options, encourages competition and innovation, and provides redundancy.

Digital and built infrastructure

While both digital and built infrastructure is necessary for MaaS functionality, public transportation infrastructure should be considered the nucleus of any MaaS environment, with all other mobility options serving as extensions to it. Hard, tangible infrastructure, like rail lines, bus lanes, bus fleets, and rail cars will all require prioritized maintenance and planning for expansion to meet the growing demand that MaaS will bring as it prioritizes public transportation to maximize people throughput within the system. The shift away from personal vehicle ownership with the rise of AVs and uptake of MaaS will greatly reduce demand for parking, spurring the reuse of those spaces for bike facilities, bus infrastructure, or expanded sidewalks to encourage walking.

While the hard infrastructure is where the rubber meets the road, the digital infrastructure establishes the backend framework that connects people with the appropriate mobility options at the touch of a button. While it will appear simple and seamless to the user, the digital infrastructure required to make MaaS run is incredibly complex. Done right, it brings together the fee structures, policies, and schedules of multiple transportation providers, both public and private. A collaborative approach between public and private sectors will allow the MaaS platform to deliver benefits to residents while meeting larger community goals around the economy, the environment, and equity. Of course, this digital infrastructure will be built on data, requiring sharing protocols among operators to manage historic and real-time data and estimate predictive data.

Management and investment mechanisms to support demand

It is fundamentally complex to deliver mobility in the public realm. At a basic level, our system and culture has been inclined toward the automobile for so long that achieving alternative transportation projects is challenging both politically and financially. The level of subsidy needed to make public transportation costs competitive with cars is often impossible for municipalities to achieve, and then on top of that, low farebox recovery forces most transit systems to operate at a deficit. MaaS success depends on the availability and functionality of public transportation infrastructure, meaning that dedicated funding streams will be needed for both maintenance and operations and expansion of public transportation. MaaS should steer people back toward public transportation as a key component of travel, bringing desperately needed funds back into the system. But the farebox alone is not enough to make MaaS work.

States struggle each year to patch together a funding quilt to cover basic infrastructure needs and have a deep reliance on the gas tax, which has diminishing returns as more drivers turn to electric or more fuel-efficient vehicles. In considering the future with AVs and MaaS, it is imperative that we reimagine our funding future as well and put in place mechanisms to charge those who use infrastructure through tolls and fees like road charging, particularly those private mobility services who rely on public resources—like roads—for their business models. In addition, federal, state, and regional funds will be needed for the significant undertaking that is developing a digital platform, coordinating agencies and companies to build out the system, and building out the regional vision for MaaS to occur. Ongoing funding will be needed to manage and iterate MaaS as technology advances in the years ahead.

The payoff: a quadruple bottom-line

With MaaS, the potential for a more sustainable transportation system is profound. Sustainability as a concept is based on the triple bottom-line: social, environmental, and financial. A fourth bottom-line should be considered for new mobility: user experience. This section explores the desired outcomes of a seamless mobility system.

Society

An autonomous future will have profound impacts on *public health*. First and foremost, AVs will only see widespread adoption if they are significantly safer than human drivers, meaning that nearly forty thousand lives could be saved each year in the United States alone. Less noise and less stress would also provide health benefits, as could improved access to health care and other social services.

Managed correctly, new mobility will result in *improved accessibility and equity*. According the Bureau of Transportation Statistics, about 15 percent of adults over the age of sixteen do not hold driver's licenses (U.S. DOT 2015). New, lower cost, and accessible travel options will increase access to opportunity for non-drivers and residents of areas with limited public transit. This is particularly critical given the trend toward the suburbanization of poverty (Kneebone 2017). For example, on-demand shared mobility services (e.g., autonomous Lyft Line) will be much better suited to the lower-density suburbs than fixed-route bus services.

Autonomous vehicles could also result in *more vibrant, affordable cities*. Parking takes up a significant amount of valuable land in our cities. Los Angeles County is estimated to have 14 percent of its area (two hundred square miles) devoted to parking, or about the same amount of land as the entire city of Chicago (Chester et al. 2015). Mobility-on-demand will likely reduce car ownership and with it the need for parking, potentially by as much as 90 percent (Rodier 2018). This land could be repurposed for housing, pedestrians, bicyclists, public transit, parklets, and open space. Construction costs for housing would also be reduced by lowering the burden of parking construction.

Environmental

Autonomous vehicles are truly an environmental wildcard, with the potential for increased demand to outpace gains in efficiency and electrification (Wadud et al. 2016). Taking an optimistic view, AVs could help *lower greenhouse gas and other emissions* by accelerating the transition to electric vehicles (EVs). According to Bloomberg Philanthropies, "The fate of AVs and EVs will only grow more intertwined in the coming decade" (Bloomberg Philanthropies 2017). Fleets are likely to be early adopters of electric vehicles, taking advantage of lower maintenance and fuel costs, such as off-peak electric charging. Smoother driving, platooning, and rightsizing vehicles for specific trips could help to *reduce energy use* (Bloomberg Philanthropies, 2017). High levels of EVs and improved vehicle-to-grid integration could leverage the temporal use patterns of vehicles and their power storage capacity to help load balance the grid with increased use of *renewable power* sources.

Financial

The potential for financial gain and economic development with new mobility is staggering. Intel Corporation and research firm Strategy Analytics estimate that "Autonomous driving technology will enable a new Passenger Economy worth US$7 trillion in 2050" (Strategy Analytics 2017). The potential for *massive financial returns*, as well as hedging against potential disruption to traditional transportation industries, is evidenced by the billions of dollars being invested by a wide range of companies, including established automobile manufacturers (e.g., GM), major technology companies (e.g., Google, Intel), mobility services (e.g., Uber), and startups of all sizes (e.g., Zoox).

Entire *new industries and business models* could be created to leverage new mobility. While approximately four million Americans make their living as drivers (U.S. DOT 2017a), the Rand corporation notes that "While the types of jobs that are likely to be lost are readily apparent, like other technological revolutions before it, the autonomous vehicle future will create new types of jobs" (Kalra 2017). Perhaps most fascinating is what we cannot predict. Much as the smartphone disrupted and spawned industries, so too will autonomous vehicles.

The seamless mobility future could also have financial benefits by *increasing productivity*, through less time behind the wheel and in congestion.

As noted previously, a future mobility system must be underpinned by an effective and *sustainable transportation infrastructure funding* mechanism. We will therefore be able to build and maintain high-quality roads, bridges, sidewalks, bicycle routes, and public transit. As the American Society of Civil Engineers reports: "The Federal Highway Administration estimates that each dollar spent on road, highway, and bridge improvements returns $5.20 in the form of lower vehicle maintenance costs, decreased delays, reduced fuel consumption, improved safety, lower road and bridge maintenance costs, and reduced emissions as a result of improved traffic flow" (Kalra 2017).

User experience

The end users of transportation—travelers and consumers—stand to benefit from MaaS on several fronts. The underlying benefit will be more mobility choices for people and goods as new modes, services, and business models are added to the MaaS ecosystem. More choices and enhanced information will enable better decision-making, tailored to optimize each individual trip. Limited options with large sunk costs (e.g., purchasing a car) will evolve into a wide spectrum of choices without fear of being stranded: take a larger autonomous vehicle to run errands with kids, use a shared microtransit service for commuting, rent a shared bike for a workout on the ride home, summon a luxury vehicle for a special night out.

New mobility also brings the promise of *lower transportation costs*. Labor costs make up nearly two thirds of the cost to operate public transit (American Public Transportation Association, 2018) and over 40 percent of the operating cost for trucking (American Transportation Research Institute, 2017). Private vehicles inherently include the cost of the driver's time, which could be reclaimed for more productive uses. The costs to use robotaxi services in the future are uncertain and debatable, but UBS forecasts costs could be 80 percent less than what ride-hailing platforms cost today, making them significantly cheaper than owning a private car for most people (UBS Group 2017).

Future mobility also holds promise that passengers will *save time*. Former drivers can engage in other activities while in motion: working, sleeping, socializing instead of being focused on the stress of driving. Several sources indicate that the average American driver spends about one hour a day behind the wheel, or about two full years over a fifty-year period of driving (U.S. DOT 2017b).

Table 2.1 An action plan for positive results

Learn: Research, pilot programs, and knowledge sharing are essential to inform policy decisions. **Prepare:** Take advantage of the pace of development to be proactive. Lay the groundwork with forward-looking regulations, investment decisions, and urban design. **Leverage:** Consider ways to build AV technology into existing systems and policies to leverage the technology to help realize larger community goals around MaaS. **Leverage:** Consider ways to build AV technology into existing systems and policies to leverage the technology to help realize larger community goals around MaaS.	**Partner:** The winning solutions will require collaboration amongst a wide range of stakeholders, including private corporations, public sector entities, advocacy groups, nonprofits, and academia. **Lead:** Difficult decisions, including public policy changes from the status quo, will be required. This will necessitate political leadership across a broad spectrum. **Adapt:** Recognizing that AV technology will be rolled out over many years, or even decades, public policy and business models will be necessarily iterative. Adaptability and flexibility will be critical.

Users will also benefit from *improved convenience* and *increased certainty*. Seamless mobility will be available at the touch of a button, free from the stress of driving, the hassle of owning and maintaining a vehicle. MaaS platforms will aggregate mobility options into a single user interface and point of sale. Better data will provide more accurate insight on travel times before and during the trip. Fewer collisions will reduce the unreliability associated with incidents.

Action plan

As other places in this book suggest, this optimistic future is far from certain. Achieving positive results on the quadruple bottom-line while navigating the substantial risks will require thoughtful action. Now is the critical time to act, when we can see the potential benefits and costs, but before the technological transformation is in full swing. Table 2.1 provides an overall action plan.

Conclusion

This vision for mobility as a service allows us to work toward a future in which big data and focused investments facilitate a seamless orchestration of mobility options within cities, adding tremendous value to society, the environment, and the economy. AV technology makes this shift possible by adding a new tool to the transportation network and bringing with it the potential to change the whole ecosystem of cities, including the role of the public sector, the future of public transit, land-use patterns, and entire economies. Success of such a future hinges on a total and complete paradigm shift in the transportation space. The work needed to realize this vision will require radical leadership at a regional scale, unwavering collaboration between and among private and public entities, and huge amounts of capital and innovation to augment our current transportation network and develop the resources to make seamless mobility work. In short: it will be an extraordinarily messy process. But the payoff could be huge.

This chapter focuses on the promise of new mobility: an optimistic look toward the future where there are opportunities to dramatically improve our transportation system. What is not covered is the potential harm and great risk that may arise in the face of new technology. With so many players vying for relevancy and a foothold in the new transportation landscape presented by AVs, many metropolitan areas are like the Wild West when it comes to emerging mobility options. Local planners and policymakers now find themselves in uncharted waters and must strike the balance between regulating these new tools and technology and capitalizing on their potential to help achieve community goals, and so far without a broad strategic vision. What follows is a more robust conversation about the perils of new mobility, and how, using the best available information, we might put in place the policies and plans that help prepare for risks and opportunities presented by AVs, but that also achieve desired outcomes regardless of technological shifts.

References

American Institute of Civil Engineers. 2017. "Infrastructure Report Card." Retrieved from: https://www.infrastructurereportcard.org/cat-item/roads/.

American Public Transportation Association. 2018. 2017 "Public Transportation Fact Book." Retrieved from: https://www.apta.com/resources/reportsandpublications/Documents/2017-APTA-Fact-Book.pdf.

American Transportation Research Institute. 2017. "An Analysis of the Operational Costs of Trucking: 2017 Update." Retrieved from: http://atri-online.org/wp-content/uploads/2017/10/ATRI-Operational-Costs-of-Trucking-2017-10-2017.pdf.

Bloomberg Philanthropies. 2017. "Taming the Autonomous Vehicle, A Primer for Cities." Retrieved from: https://www.bbhub.io/dotorg/sites/2/2017/05/TamingtheAutonomous-VehicleSpreadsPDF.pdf.

Chester, M., A. Fraser, J. Matute, C. Flower, C., and R. Pendyala. 2015. "Parking Infrastructure: A Constraint on or Opportunity for Urban Redevelopment? A Study of Los Angeles County Parking Supply and Growth." *Journal of the American Planning Association*, 81(4): 268–286.

Cookson, G. 2018. Inrix Global Traffic Scorecard.

Greenfield, A. 2014, July 10. "Helsinki's Ambitious Plan to Make Car Ownership Pointless in 10 Years." *The Guardian*. Retrieved from: http://www.theguardian.com/cities/2014/jul/10/helsinki-shared-public-transport-plan-car-ownership-pointless.

Kalra, N. 2017, August 29. "What Autonomous Vehicles Could Mean for American Workers. The Rand Blog." Retrieved from: https://www.rand.org/blog/2017/08/what-autonomous-vehicles-could-mean-for-american-workers.html.

Kneebone, E. 2017, February 15. Testimony before the House Ways and Means Committee, Subcommittee on Human Resources.

Rodier, C. 2018. "Travel Effects and Associated Greenhouse Gas Emissions of Automated Vehicles." National Center for Sustainable Transportation.

Siddiqui, F. 2018, March 24. "Falling transit ridership poses an 'emergency' for cities, experts fear." *The Washington Post*. Retrieved from http://www.washingtonpost.com.

Strategy Analytics. 2017. "Accelerating the Future: The Economic Impact of the Emerging Passenger Economy." Retrieved from: https://newsroom.intel.com/newsroom/wp-content/uploads/sites/11/2017/05/passenger-economy.pdf.

UBS Group. 2017, September 27. How disruptive will a mass adoption of robotaxis be? Retrieved from: https://neo.ubs.com/shared/d1gAiLhfW3FA/

United States Department of Transportation, Bureau of Transportation Statistics. 2015. "Licensed Drivers." Retrieved from: https://www.bts.gov/content/licensed-drivers.

United States Department of Transportation, Bureau of Labor Statistics. 2017a. Occupational Employment and Wages. Retrieved from: https://www.bls.gov/oes/current/oes536099.htm

United States Department of Transportation, Volpe Center. 2017b, December 11. "How Much Time Do Americans Spend Behind the Wheel?" Retrieved from: https://www.volpe.dot.gov/news/how-much-time-do-americans-spend-behind-wheel.

Wall Street Journal Staff, The. 2015, October 19. "Apple CEO Tim Cook Talks Music, iPhone Innovation and More at WSJDLive 2015." *The Wall Street Journal*. Retrieved from: https://blogs.wsj.com/digits/2015/10/19/apple-ceo-tim-cook-talks-new-frontiers-at-wsjdlive-2015-live-blog/.

Wadud, Z., D. MacKenzie, and P. Leiby. 2016. "Help or Hindrance? The Travel, Energy and Carbon Impacts of Highly Automated Vehicles." Transportation Research Part A.

Winston, C. 2013. "On the Performance of the U.S. Transportation System: Caution Ahead." Brookings Institute. Retrieved from: https://www.infrastructureusa.org/wp-content/uploads/2013/10/performance-transportation-system-caution-ahead-winston.pdf.

3 Balancing promise with peril

Ronald T. Milam and William Riggs

Introduction

How can we balance promise and peril in the new mobility future? In the first two chapters, we dialogued the positive and negative implications of disruptive transport. This chapter talks about the tools and information that planners and policymakers use to consider development. We focus on the ways travel behavior is changing and how we can achieve the benefits of new mobility and avoid the pitfalls. This concludes with suggestions and policy principles that guide cities to more sustainable and livable futures.

Given that we focus on how many private-sector market forces are changing travel decisions and behavior, it is important that we outline and underscore these as a starting point. These factors include:

- Reduces the cost of vehicle travel (in both money and time). The concept of mobility or transportation as a service (MaaS or TaaS) relies on only paying for the cost of travel when a trip is made. Sharing trips can further reduce individual traveler costs and is made convenient by app-based technology through smart phones.
- Eliminates burden of driving. Autonomous vehicles (AVs) complement the MaaS model by removing the driver from transportation network company (TNC) services or by allowing private vehicle owners to avoid the driving task. For TNCs, eliminating the driver lowers the cost of service. For private individuals, time otherwise spent driving is now available for other purposes.
- Reduces potential for collisions. AV technology offers the potential of computer- and sensor-aided travel that is designed to avoid collisions. If connected vehicle (CV) technology is also included, vehicle travel can occur with even greater awareness of environmental conditions to minimize the risk of collisions.
- Vehicle travel made more convenient. TNCs today provide door-to-door service, eliminate the chore of parking, and offer a variety of vehicle choices and services including wheelchair assistance and Spanish-speaking drivers. However, TNC trips are expensive enough that few people that rely on

vehicle travel are willing to forgo owning their own vehicles. The transition to AVs will change the cost equation, and vehicle design flexibility may result in even greater vehicle and service choices, in addition to providing more travel options for the young, elderly, and those with a range of disabilities.

These changes create decision points in how we manage roadways and curb space but also how we do transportation demand management. Given this we also explore the influence of the trends on travel behavior and consider government policy and regulatory responses (Rodriquez 2017).

To summarize, although some local municipalities like New York and London have limited new mobility services, most federal and state governments have accommodated disruptive transport. This can be seen in the explosive growth of TNCs and the openness to AV testing on public streets, even in states such as California, where recent laws are focused on reducing vehicle travel and encouraging more active transportation. In light of this, *a key policy question is what motivates this accommodation? Is it due to current lobbying and other political influence? Or, is it due to the potential for greater sharing of vehicles and trips that is necessary to achieve important government objectives from reducing congestion and emissions to increasing travel choices for everyone?*

This is a central concept because without government action, the private-sector business model for TNCs and MaaS generates revenue based on miles of travel, minutes of travel, and choice of vehicle/service. Hence, the private sector is currently incentivized to increase the use of vehicles while the public sector in states like California has spent the past couple of decades focused on reducing vehicle miles of travel (VMT) to improve sustainability. This has come in the form of encouraging efficient land-use patterns; building transportation networks that support walking, bicycling, and transit; and discouraging vehicle travel that requires substantial energy consumption.

To grapple with this dichotomy between what the market wants and the sustainable and equitable vision that many cities are trying to achieve, we first take a detailed look at the transportation planning context. This is something that is alluded to in the first two chapters, but we put an engineering approach on it. We then model potential new mobility outcomes and what they mean to land-use and transportation trends. We then dialogue what this means for potential policy responses.

Transportation planning context

To ensure a common understanding about how transportation professionals view transportation planning with respect to growth, land-use development, and transportation networks, some key planning terms are defined below.

- Mobility: the ease of moving on the transportation network.
- Accessibility: the ability to reach goods, services, and destinations (Caltrans 2010).

When evaluating effects of land-use changes associated with development proposals or proposed modifications of the transportation network, mobility and accessibility are central considerations for transportation professionals. For example, adding more residential development on an infill lot in a crowded downtown will tend to reduce mobility by exacerbating the effects of crowding or congestion, especially when congestion is simply measured based on vehicle speeds or delay. However, by placing more people closer to downtown destinations (i.e., places to work and shop), accessibility has increased because more people can reach the available goods and services in this area. Understanding how disruptive trends influence the mobility and accessibility dynamic is an important part of evaluating future transportation system changes.

Common to both measures is the influence of travel speed. It measures mobility directly and influences the cost of accessing goods and services in terms of money and time. Over the long-term, speed even influences the distribution of land use. In ancient cities, land uses remained concentrated because travel speeds were limited to walking or riding a horse. As new travel modes and energy sources emerged to power travel, speeds increased and so did the distribution of land uses.

With today's dispersed land uses, global citizens consume more of our time in travel and more energy compared to concentrated land-use patterns. When this energy is in the form of fossil fuels, we generate undesirable air pollution and greenhouse gas (GHG) emissions. Travel costs tend to also be higher for providing accessibility to communities with dispersed land use forms and the overall transportation infrastructure is expensive to operate and maintain. With heavy reliance on large personal vehicles for high-speed travel, substantial land area has been consumed to accommodate driving and parking. This continues to result in vast spatial inequity and numerous collisions, injuries, and fatalities.

Given the undesirability of these trends, focusing on land use and transportation has been a potential solution. Placing future land use development close to existing land uses and developing a supporting transportation network that better accommodates low-speed travel such as walking, bicycling, and scootering can help in this.

While some urban areas pursue this strategy, many local, regional, and state transportation plans continue to be filled with projects to expand the network supply (i.e., widening roadways). This strategy has failed to increase speeds and reduce travel times due to the recognized effects of induced vehicle travel (Milam et al. 2017). More effective alternatives, such as pricing travel demand as recommended by economists, consistently run afoul of political acceptability but are always just around the corner (Taylor 2018).

With this logjam of ineffective solutions as background, new innovative technology solutions such as AVs are being proposed to disrupt and improve today's transportation system. Continuing to define transportation problems as speeds are too slow (i.e., congestion) is contributing to new solutions that remain focused on increasing speeds or creating new travel choices that do not require our attention to tasks such as driving. TNCs such as Uber and Lyft remove the task of driving while bikes, electric bikes (e-bikes), and e-scooters in shared platforms are providing faster travel times on crowded downtown streets (and sidewalks) where vehicle speeds have dropped close to walking speeds (Agrawal 2018).

These new travel choices have also disrupted the status quo for transit where ridership across U.S. metropolitan areas has declined since about 2015 despite increased employment and a growing economy. This outcome is attributed in part to the expansion of TNCs but also lower fuel prices and increased car ownership (Siddiqui 2018). AVs have the potential to further reduce the cost of using vehicles and grabbing even more of the travel market—and that is without considering the potential for new innovations in aerial travel (i.e., Uber Elevate) and rail (such as HyperLoop).

As we enter a new era of transportation, mobility and accessibility will remain a central focus. The fundamental question for transportation professionals is, "How will disruptive trends affect the basic measures of mobility and accessibility, most notably, speed, travel time, and travel cost?" These metrics play a strong role in modal preferences that have consequences for sustainability, equity, return on transportation investments, and long-term land use. Other factors will also need to be considered including how the comfort and convenience of travel may change and how human behavior could be influenced by anchoring inertia, peer influence, and mental accounting that have been exposed through behavioral science research (Thaler & Sunstein 2009).

To understand just how much disruptive trends could change the status quo, we now focus on how new mobility and the transition from transportation network companies like Uber and Lyft to self-driven cars could dramatically influence future travel behavior and demand. We use travel-demand forecasts to help understand the direction and magnitude of change that could occur without the influence of new government policies and regulations.

Modeling disruptive trends

Disruptive trends extend beyond just the technology changes in transportation. While not a complete list, we identified sixteen factors related to trends including, but not limited to, job market health, fuel prices, social networking, vehicle ownership, AVs, and internet shopping. The potential outcome for the future travel associated with these sixteen factors is difficult to predict because of:

- Government regulation of AVs, TNCs, and new modes.
- Public transit agency responses to TNCs and AVs.
- Public acceptance and use of AVs and sharing them for regular travel.
- Public acceptance and use of new modes such as e-bike and e-scooters.

Despite the unknowns, these forecast models are very important. Transportation planners use models to help test future scenarios and to provide insights about potential future outcomes. Travel forecasting models, in particular, are constructed to predict travel behavior outcomes when inputs such as land use, demographics, or transportation network components are changed. In the United States, each metropolitan planning organization (MPO) typically develops a travel-forecasting model to comply with federal requirements to provide travel-demand forecasts associated with its regional transportation plan (RTP).

These forecasts help evaluate plan performance for VMT, transit ridership, and emissions. The models use observed travel behavior in response to existing land-use patterns, socio-economic conditions, and transportation systems. As such, if a disruptive trend is likely to change one of these elements directly or indirectly, a travel-forecasting model can be used to provide insight on how that change may manifest itself in terms of travel-demand changes. Limitations do exist in these applications, especially when trends influence factors not included in the models, but they provide a starting point to help anticipate change versus waiting for the change to occur—something Riggs and Boswell advocate for in this book.

In our case, we tested these scenarios using the travel-demand models of seven regions across the United States combined with similar test results from two additional regions. All model runs include full market penetration of AVs in the horizon year of the models, which was 2035 or later. This used the following travel-forecasting model variables related to travel behavior.

- Terminal time: Travel models define the time needed to park your car and walk to a destination as "terminal time." The higher a terminal time, the less likely a person will choose an auto for a particular trip. AVs are likely to reduce terminal times by eliminating the need to park and providing on-demand door-to-door service. The amount of reduction though will depend on how cities prioritize curb space use and their curb space management policies.

- Parking cost: Most models include a variable for parking cost in areas where costs are imposed. AVs have the potential to lower or even eliminate these traditional parking costs. However, cities in the future may impose pick-up and drop-off costs for AV use depending on location to help manage peak-period traffic demands.

- Value of time: Travel models also incorporate the value of time, but in different ways. Travelers using AVs will have lower values of time because the opportunity cost of driving will be reduced.

- Auto availability: Models generally have variables tied to trip rates and auto availability. AVs may increase trip rates due to their greater convenience and ready availability. Greater convenience could lead to more discretionary vehicle trips for shopping, social, leisure, or recreational purposes. Additionally, people not licensed to drive will be able to make vehicle trips. Vehicle availability will increase for many households and at workplace locations—especially those in urban areas.

- Roadway capacity: As vehicles become more automated and connected, they offer greater potential to increase roadway capacity especially on freeways. The increase in capacity will come from shorter headways, less weaving, and more stable traffic flows. Roadway capacity will increase first on freeways and expressways, then on major arterials. However, the potential exists that freeway interchange off-ramps where vehicles transition to the arterial system may become significant bottlenecks. The increases in freeway capacity could substantially increase the peak-hour flows reaching off-ramps that will not have sufficient capacity to accommodate those higher flows having been designed for much lower peak-hour volumes.

- Auto operating costs: Vehicle travel has costs associated with purchasing or leasing, operating, and maintaining the vehicle. Travel decisions tend to focus on the operating costs, such as fueling the vehicle, and can be expressed in a model as a per-mile cost to capture higher costs for longer-distance trips. For AVs, operating costs will depend on whether the vehicle is owned or offered through a TNC or MaaS-type platform. For individual travelers, it will also matter whether a trip is shared with other passengers. Nevertheless, the miles traveled will be a key factor in determining the cost of a trip.

- Auto occupancy: Auto occupancy is the number of persons per vehicle, and it has a substantial effect on the number of vehicle trips and related effects on how the roadway network operates. In traditional auto travel, the autos all have one or more people. With AVs, zero-occupant travel may occur. These "ghost trips" are largely associated with "vehicle balancing," such as getting to the next passenger, and have the potential to reduce auto-occupancy levels below 1.0.

The general expectation from testing AV effects was that vehicle travel would likely to increase and transit ridership would decrease for the main reasons cited at the beginning of this chapter.[1]

- AVs will reduce the cost of vehicle travel (in both money and time).
- AVs will eliminate the task of driving.
- AVs will reduce the potential for collisions.
- AVs will make vehicle travel more convenient.

The future of transportation disruption

The model results confirmed the expectations noted above, but the magnitude of the effects may be surprising. In sum, the long-term effects of AVs could include more dispersion of land-use growth (especially residential) and a greater willingness to make longer-distance trips because of associated decisions to live further away from destinations. Figures 3.1 and 3.2 show the range of effects captured by the models for vehicle travel and transit use. Each dot in the chart represents the results from an individual model, and the tests included both private ownership of AVs similar to automobile ownership today plus a scenario where 50 percent of drive-alone (i.e., single-occupant) trips were shifted to shared vehicles (i.e., carpools). The models were not capable (without substantial modification) of capturing the zero-occupant vehicle trips that would occur as AVs travel between different passengers or to final parking locations when not in use. Also, long-term land-use changes were not accounted for in these model applications. So, higher levels of VMT are possible.

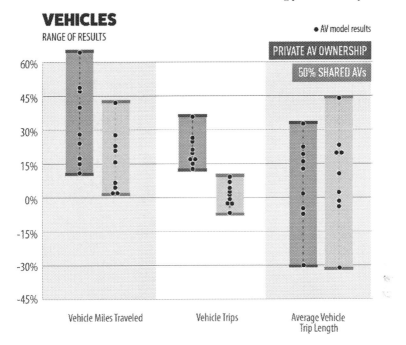

Figure 3.1 AV effects on vehicle travel

Source: Authors.

Clearly there are a range of impacts given the uncertainty and change in the transportation sector, so these results are best used by focusing on the range of potential effects. That said, some more specific summary bullets are provided below.

- Vehicle trips increase by an average of 20 percent without any shared-use regulation. That increase is virtually eliminated (on average) with 50 percent of the AVs required to be shared rides.
- VMT increases by an average of 31 percent without any shared-use regulation. That increase is halved (on average) with 50 percent of the AVs required to be shared rides.
- Transit trips decline by an average of 29 percent without any shared-use regulation, which grows to 35 percent with 50 percent of the AVs required to be shared rides.
- On average, bus and transit trips less than five miles decrease more than rail and transit trips greater than five miles.

In comparison to other research we see that these results may be highly relevant. For example, a unique experiment involving the provision of 60 hours of free chauffeur service for one week (Harb et al. 2018) and showed a VMT increase of 83 percent for those participating. While this experiment was conducted using

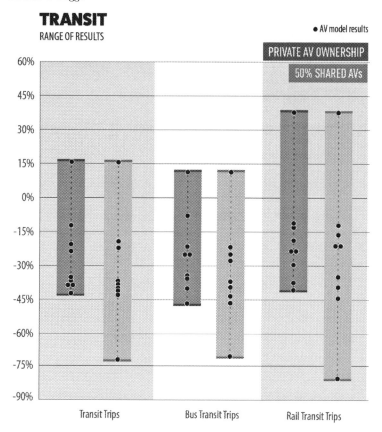

Figure 3.2 AV effects on transit ridership

Source: Authors.

a small sample of thirteen test subjects from the San Francisco Bay Area, it underscores the significance and importance of our modeling.

We do not claim that the model captures all induced growth and induced vehicle travel effects. Yet it provides (and was designed as) a "stress test" to better understand potential effects of disruptive transport. Our hope is that they help frame future behavior and transportation trends, and help inform future research and analysis.

Conclusion: future outcomes and policy

Given that these modeling results provide a framing, they also underscore the policy import. The actions of government can have a dramatic effect on these outcomes. Policy or regulatory responses can change costs of a ride or the number of people in a vehicle. Governments can use policy and regulation to balance the desires of private companies with the public good.

With that context in mind, we provide a brief list of potential policy and regulatory responses designed to offset the effects revealed by the modeling tests. In general, the responses include: increasing public transit competitiveness; increasing the occupancy of new mobility vehicles, decreasing their size, and increasing the cost of zero- or low-occupancy vehicle travel; and using land-use policy.

Transit competitiveness

Part of the explanation for the decrease in transit ridership is that transit travel times are much slower than automobile travel especially if delivered in a TNC or MaaS platform door-to-door. Today, TNC passengers have very short wait times, often less than five minutes, and in-vehicle travel times are similar to using a private auto. AVs could improve upon the wait time and possibly the in-vehicle travel time due to capacity increases. AVs will also reduce the cost of vehicle travel. In response, transit travel experiences and travel times need to improve to remain competitive as outlined below.

- Increasing frequency of service: Frequency directly influences wait times and provides flexibility to system users to come and go from destinations without having to worry about schedules. Increased frequencies become possible within transit operating budgets if AV transit technology reduces labor costs.
- Extending operational hours: To compete with vehicle travel offered through TNCs, MaaS, or private vehicle ownership, operational hours need to cover most of the day. Extending hours and geographic range of service become possible with transit vehicles and services that are "right-sized" to market demand based on land-use context as illustrated in Figure 3.3.
- Providing transit-only lanes: Similar to operational hours, in-vehicle travel time on buses needs to be faster to compete with vehicle travel. Transit-only lanes (during peak periods) improve roadway space efficiency and utilization and lower current in-vehicle travel times. With autonomous transit vehicles tailored in size and frequencies to match demand, these lanes can increase productivity.
- Automating transit service: Buses on fixed routes are one of the first opportunities for autonomous vehicle use. Fixed routes are easier to navigate than an open network, and the switch to autonomous operations reduces labor costs. Savings could be redirected to expanding core services, especially rail service, which would minimize the impact of driver reductions by increasing other operational and maintenance jobs. Savings could also be translated into reduced fares, with the possibility of offering free transit service that could stimulate a virtuous cycle of attracting more ridership and reducing cost per rider such that service could be expanded to attract even more riders. If automated operation is combined with technology for matching riders and vehicles, then autonomous rapid transit (ART) service could be offered. This type of service would operate in transit-only lanes but have

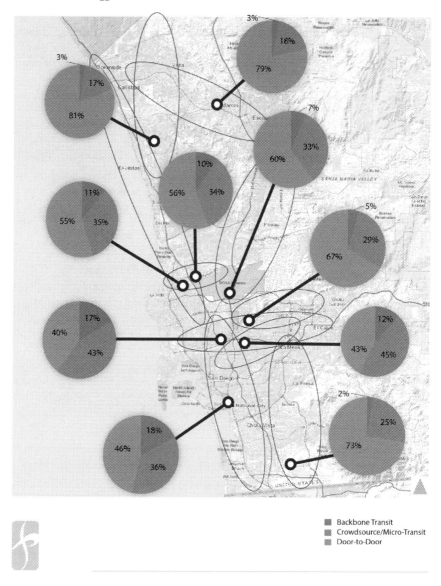

Figure 3.3 Right-size transit—matching demand to transit service type

Source: Authors.

the benefit of matching riders with common destinations together in transit vehicles. This type of matching similar to Uber Express Pool would allow the automated transit vehicles to skip some stations once the vehicle is full thus improving in-vehicle travel times compared to conventional bus or bus rapid transit (BRT).

- Better match or "right size" transit demand to type of service – TNCs, MaaS, and AVs offer expanded options for demand-responsive and crowd-sourced transit in low- to medium-density areas whether service is provided by the public or private sector. Private-sector TNC platforms benefit from costs only being incurred when a trip is made. Public agencies could benefit if allowed to operate this type of on-demand door-to-door service using a similar platform or by contracting for this type of cost-effective service when traditional fixed-route bus productivity would otherwise be low (e.g., less than ten riders per hour).

  As density and transit productivity increase, crowd-sourced transit service could be offered similar to Uber Express Pool or Chariot. The main idea is to provide a route-deviation service using micro-transit or small-transit vehicles that rely on real-time demand-responsive adjustments from crowd-sourced app technology. For truly dense corridors with the potential for high transit productivity, backbone or traditional fixed-route high-frequency rail and bus service operating in exclusive or managed rights-of-way would be provided.

  The maps in Figure 3.3 show the potential transit-market demand and associated types of transit service for trips in San Diego County. The first map reflects an assessment of potential transit market demand with the darker shading indicating areas with higher potential demand. The second map reveals how this demand could best be matched to the three types of services described previously: backbone, crowd-sourced, and door-to-door. Only select corridors are appropriate from a demand (and cost effectiveness) perspective for backbone transit service involving fixed routes. Much of the county, would be more cost effectively served with more flexible crowd-sourced and door-to-door type service especially if cost of service only occurs when trips are made. This type of service also has the best potential to attract new riders.

- Service performance and equity: A key challenge in ensuring that MaaS and TNC-type transit platforms are equitable is that they are market driven. While some data have shown that they can increase access to transportation resources, analyses have only been done in urban locations that have a fair degree of density. Planners and engineers do not yet know what the implications for more rural and poor areas might be. It could be that they would require subsidy or mandatory service standards for operations, to make sure that private providers maintain safe and reliable service access. This may be an important step since private providers serving in collaborative public roles, might need regulation so they do not suddenly pull from a market or deny rides and access.

Increasing occupancy or decreasing size

In terms of AVs, absent government regulations, initial implementation will likely occur through TNC or MaaS platforms (although companies like Tesla may offer AV technology through a traditional private-ownership model). While AVs offer potential benefits, such as reducing collisions, they also make vehicle travel more attractive. Increases in vehicle use could exacerbate current problems associated

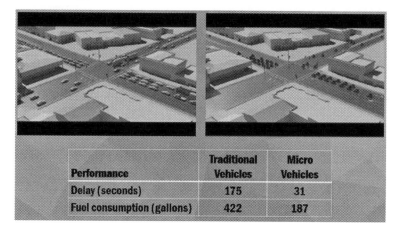

Performance	Traditional Vehicles	Micro Vehicles
Delay (seconds)	175	31
Fuel consumption (gallons)	422	187

Figure 3.4 Vehicle size effects on traffic delay and fuel consumption

Source: Fehr & Peers, 2018.

with congestion and emissions especially if vehicle sizes remain large and occupancy levels remain low. The following actions are intended to minimize adverse effects of greater vehicle use.

- Require AVs to be electric: Using electric power generation would minimize the emissions associated with AV travel.
- Support small or micro-sized AVs for personal use: Figure 3.4 shows how vehicle size influences intersection delay and fuel consumption. Today's large vehicle sizes (combined with low occupancies) consume substantial physical space, capacity, and green time at signalized intersections. Reducing vehicle sizes improves network performance.
- Manage or price AV travel to encourage high-occupancy levels: Various studies of AV effects emphasize that the only way to prevent substantial increases in vehicle use (i.e., VMT) is to require AVs to operate as taxis carrying multiple passengers. Building pricing into AV use early can help shift ground transportation toward more efficient travel outcomes and to partially offset transportation revenue losses from parking and citations. Instead of peak-period travel demand routinely overwhelming available roadway supply, demand-responsive pricing of AVs especially in TNC or MaaS platforms could help manage fleet sizes and roadway space utilization. This policy response is not simple, though, and would require addressing numerous issues typically raised for any U.S. road-pricing proposal. Notably, equity of any change given current system is publicly owned and perceived as "free" by users, absence of an existing market (creating prices does not necessarily create a market), use of revenues to ensure efficient outcomes, limited ability to transfer payments from those willing to pay for travel to those willing to forgo travel, and whether revenue transfers must account for who paid the taxes to build the current network.

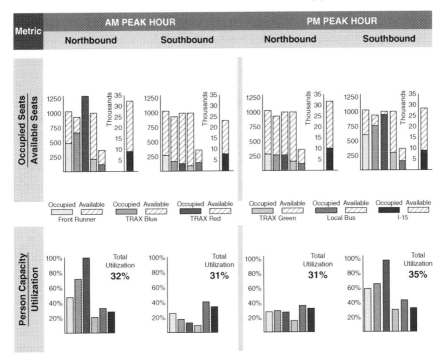

Figure 3.5 Seat utilization measurement—wasatch front central corridor study

Source: Authors.

Despite those issues, it is important to recognize that vehicle travel on today's roadway networks is characterized by very low seat utilization. As shown in Figure 3.5, freeways such as I-15 in Salt Lake City, Utah, have seat-utilization levels below 35 percent. This means that over 65 percent of the seats on the freeway during the peak period are empty. The United States suffers from congestion (i.e., slow-moving vehicles) because the combination of public and private sector incentives and disincentives for travel fails to fill existing seats. This is in sharp contrast to air travel where planes operate with very high levels of seat utilization. The lack of a market for vehicle travel and associated roadway pricing is directly related to this outcome. Absent a change to vehicle travel markets and pricing, AVs could potentially lower existing seat utilization levels due to zero-occupant trips.

Land use

As explained previously, new mobility and autonomous vehicles have the potential to contribute to more dispersed land-use patterns. Greater land-use controls, such as those on the following list, may be necessary to offset undesirable expansion of land-use development.

- Urban growth boundaries: AVs and new mobility may extend the distance people are willing to travel between their home and major destinations, such as employment and education centers. Urban growth boundaries are one mechanism for directing growth to help minimize undesired expansions of urban-area footprints.
- Zoning changes: AVs and new mobility may increase development pressure on land areas and parcels that previously were not envisioned for residential development. Some cities and counties allow residential development under a wide variety of zoning classifications. With housing supply constraints in many major U.S. cities, AVs may extend travel distances as noted above, which could increase demand to build residential homes on parcels originally intended for other uses.

In sum, this chapter began with the question, "How will disruptive trends affect the basic measures of mobility and accessibility, most notably, speed, travel time, and travel cost?" The evidence presented highlights that new mobility has the potential to increase the use of vehicles and extend regional accessibility by lowering the costs (money and time) of vehicle travel. Offsetting potential undesirable effects is possible but requires government actions. As we alluded at the start, and is reinforced throughout this book, the objectives of the private market to incentivize vehicle use may generate outcomes misaligned with important government objectives to reduce vehicle travel.

The private market will likely generate revenue from new mobility services and self-driving cars based on miles of travel, minutes of travel, and choice of vehicle/service. This structure does not guarantee that these vehicles will be shared. Instead it creates competition between service providers to reduce costs and increase choices to attract more riders. More miles and minutes mean higher revenue, and in this light, policy is needed to balance private-market interests with government goals such as reducing VMT, reducing emissions, and increasing active transportation. Uncertain outcomes create an opportunity for action—so that we can achieve the promise and avoid the peril of new mobility.

Note

1. While the nine regional models tested relied on different structures, software, quality of data inputs, etc., they represented a cross section of the current state of the practice. Further, additional models will continue to be tested and updated results will be posted to the following web page. http://www.fehrandpeers.com/autonomous-vehicle-research/.

References

Agrawal, N. 2018. "The Average Speed of Traffic in Midtown Manhattan Is 4.7 Mph. New York Thinks It's Found a Solution. *Los Angeles Times*. http://www.latimes.com/nation/la-na-new-york-traffic-manhattan-20180124-story.html.

Caltrans. (2010). *Smart Mobility 2010: A Call to Action for the New Decade.* Sacramento, CA. Caltrans.

Harb, M., Y. Xiao, G. Circella, P. Mokhtarian, and J. Walker. 2018 *Projecting Travelers into a World of Self-Driving Vehicles: Estimating Travel Behavior Implications via a Naturalistic Experiment.* Transportation Research Board.

Milam, R., M. Birnbaum, C. Ganson, S. Handy, S. and J. Walters. 2017. *Closing the Induced Vehicle Travel Gap Between Research and Practice.* Transportation Research Record: Journal of the Transportation Research Board, Volume 2653, 10–16.

Rodriguez, G. 2017. *Automated Vehicle Regulatory Challenges: Avoiding Legal Potholes through Collaboration.* League of California Cities.

Siddiqui, F. 2018. "Falling Transit Ridership Poses an 'Emergency' for Cities Experts Fear." *The Washington Post.* https://www.washingtonpost.com/local/trafficandcommuting/ falling-transit-ridership-poses-an-emergency-for-cities-experts-fear/2018/03/20/ ffb67c28-2865-11e8-874b-d517e912f125_story.html?noredirect=on&utm_term=. 1f012b416b43

Taylor, T. 2018. "The Stockholm Congestion Charge." *BBN Times.* https://www.bbntimes. com/en/global-economy/the-stockholm-congestion-charge

Thaler, H. and C. Sunstein. 2009. *Nudge. Improving Decisions About Health, Wealth, and Happiness.* Penguin Books.

Part II
Going small: Changes at the city scale

4 Shaping urban environments around transportation innovation

Michael Johnson and William Riggs

Introduction

The way we plan and experience our cities has been dictated by the automobile for the better part of a century. Thankfully, those paradigms are all being challenged by incredible opportunities associated with the new mobility future. As discussed in other chapters in this book, autonomous and connected vehicles will offer new ways of thinking about street right-of-way and provide new equitable forms of mobility to all. At the same time, these opportunities are also connected to challenges. Making personal automobile travel easier and more attractive could increase the number of trips taken and the distances people are willing to take trips.

As planners, designers and citizens, we must creatively re-think, adapt, and improve our cities to prioritize human contact and health, advance sustainability and resiliency while also minimizing the negative impacts of the new automobile travel. One way to start is to focus on new flexible ways to shape land and buildings. This chapter focuses on how we can address challenges at the local scale. These include things that we encounter everyday, such as how we use land, plan for open space and infrastructure and design for our streets. Technology related to automobiles is changing rapidly, causing an extreme sense of urgency, and we must act now to ensure that the design of our cities is ahead of technological innovation.

Three principles

To address new technological innovations in mobility and transportation, we suggest three core principles that should guide our thinking as planners and designers. These ideas are not new and unique, and are rooted in the works of those that have come before us like Christopher Alexander, Ian McCarg, and Jane Jacobs:

1 **Adapt spaces for people first.**
   Our cities should be built and adapted for people first, emphasizing health outcomes and human-powered movement and replacing space for cars with places for human contact.

2 **Create truly sustainable + resilient places.**

Cities represent the most sustainable form of development, but still fall short of goals to not only do less environmental harm but also mitigate climate change, respond to chronic streets and acute shocks, and generally improve quality of life. Along with technological advances, cities must emphasize systematic, sustainable, and resilient connections with nature to ensure success for generations to come.

3 **Be action-oriented.**

Our cities must establish a new paradigm-shifting relationship with automobiles. We do not need to wait for AV's to reduce or remove zoning parking minimums, decouple proximate requirements for parking from land uses, and recapture space for affordable housing, food growth, and other uses to ensure that our cities are inclusive and affordable to all. We must lead with flexible and forward-thinking solutions and policies. And we must start now.

We use these principles to frame our discussion on how we can shape the built environment around new innovations in transportation.

Adapt spaces for people first

The design and adaption of our cities must embrace and celebrate what it means to be human. Technology in our cities will continue to evolve, but our cities must first and foremost continue to exist as places for human contact, collisions, and innovation through improved land-use policy, open-space design, infrastructure, and streets.

For the first time in human history, more people live in cities than in rural areas. And while these cities occupy just 3 percent of global land area, it is within cities that we produce 80 percent of global GDP and generate 90 percent of innovation (Cox 2017; World Bank 2018). Yet, approximately 25 to 50 percent of a typical city is occupied by road right-of-ways generally dominated by personal automobiles. We should reprioritize the use of this valuable land to facilitate "collisions" between different kinds of people. It is not that hard to imagine the intentional redesign of our public realm to encourage more chance meetings, mixing of people of diverse backgrounds, and new kinds of meet-up spaces that not only improve our quality of life and enhance our human spirit, but also propel innovation.

Our city spaces should also be adapted to prioritize human health. At the most basic level, it is widely known that increased walking is directly connected to improved human health. And for many years our cities have been designed to discourage walking. To be sure, examples of human-scale walkable urbanism have continued to flourish in pockets. Many memorable and benchmark examples exist, from the medieval streets of European cities (celebrated by Allan B. Jacobs in *Great Streets*) designed far before the car, to the active city blocks of Manhattan that Jane Jacobs fought to preserve. From college campuses to main streets all over the world, walkability has persisted despite design practices and policies that have prioritized and emphasized the automobile.

But walkability in our cities is not as pervasive as it should be. A recent article on "Imagining the Driverless City" by the Urban Land Institute underscores that autonomous vehicles could be a boost to walkable urbanism (Kiger 2015). Despite the contemporary elevation of walkability as a popular buzz word, with metrics and websites like walkscore.com, and the linking of walkability to increased real estate values and quality of life, the redesign of our cities to truly emphasize walkability has not gone far enough.

Now, with the promise of AV's that will use less street right-of-way, and the potential to decouple parking from land uses in our cities, the time is now to take back spaces to serve people first, prioritize walkability, and improve human health outcomes. We must actively rethink the land-use implications, open-space networks, infrastructure systems, and street-design frameworks to ensure immediate health-oriented change in our cities. The design implications will vary wildly across geographic regions, but dedicating less space to personal automobiles and more space to people has the potential to improve public safety, increase opportunities for social interaction, provide accessible spaces for fitness, physical activity and exercise, and enhance emergency preparedness and resiliency.

Land-use policy

In a world of new and emerging transportation technology, there are myriad existing land-use policies that would not be eliminated (or subordinated) for the sake of emerging technology. Though there is currently very little land-use policy focusing on AVs, the emergence of this technology is not happening in a policy vacuum. Land-use plans, for instance, still control development in cities and regions. Housing and transportation plans and, in some cases, greenbelt policies still guide regional development in many parts of the country.

Yet these same land use policies in the United States have been dominated by Euclidian zoning principles, which emphasize single-use areas within our cities and intentional separation of places where we live, work, shop, and play. These principles directly fight against human contact and health outcomes. Euclidian zoning practices could not have perpetuated without the advent of the personal automobile, as individual everyday uses could spread across the city and out of walking distance. This, of course, has led to increased traffic and a challenging work-life balance, amongst others.

Current trends in land use and zoning regulations have emphasized more form-based solutions. These types of codes go back centuries but continue to gain popularity as they seek to control the physical form of our cities without micro-managing use. Form-based codes emphasize the relationship between building facades and the public realm, the form and mass of buildings in relation to one another, and the scale and types of streets and blocks.

However, like Euclidean mechanisms, form-based mechanisms make assumptions about personal automobiles that will be outdated, and do not truly emphasize human health and human contact. Our cities should emphasize the kind of social, physical, and individual environments that positively impact the social determinants of health. From dense urban cores to suburban environments, our health-centric approach to city building must demand and prioritize the following outcomes, accounting for nuanced regional differences and local priorities.

What can we do with land use to promote sustainability, in a world of smart, connected, and autonomous vehicles? First, adjustments to greenbelts and exurban growth controls might need adjustment to disincentivize long-haul commuting, but the policy groundwork and regional thinking for such changes are already in place. Many communities have already developed sophisticated methods for allowing sustainable (and climate-conscious) growth. Furthermore, some locations have devised strategies to incentivize smart growth by providing funding. For example, the grants stemming from programs like California's Affordable Housing for Sustainable Communities program, funded from the carbon market established by the California Global Warming Solutions Act of 2006 (the landmark reduction strategy by the state; also called Assembly Bill (AB) 32), can be applied to affordable and transit-connected housing units in the urban core.

Existing water and utility policies could also limit extreme commutes. In many communities, these policies limit suburban development—especially in an era of extreme weather and heat events. Likewise, moves by transportation engineers and planners to begin quantifying the environmental impacts of development projects based on vehicle miles traveled (VMT) rather than level-of-service (LOS) at intersections provides an additional regulatory tool to slow the rise of a cadre of super-commuters, traveling ever-increasing distances as AVs become more widely adopted.

Open-space design

Access to open space and park space is proven to improve mental health, reduce cardiovascular morbidity and mortality, reduce obesity and the risk of type 2 diabetes, and improve pregnancy outcomes. These spaces are directly linked to psychological relaxation and stress alleviation, increased physical activity, and reduced exposure to pollutants, noise, and heat (Ulrich et al. 1991; Wolch 2007; World Health Organization 2016). The concept of biophilic cities goes even further, suggesting that people have a physical and psychological need for nature and natural areas in their daily life. In his breakthrough 2011 book, Tim Beatley describes a biophilic city as a place "that puts nature first in its design, planning, and management; it recognizes the essential need for daily human contact with nature as well as the many environmental and economic values provided by nature and natural systems" (Beatley 2011). The opportunity to rethink the spaces in our cities once occupied by personal automobiles to provide these human health benefits is empowering. However, we have a long way to go.

Open spaces and park spaces in our cities is generally undersized already. The World Health Organization (WHO) suggests a minimum of nine square meters (ninety-seven square feet) per open space per capita in our cities, but this assumes that open space is safe, functional, and accessible. According to the study, a more appropriate number would be in the range of twenty-five to fifty square meters per capita. Our most densely populated global cities, where the most growth is projected, do not even come close to meeting this target. This includes Buenos Aires at roughly two meters per person (twenty feet), Tokyo at three meters m^2 (roughly thirty feet), Istanbul at five meters (fifty-four square feet), and Toronto at just over twelve meters or one-hundred-thirty-five square feet per person.

Setting an even more ambitious goal, the National Recreation and Park Association (NRPA) recommends ten acres per thousand residents, and that all residents be within a five-minute walk to access it. When considering this proximity between people and parks and open space, even fewer urban and suburban cities meet the mark. But there is hope. The Trust for Public Land owns over three million acres of open space and has built its mission around providing park spaces within a ten-minute walk of every resident in the United States. Also, while one in three residents lack access to a park or natural area (TFPL 2018), in many U.S. cities, including some of our densest cities, like Washington, D.C., New York City, and San Francisco all meet or exceed this metric.

As we rethink our cities in the context of AV and technological advances, we must simultaneously adapt our urban land to ensure improved health outcomes and access to open spaces that improve our mental health and cognitive functions, reduce diseases and mortality risks, improve social interactions, enhance physical activity and reduce obesity, improve air quality, and mitigate climate change (World Health Organization 2016).

Streets and infrastructure

Infrastructure in our urban environments has emphasized centralized approaches to provide power and clean water, remove and treat wastewater, and reduce flooding by conveying stormwater away as fast as possible. These "pipes and wires" of our cities have historically been buried underground and kept out of site or have been strung overhead in ways that leave them overexposed. Time after time these water and energy systems have broken down under the pressure of chronic stresses and the acute shocks of natural disasters, often with catastrophic implications for human life.

New technologies have allowed us to think differently about infrastructure in our cities. Advancements in renewable energy production and storage technologies that harness the power of the sun, wind, earth, and water, coupled with the opportunity to create more resilient, less centralized micro-grids, will reshape the way our cities are powered in the future. Similarly, water management in our cities is undergoing similar innovations emphasizing more local, district, and site-based systems and solutions. As defined by the American Society of Landscape Architects, green infrastructure is the overarching term that has been used to describe nature-based solutions in our cities to absorb and sequester atmospheric carbon dioxide (CO_2), filter air and water pollutants, stabilize soil, provide habitat, reduce energy use, improve water quality, and provide flood mitigation. Green infrastructure is crucial to combating climate change, while creating healthy built environments, and improving quality of life (ASLA 2018). When combined with advancements in technologies, specifically MaaS and AVs, there is an incredible opportunity to rethink the way spaces in our cities are used.

As an important and ubiquitous infrastructure element in our cities, streets form the connective backbone to land use, open space, and infrastructure systems. Streets provide a platform and language for global cities, small towns, and suburban areas alike. Regardless of geographic region, location, or density, streets represent a significant amount of space in the built urban environment (25 percent-50 percent of total urban land area). When we add space currently occupied by parking to the space dedicated to streets, the proportion of our cities dedicated to movement and storage of personal vehicles in relation to density is nothing sort of astonishing. The proportion of the space required has continuously grown along with increased automobile use. The result is that, for the better part of the last century, the space requirements for automobiles have competed with, cut off, and gotten in the way of spaces for human use. The design of our streets has perpetuated this imbalance. Reshaping urban innovation in our cities will begin with smarter use of our streets. General principles for the holistic design of our streets in coordination with AV technologies include:

- Provide less space for vehicles in the future and more space for people
- Emphasize human and active modes along our corridors
- Increase access to nature and vegetation in the right of way
- Mitigate flooding and improve water quality through green infrastructure
- Incorporate mixed-uses and density for affordable housing/equity along our streets
- Design our streets for flexibility
- Design our streets for adaptability
- Prioritize human safety and well-being

Because new mobility will be managed in ways that today's traffic cannot, we will have new opportunities to design and adapt our cities using a people-first mentality and encouraging reduced dedicated space for the automobile and new urban forms that were not possible before. While Chapter 5 dives deeper into the detail what the future street can be, in sum, our streets are the most important platform for this change. In addition to an emphasis on multimodal travel on streets—integrating public transit, bicycles and other modes of transport with AVs, cities must consider the reduction of dedicated pavement, the shared use of streets, and pedestrian-only environments.

Many cities are already planning for mobility with these principles in mind. Stockholm and Amsterdam have been wildly successful in bringing bicycles into the urban fabric. In its planning for the future, Stockholm is promising to go even further by promoting a dense and mixed-use urban environment that reduces travel needs and distances, while also connecting districts with multimodal linkages (City of Stockholm 2012; O'Sullivan 2017). Cities like Detroit are taking a more grassroots approach toward change. A group has built a movement around the city's burgeoning bike culture and organized a massive Slow Roll event in the

Motor City, with over five thousand cyclists taking to the city's oversized streets every Monday evening to ride through spaces once occupied solely by automobiles (Slow Roll 2018).

New disruptive transportation might not only reduce the need for parking but also the size of space on roads occupied by vehicles. Wide city streets could be narrowed, adding more space for landscape elements or even new buildings in some circumstances. In dense cities like Washington, D.C. or San Francisco, right-sizing roadways could create additional space for residential or retail development, similar to Las Ramblas in Barcelona. In overbuilt cities such as Detroit, green infrastructure or multi-use paths could continue to take the place of some roadways and unused parcels of land. The city of Indianapolis, Indiana, in the United States has created a cultural trail, taking road right-of-way to create a robust pedestrian and bike route that connects major cultural destinations throughout the city.

Create truly sustainable + resilient places

The process to rethink cities to incorporate AVs must be a built in an environment that takes sustainability and resilience seriously. Future advances in renewable energy production and storage, combined with efficiencies provided by automation and technology, have the potential to create urban environments that are less wasteful and destructive to the environment and to human health than today's cities.

In many ways, cities already represent our most sustainable models of development. But cities still produce 50 percent of our global waste, consume 70 percent of our natural resources, and account for 80 percent of global greenhouse gas emissions annually. By 2050 cities will be home to two-thirds of the world's inhabitants, making it imperative that we find innovative ways to reduce our environmental impact at a city scale.

Resilience is generally defined as the capacity to prepare for disruptions, recover from shocks and stresses, and adapt and grow from a disruptive experience. The need for designing this capacity in the built environment has never been more pressing. The costliest year on record for natural disasters within the United States was 2017, with total damages amounting to $306 billion—an incredible 40 percent increase above the previous record. Compounding this is the widening gap between insured and uninsured losses to disaster damage, a gap that also grew to a record $193 billion worldwide in 2017. The reliance on insurance to manage risk and recover from disruptive events is failing in the era of climate change. It was reported that about 80 percent of victims of hurricane flood damage in the United States were uninsured.

It's not the first time we've seen these headlines—or the data that indicates that weather and climate-related disasters are increasing in frequency and severity worldwide. We also continue to learn that our planning policies and decisions have disproportionately increased the impacts of these disasters, especially for our poorest residents and communities. We are not only inadequately prepared to withstand and quickly recover from these growing risks, but our building codes, our regulatory policies, and the way we build and develop our communities frequently exacerbate the problems we are facing.

The shift to new mobility and AVs plays a big role in our ability to create more sustainable and resilient cities that use less energy, convert infrastructure into green space, and address the vulnerabilities posed by both chronic stresses and acute shocks. Our rethinking of urban spaces and infrastructure vacated by personal vehicles in an AV-led future can help us close the growing gap between risk and our ability to manage that risk through forward-looking planning and design. This may also be our best shot to proactively adjust to climate change and reverse destructive trends looming over our cities. The Landscape Architecture Foundation (LAF) has made this explicitly clear in their recent call to action:

> After centuries of mistakenly believing we could exploit nature without consequence, we have now entered an age of extreme climate change marked by rising seas, resource depletion, desertification and unprecedented rates of species extinction. Set against the global phenomena of accelerating consumption, urbanization and inequity, these influences disproportionately affect the poor and will impact everyone, everywhere. The urgent challenge before us is to redesign our communities in the context of their bioregional landscapes enabling them to adapt to climate change and mitigate its root causes (Landscape Architecture Foundation 2016).

The mitigation of climate change is a complex issue that many see reaching an irreversible tipping point. However, we cannot allow a sense of fatalism to stop us from doing what we can to do reduce and sequester carbon. New mobility and transportation solutions represent one of our biggest opportunities for positive gains. The transportation sector in the United States generates the largest share of greenhouse gas emissions (28 percent). Greenhouse gas emissions from transportation primarily come from burning fossil fuel for our cars, trucks, ships, trains, and planes (U.S. EPA 2015).

We need immediate prioritization of policies that require reduction of greenhouse gas emissions from the transportation industry. And we need to rapidly increase carbon sequestration in our cities. Sequestration can take many complex forms, but something we can all do can be as simple as planting more trees in our parks, open spaces, and along our city streets. For example, the city of Ann Arbor, Michigan (population 120,000), has over 1.45 million trees that remove 405 tons of pollution per year, which is equivalent to the pollution produced by 358,000 automobiles annually (City of Ann Arbor 2018). Already affectionately known as "TreeTown," the city's recent forest management plan demonstrates a commitment to strengthening the health of its canopy and planting over 1,100 new trees every year on public and private lands. But is that enough? How can we use our street right-of-way at a city scale to exponentially increase the number of trees we plant? The city of Beijing has recently taken a more extreme approach to tree planting, recently announcing plans to create a "green necklace" of trees to clean the city's air (Wong 2017).

Tree plantings are an achievable and economically sustainable solution. In a study of five U.S. cities, each dollar invested in urban trees returned between $1.37 and $3.09 in benefits. Benefits measured include energy savings, atmospheric CO_2 absorption, air-quality benefits, stormwater runoff reduction, and aesthetic and other benefits gauged by measuring increases in real estate values (McPherson et al. 2005).

In the context of AVs and potential sustainable and resilient impacts, our primary and immediate responsibility is to help cities evaluate and capitalize on the unrealized opportunities in their outmoded facilities, strained infrastructure, and underutilized properties—most of which were built around the automobile. This adaptive approach can bring resourceful transformative potential to gridlocked streets, tired public spaces, cut-off neighborhoods, abandoned industrial sites, and contaminated urban streams.

Be action-oriented

Despite literature that suggests new mobility and autonomous vehicles will require less street width and fewer parking spaces, there is a danger that our cities will end up dedicating even more urban space to AV's in order to adopt them. This issue is especially important to address during the critical transition period over the next 20-30 years when AV's will need to co-exist with human-driven automobiles and all other transportation modes. As planners, designers and citizens, we cannot afford to wait and see what will happen to our streets and parking resources as vehicle technology rapidly changes. Because as we do, even our most dense cities like New York are already considering strategies that prioritize adding additional dedicated street real estate for privately-owned AVs, which would take us down the same car-centered design road of the past (Schneider 2017). We cannot let car-driven thinking dictate the design of our cities again. We need to ensure that the physical design of our streets and urban environments is out in front of the rapid advances in vehicle technology.

While AV's are already being tested on many of our streets, it may take decades for the benefits of AV's to be fully realized in our cities. Now is the time to plan, design, and implement flexible street environments to ensure that AV's do not further destroy our cities by putting efficient automation before people. As AV technology continues to advance, cities must maintain relevance by doing what they have always done best: celebrating people and emphasizing human connection, interaction, and commerce. This does not require expensive design and high-designed environments. Nor does it require complete re-writes of our zoning codes and street design manuals. We can and should start immediately, embracing the "pop-up" design movement that has started to take back our streets and public spaces.

The American Society of Landscape Architects (ASLA) started a grassroots movement, dubbed "(Park)ing Day," in which parking spaces are converted to small urban parks for a day. Open Streets programs have been employed in cities across the United States, temporarily opening streets to people by closing them to cars. Pop-up programming usually accompanies these events as communities rally around the idea of taking back their car-dominated streets for more productive functions and benefits. For example, Open Streets Detroit is a collaborative public/private effort that closes nearly four miles of Michigan Avenue, one of the city's key arterials, in Corktown one day a year (Runyan 2017). This kind of tactical urbanism has been extremely successful helping people envision a future for their streets that is not built around the automobile. There is no reason why these conversions cannot be more permanent, like New York City has done with Broadway (PPS 2018).

Detroit has taken an even more provocative and tactical approach as part of a Knight Foundation funded effort dubbed Mix Tape Zoning. To encourage more small scale-development along the city's hundreds of miles of desolate commercial corridors, Detroit is employing a series of "Pink Zones" along key commercial corridors to test zoning changes. This lightening of regulatory red tape encourages reduced parking requirements, more pedestrian space, by-right opportunities for housing that did not exist before, and improved treatment of stormwater. Much of this is being phased in such a way that the initial investment is done via pavement reduction, use of permeable pavers, and street paint.

Parking management in our urban environments should also be an immediate target for positive change. Because parking lots are controlled environments, AV technology could be quickly deployed there, thereby rapidly freeing up valuable, former parking land on and off the streets. Adaptive reuse of parking spaces could facilitate redevelopment of that land to other important uses.

For example, parking in Houston's Central Business District makes up over 21 percent of land use. How might this land be reenvisaged in the future? What are the things we can do right now to better utilize portions of this valuable resource? Adding more parks to reduce impervious surfaces might improve stormwater runoff, urban ecology, and human wellness. New development in these parcels could be incentivized to promote affordable housing. Parking structures could be reimagined for a variety of uses including improved e-commerce delivery, event venues, and even shared working or living spaces.

Now is the time to act, to ensure that we, as planners and designers, can get ahead of the rapidly changing technologies of automobiles. We do not have to wait and be reactive to that technology, and we do not have to wait to rewrite entire zoning codes. Tactical urbanism provides a low-risk platform to rapidly test and prototype ideas in real-time, providing extensive outreach and allowing for appropriate buy-in from skeptical community members and stakeholders. And who knows, maybe some of it will stick!

Conclusion

In sum, while emerging forms of transport may bring about new challenges in transportation accessibility, as was dialogued to start this book, they also provide great promise. They herald opportunities to reshape the way we configure our cities, from land use to design, and with appropriate policy constructs to limit their negatives, can help lead to a more sustainable and just urban future. While things like sprawl and uncontrolled growth should still be considered, they present a decades-old challenge that continues to require a balanced approach to how, and where, communities grow. It is important that cities become more experimental with all the land they own—most importantly their streets. AVs may present a challenge to questions about growth, but they also present an opportunity to optimize travel within existing urban areas and for individuals underserved by current transportation infrastructure.

References

ASLA. 2018. "Green Infrastructure." *American Society of Landscape Architects*. 2018. https://www.asla.org/greeninfrastructure.aspx.

Beatley, T. 2011. "Biophilic Cities: What Are They?" In *Biophilic Cities*, 45–81. Island Press: Washington, D.C.

City of Ann Arbor. 2018. "The Urban Forest." https://www.a2gov.org:443/departments/forestry/Pages/The-Urban-Forest.aspx.

City of Stockholm. 2012. "Urban Mobility Strategy." Stockholm: City of Stockholm.

Cox, W. 2017. "How Much of the World Is Covered by Cities? | Newgeography.Com." http://www.newgeography.com/content/001689-how-much-world-covered-cities.

Kiger, P. 2015. "Imagining the Driverless City." *Urban Land Magazine*. October 2, 2015. https://urbanland.uli.org/industry-sectors/infrastructure-transit/imagining-driverless-city/.

Landscape Architecture Foundation. 2016. "The New Landscape Declaration." Philadelphia. https://lafoundation.org/myos/my-uploads/2017/02/03/laf-new-landscape-declaration.pdf.

McPherson, G., J. R. Simpson, P. J. Peper, S. E. Maco, and Q. Xiao. 2005. "Municipal Forest Benefits and Costs in Five US Cities." *Journal of Forestry* 103(8): 411–416.

O'Sullivan, F. 2017. "Stockholm Starts a Friendly Rivalry Over Car-Free Planning." CityLab. 2017. https://www.citylab.com/design/2017/05/stockholm-pedestrian-downtown-plans-oslo/526464/.

PPS, 2018. "Broadway Boulevard: Transforming Manhattan's Most Famous Street" Project for Public Spaces. https://www.pps.org/article/broadway-boulevard-transforming-manhattans-most-famous-street-to-improve-mobility-increase-safety-and-enhance-economic-vitality

Runyan, R. 2017. "Open Streets Detroit to Include Dancing, Fitness, Art, and More [Updated]." *Curbed Detroit*. September 15, 2017. https://detroit.curbed.com/2017/9/15/16313514/open-streets-detroit-activities.

Schneider, B. 2017. "Don't Let Autonomous Vehicles Revive Car-Centric Planning." CityLab. 2017. https://www.citylab.com/transportation/2017/07/will-autonomous-vehicles-lead-to-a-resurgence-of-auto-centric-infrastructure/534804/.

Slow Roll. 2018. "Slow Roll–Home Page." 2018. http://slowroll.bike/index.php.

TFPL. 2018. "Trust for Public Land." The Trust for Public Land. 2018. https://www.tpl.org/ourland#sm.0000118u3n02lxec4vqo8a78xugy7.

Ulrich, R. S., R. F. Simons, B. D. Losito, E. Fiorito, M. A. Miles, and M. Zelson. 1991. "Stress Recovery during Exposure to Natural and Urban Environments." *Journal of Environmental Psychology* 11(3): 201–230.

U.S. EPA, OA. 2015. "Sources of Greenhouse Gas Emissions." Overviews and Factsheets. U.S. EPA. December 29, 2015. https://www.epa.gov/ghgemissions/sources-greenhouse-gas-emissions.

Wolch, J. 2007. "Green Urban Worlds." *Annals of the Association of American Geographers* 97(2): 373. https://doi.org/10.1111/j.1467-8306.2007.00543.x.

World Bank. 2018. "Urban Development." Text/HTML. World Bank. http://www.worldbank.org/en/topic/urbandevelopment/overview.

World Health Organization. 2016. "Urban Green Spaces and Health." Copenhagen. http://www.euro.who.int/__data/assets/pdf_file/0005/321971/Urban-green-spaces-and-health-review-evidence.pdf?ua=1.

Wong, E. 2017. "China to Plant 'Green Necklace' of Trees Around Beijing to Fight Smog". *The New York Times*. March 23, 2017. https://www.nytimes.com/2017/03/23/world/asia/china-to-plant-green-necklace-of-trees-around-beijing-to-fight-smog.html.

5 Transforming street design

Approaches to reengineering our neighborhood streets

William Riggs, Marc Schlossberg,
Elizabeth Shay, and Adam Millard-Ball

Introduction

Global citizens get few moments to rethink streets and make decisions that will both serve the basic purposes of transportation *and* address urgent challenges like climate change, rising obesity, social isolation, and conflict—all while expanding opportunities for general happiness throughout society. Such a pivotal moment is upon us with the emergence of many disruptive transportation innovations and the coming of the autonomous vehicle or driverless car (Larco 2017). City planners, policymakers, and community residents have a unique, and immediate, opportunity to rethink their streets, and about streets can best serve the public.

In particular, autonomous vehicles present new and unique opportunities for fresh thinking about how streets are used—for whom, how, why, and to what ends. The bulk of transportation planning over the last fifty-plus years has conflated the basic purpose of transportation—providing access to destinations—with the simplistic goal of moving motor vehicles at high speeds with limited impedance (Cervero, Guerra, and Al 2017). Streets have been designed for movement of cars, with other road users treated as an afterthought—if at all (Riggs and Gilderbloom 2016).

As evidence mounts that there is no way to build our way out of congestion, and as the contributions of cars to air and water pollution become more stark, cities have begun to rediscover the benefits of walking, biking, and transit (Schlossberg et al. 2013). They also have begun the slow process of rearranging land uses and updating zoning codes to promote the fundamental purpose of transportation through these non-auto modes (Talen 2013). The general shift toward urbanism underway across the United States is making walking to many destinations easier, more enjoyable, and more widely accepted as natural and beneficial (Glaeser 2011).

At the same time, to date, progress toward sustainable transportation has been slow, but in this chapter, we show how planners and policymakers can seize on the potential of autonomous vehicles to accelerate the transformation.

History tells us that a concerted effort will be needed to channel the potential of autonomous vehicles toward sustainable transportation (Coles 2016). The last

---

What streets provide

Transport—to move people, freight, information
Accessibility to goods, services, activities
Equity of access and impact—highways that disrupt vs. streets that connect
Economic and social exchange
Space for community infrastructure—utilities and ecosystem services
Public and social—plazas, boulevards, waterfronts
Cultural and artistic canvases

---

major technological revolution in transportation—the rise of the motor car—saw parked cars spread out to fill every corner of public space, and a rising death toll as cars sped down streets that were historically places for walking, children's play, and social interaction. Cities responded through regulating curb use, installing the newly invented parking meter, moving pedestrians to the sidewalk and children off the street, and creating the new offense of jaywalking. While initial public opinion placed the blame for collisions on the car, a concerted campaign by the auto industry shifted the onus on pedestrians to stay out of the street (Millard-Ball 2016).

New mobility and AVs offer a new entryway into society-wide conversations about transportation, functions of cities, the use of streets and how all of these issues impact equity, environment, social cohesion and happiness, local economies, and more (Riggs and Boswell 2016a; Riggs and Boswell 2016b; Riggs, LaJeunesse, and Boswell 2017; Riggs and Boswell 2016c; Fagnant and Kockelman 2014; Guerra 2015). They are likely to disrupt things from city centers to suburbs to at least the urban/rural edges. They may add to the mix of transportation options, may replace some forms of transportation as we know it currently, and could influence changes to land-use systems in a wide variety of ways. That said, cities can and do control what happens on its streets and on its land and therefore still have an active role to play in determining how people move about within limited space. Ultimately, how cities regulate the use of the street will be key as competition for limited space will only increase.

Given this opportunity, it is worth taking time to consider the opportunities to rethink the physical design of the street.

Major opportunities: rethinking street space

While there are other anticipated benefits of autonomous vehicles, one of the most clear and certain outcomes is the space saved by the vehicles. Physical space allocated to vehicles, whether for storage (parking) or for movement (lanes), claims a substantial share of urban road networks. The advent of AVs presents opportunities to rethink how public street space is allocated, given potentially lower demand for parking and travel capacity.

Without delving into the details of how vehicle storage is likely to shift in space (to peripheral locations) and in time (based on peak hour needs), a shift toward AVs is likely to free up space in several ways:

- Lane *space* may be reduced, with narrower lanes for smaller vehicles.
- Lane *miles* may be cut as automation supports denser packing of traveling vehicles, and some lanes are determined to be excess.
- Parking *demand* on streets may be reduced by decreasing vehicle size, by ownership being replaced by renting or sharing models, and by the ability of AVs to drop off the passenger and then park remotely.
- Parking *supply* may be removed by policy or by market mechanisms.

Reduced demand for both storage and travel space in urban areas presents substantive opportunities to reclaim physical space for other purposes, reinforcing the conditions that require and support sustainable transportation. Examples of other uses for such reclaimed space include infill housing and small-scale retail and commerce, recreation (active and passive), and public and social purposes. Schools could extend their presence and activities into former parking or travel lanes; household gardens or community agriculture could fill small spaces; art or cultural activities—creation, performance, instruction—could find a platform. This short and generic list of potential alternative uses of space is a placeholder for the purposes a community may consider and then designate for shared goals identified through active public discourse.

The potential to reclaim urban space for existing needs and future public purposes exists regardless of how AVs are fueled (electric, fossil) or whether they are individually owned, shared, or rented. At the same time, the ownership regime will dictate the kind and level of space savings to be harvested, with a shared model offering more profound reductions in parking demand, making this question a point of interest to planners and policymakers in the run-up to and during the shift to AVs.

Focusing on the street as real estate

Given this background we focus on the primary concept of the street as space that can be repurposed, or real estate that can be allocated in similar or different ways than done currently. Cities generally refer to the space from one side of the street to the other as the right-of-way (ROW), and we focus on how this space can change to support the primary functions of a sustainable transportation system. This perspective is distinct from many other current publications and reports that have expounded on transportation innovations or revolutions that are occurring in parallel with the evolutions of autonomy and artificial intelligence (Fulton et al. 2017; Cohen and Shaheen 2017; Litman 2014; Bahamonde et al. 2016; Anderson et al. 2014; Lipson and Kurman 2016; Isaacs 2016; Airbib and Seba 2017; Firnkorn and Müller 2012; Meyer and Shaheen 2017; Brown et al. 2014).

Focusing on the physical space allows us to avoid some of the speculation about vehicle sharing and the possible over-optimism among many city planners about the extent to which a shared-use model will supplant private car ownership (Clewlow and Mishra 2017), because the ROW will be impacted in either case. Further, although there are some assumptions about the shared nature of vehicles elsewhere in this book, questions of buying vehicles or buying rides are largely out of the control of cities, and in the domain of automakers (sometimes called OEMs, or original equipment manufacturers) or transportation network companies (e.g., Uber and Lyft). Hence we focus on physical space.

The opportunities of lanes and parking

While safety is often cited as a primary anticipated benefit of autonomous vehicles, one of the other clearest socially beneficial outcomes is the potential space saved by smaller vehicles traveling more closely together and in service for more hours. Without delving into the details of how vehicle storage is likely to shift in space (to peripheral locations) and in time (based on peak hour needs), we can anticipate that AV penetration will free up street space in two ways:

1 **Lanes**—both *number* and *space*—may be reduced, as many AVs will be narrower, require less space between vehicles, and will be capable of sharing opposite-direction lanes as available. If the AV future is substantially populated by shared fleets instead of individual ownership, then the actual number of vehicles on the road may be substantially lower, with the follow-on effect of requiring still less lane space.
2 **Parking** *demand* on streets may be reduced by decreasing vehicle size, by ownership giving way to renting or sharing models, and by a shift to curb passenger delivery paired with remote storage. Parking *supply* may be removed by policy or by market mechanisms—reducing the need for on-street parking to store vehicles.

Reduced demand for both storage and travel space in urban areas presents a rare opportunity to reclaim physical space for other purposes. How might that liberated space be reallocated? Non-auto transportation, infill housing, small-scale retail and commerce, urban ecological corridors, recreation (active and passive), and other public and social purposes all merit consideration. Schools could extend their presence and activities into former parking or travel lanes; household gardens or community agriculture could fill small spaces; art or cultural activities—creation, performance, instruction—could find a platform. When given a newly blank canvas, our communities may be quite creative with imagining how to fill it.

This potential to reclaim public space currently dominated by the movement and storage of vehicles exists regardless of how AVs are fueled (electric, fossil) or whether they are individually owned, shared, or rented. At the same time, the ownership regime will dictate the kind and level of space savings to be reaped, with a shared model offering more profound reductions in parking demand—making this a particular point of interest to planners and policymakers in the run-up and transition to AVs.

With our focus on the ROW and possible alternative uses that may become possible with the rise of AVs, there may be different visions for what a street can be in the future—within different urban places. The following section delineates a series of hypothetical street sections for both a prototypical urban and a residential street, using the ReStreet design tool (Riggs, Boswell, and Ross 2016; Riggs 2017; Riggs 2018).

Urban street design

Four-lane streets with on-street parking are a common urban street type in these neighborhoods. Such streets juggle the competing demand of moving large volumes of traffic, providing parking, and providing pedestrian access to local businesses. A typical design has two lanes for vehicles in either direction, on-street parking, sidewalks, and perhaps a center turn lane or some space for trees or other amenities.

As we "deconstruct" the street section, as shown in Figure 5.1, we explore how the valuable right-of-way resource can be transformed in an AV future. For example, as on-street parking and other street ROW becomes available (proactively or by default), there is a small set of critical basic street design elements that may be implemented in ways that maximize walking and biking as a first priority, then to support transit, and finally to accommodate AVs. These basic building block of street cross sections include:

- Building facades (front, street-facing elevations)
- Sidewalks and paths
- Protected bikeways
- Curbs and other edges
- Transit lanes, stops, and drop-off zones
- Vehicle lanes—travel and parking

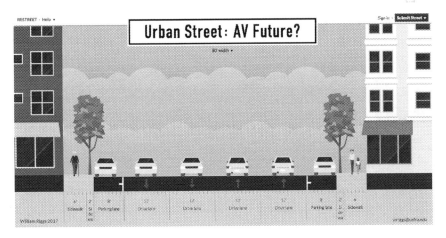

Figure 5.1 A typical urban street

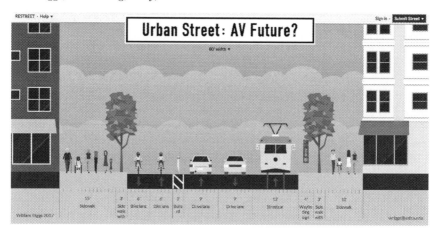

Figure 5.2 A typical urban street in an AV future

Increasing auto-free zones is also a useful goal, as indicated in Figure 5.2, insofar as they are implemented in ways that increase vitality and efficiency of the ROW and convey environmental benefits. Driveways can be expected to decline—in number and in size—as the need to accommodate building-adjacent parking drops substantially, simultaneously enhancing the pedestrian and bicycling environment. Driveways will be used primarily for freight/goods access, with attendant decreases in frequency and increases in flexible control over use.

A long-run goal for a street that incorporates these principles as a car-free downtown area, is depicted in Figure 5.3.

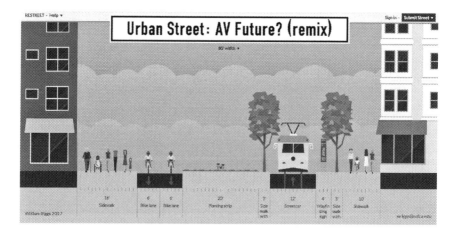

Figure 5.3 A radical urban street in an AV future

Suburban/residential street design

A typical residential street cross section, as shown in Figure 5.4, includes on-street parking on both sides of the street and usually enough street width to accommodate three lanes of moving vehicles, although only a single "lane" in each direction is used. In most residential streets, it is a rare event to have two opposite-moving vehicles pass each other on any given block. Moreover, since most properties are required to have off-street parking, most residential streets can already be considered significantly overbuilt in terms of vehicle infrastructure. The rise of autonomous vehicles will only make this mismatch between supply and demand more apparent, raising opportunities for creative retrofit—maybe even streets that are turned in to gardens or play spaces.

Like urban streets, residential streets in some neighborhoods have the potential to be completely different in the future. Reducing and combining lanes has the potential to make the public right of way safer and accessible to more people for more uses. Sidewalk- or bikeway-adjacent lanes, which previously may have served as parking lanes, may be repurposed for other uses—or they may serve as intermittent catchment zones as AVs move through and respond to the environment, and need extra space to load, unload, or pass.

Thus, residential streets offer even more exciting possibilities to repurpose street space, given that the primary purpose of such streets is usually access, rather than through movement. Similar to the urban prototype and as is depicted in Figures 5.5 and 5.6, as space previously allocated to lanes and parking becomes free, it can be apportioned to other travel modes. Parking needs in residential areas also can be expected to decrease and may result in re-purposed private driveways and garages, while former on-street parking becomes publicly available for reuse.

Again, could this be for the reimaging of the street as a park or public greenway? It could be that we transition not only to safer streets but that the street begins to erode away—dissolving into or even becoming a part of the natural landscape.

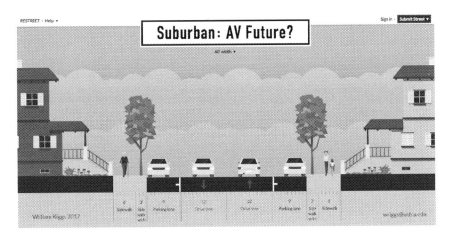

Figure 5.4 A typical suburban street

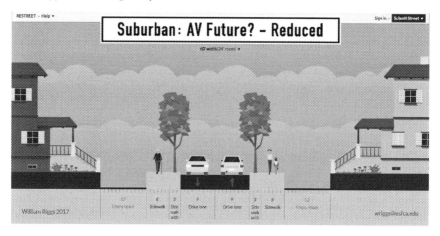

Figure 5.5 A typical suburban street in an AV future

Principles for practice and research

The technology to guide AVs is still emerging. Detection, prediction, and response of vehicles to the environment—both static and moving (e.g., people, animals, and other vehicles)—will create a dynamic travel environment in streets, which may carry over the space currently dedicated to parking. Sidewalk- or bikeway-adjacent lanes, which previously may have served as parking lanes, may be repurposed for other uses—or they may serve as intermittent catchment zones as AVs move through and respond to the environment, and need extra space to avoid collisions.

The evolution of new street cross sections, as AVs first emerge as a minor mode and ultimately come to dominate, is likely to involve changing behavior among

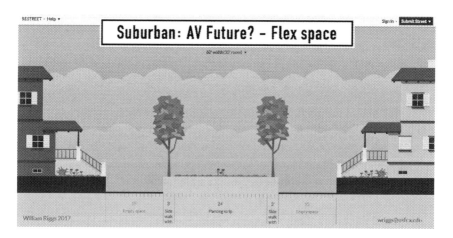

Figure 5.6 A radical suburban street in an AV future

travelers (pedestrians and cyclists, as well as human drivers), shifting policies, and new tools by planners to shape the travel environment to benefit travelers of all modes. And, in light of these changes and shifts we offer five principles for both practice and research.

Five principles for engineering and planning practice

1 **Stop expansion and start deconstruction**

As a recent work has suggested, there is not room for a business-as-usual approach in an autonomous future (Riggs & Boswell, 2016a). Automotive roadway capacity should not be increased, and roadway expansion or widening projects should be eliminated, so as not to result in "stranded assets." Conversely cities, need to begin considering eroding the vehicular ROW, starting with road diets and lanes with reductions and parking removal—as we have illustrated in our deconstruction exercise, streets. Additional ROW can be dedicated to pedestrians, bicycles, and transit—modes consistent with sustainable transport goals.

2 **Re-rethink streets**

Streets are a public resource and often a city's biggest asset and must be utilized in ways that maximize the public good. Cities can and should dictate modal priorities, act in regard to width and speeds to achieve local and global goals, and utilize this previous pace to meet both transportation needs and non-transportation functions such as ecological health, social interaction, public health, and community happiness. Autonomous technology offers a chance to rethink both the form and the function of how roadways are purposed, and cities must rethink the street before AV technology does it for them.

3 **Prioritize human travel**

In programming the right of way, cities should prioritize non-automotive uses first, followed by transit and then AVs. This follows a modal priority hierarchy that values sustainable modes first and gives priority to pedestrians, cyclists, and transit over AV traffic. Access for AV also should be conditioned not only to ensure the safety of pedestrians and cyclists, but also to avoiding criminalizing or deterring walking or biking. Walkers and cyclists have the right to be unpredictable. *It is critical that AV technology account for this as a condition to roadway operation in cities.* Specific policies might include:

   a Reduce auto-lane width and quantity and use space for bike/ped
   b Dictate local, regional, or state AV operational standards that ensure maximum pedestrian and cyclist safety and comfort
   c Manage and repurpose ROW to increase dedicated bicycle/pedestrian space; include parking and lane reduction spaces
   d Integrate bicycle and pedestrian amenities that serve ecosystem functions as part of street transitions

e   Provide drop-off zones at edges of bikeway; prevent vehicles from crossing bicycle or pedestrian infrastructure

f   Expand high-quality bike parking—safe, secure, convenient, affordable

4   **Embrace economics**

As we begin to consider streets as an asset or a utility, it is important to think about how we can use that asset most efficiently. For many years planners have discussed using pricing to make parking more efficient (Shoup 2005; Willson 2013). As we enter the autonomous future, pricing parking becomes ever more urgent. We must continue to reduce parking and develop broad pricing programs. We also must have bold dialogues on how we charge for street access and account for inefficient versus efficient use of the roadway. Because autonomous vehicles are likely to offer ample opportunities to game an economically inefficient system, we must develop broad economic policies that end spillover effects and tragedies of the commons. Specific policies might include:

a   Removing on-street parking

b   Eliminating car parking minimums

c   Pricing all parking

d   Using dynamic, use-based pricing
  i   Congestion charging (pay by location, time of day, day of week, etc.)
  ii   Charging for waste (pay per empty seat or based on car geometry)

e   Creating more robust behavioral incentive programs and integrated mobility passes that complement the sustainable travel revolution

5   **Start the evolution now: harness the AVs dialogue to build future streetscapes now**

Cities should attempt to anticipate the future and set a clear vision, then work backward to achieve those goals, planning for the types of streets, roads and development they want to see rather than having it dictated by innovation or industry. Technological changes may be sweeping and fast-paced, and while cities can harness the power of these changes, they should not embrace technology for technology's sake but work to use it to achieve city's goals and the purpose of transportation and sustainable travel goals such as accessibility, connectivity, and social equity. Cities should self-determine what their street look like as opposed to having it dictated by technological innovation such as AVs. Designs on streets should be made considering similar principles to city decisions (accessibility, spatial equity, etc.)

While AVs do not change many of these goals, they add urgency and provide a dialogue point for education and energizing multiple publics on the topic of transportation—with either anxiety or excitement. Planners and policymakers can harness this energy. Cities should take action now that meet sustainable transportation goals that are consistent with long-term deployment of AVs. What we want out of our streets has not changed. As we have illustrated in our exercise of deconstructing two street sections, most of the existing street design principles exposed by organizations like by NACTO or the ITE still hold in an autonomous future—and we believe may have more importance in an AV future. Streets are ecosystems that can evolve and we believe this evolution should start now.

Cities and citizens should experiment with their streets and partner with researchers to investigate interventions and opportunities. Planners should not wait on the certainty of how technology will develop but deploy sustainable transportation solutions now. These can be either incremental or broad-reaching, but should nudge streets toward this evolved sustainable travel paradigm. Expending the effort to plan and strategize before the technology hits the streets make it less likely that other players will rush into a policy or practice vacuum and set the terms.

Principles for research and education

In addition to principles for practice, we also offer the following thoughts for research and education. In large part, we have chosen to separate many of the complex dialogues about autonomous vehicles and to narrow on one key topic— sustainable travel and the form of future streets. As mentioned earlier, this departs from some of approaches of other academics who assume multiple revolutions in transport happening at the same time, for example the transition to electric and shared vehicles. While we recognize these shifts may be happening at the same time, they in many cases beyond the scope of influence and outside of the purview of the practicing planner. At the same time, the role of research and education may be to grapple with the complex and wicked nature of these interrelated trends. As such we offer the following thoughts for academic community.

1 *Can urban planning pedagogy advocate for a sustainable transportation future? Can we train planners and policymakers who can lead city-shaping in a much different and assertive way?*

There has been ample dialogue in higher education about how sustainability can be taught at the university level and how it can be included broadly across the curriculum. At the same time, as a policy and planning community, there have been few dialogues about how research and education can (and possibly should) have an agenda of a more sustainable, equitable, and happy urban future. Might it be time to ignite a new dialogue on how sustainable transportation education and research can embrace the spirit of Krumholz and "make sustainable transportation happen"? Should the academy embrace the notion that an agenda for research is at hand and ready for activation, and that we intend to educate practitioners who can reshape our streets, communities, and planet?

We believe that this kind of dialogue holds merit in forums such as the Association of Collegiate Schools of Planning, the Urban Affairs Association and the National Academies/Transportation Research Board. How should we respond to Handy's recent idea that we just need to "get on with" addressing problems of climate and sustainable travel? Do we find it hard to get on with it because we don't recognize that we are, in fact, not unbiased actors in the process of shaping sustainable streets and futures?

2 *Can the challenge of autonomous vehicles offer a gateway for us to discuss and influence other important urban issues and dialogues?*

Our work focused on the topic of street design to facilitate sustainable transportation. This assumes that autonomous vehicles are only a part of the transportation dialogue. At the same time AVs offer a unique turning point for discussing not only the future of streets but the future of cities. There is ample debate over the impact of AVs on sprawl, and we have not dialogued that. More work is needed to understand parallel issues of regional land use, migration and travel behavior, and potential social-equity issues and growing challenges between accessible urban areas that may be AV-rich and less rural areas where the platform is less accessible (potentially heightening social equity and spatial justice issues). While some of this may to wait until more tacit cases exist, evaluating actual human behavior and choices with these vehicle systems, policy can be developed, proposed and implemented now to address some of these issues.

3 *What are the opportunities and challenges for AVs for other urban typologies and street typologies? In what environments are the barriers to AVs low and in what are they high?*

As a part of our exercise we focused on just a handful of street typologies, but more work is needed on this. They need to be varied and expanded as well as truthed through more detailed design. There is a need for practice-ready street sections and more design typologies and concepts to guide engineering. The engineering academy and TRB/NACTO should consider developing and vetting standards, collaborating with planning academics and professionals who are attempting to anticipate these changes.

Further we recognize that AVs need testing in different environments, and this is an opportunity for the policy and planning community to work with colleagues in the technology and computer science field to explore other locations and operational domains for AVs. Looking at locations beyond Michigan, Pennsylvania, Arizona, the Silicon Valley, and Singapore, where current testing of AVs is taking place, may make roads more safe for pedestrians and cyclists and emphasize their importance in the hierarchy of roadway users. We posit that some areas may be more AV-ready (based on factors such as physical, cultural, etc.) than other and some may need more intervention to eliminate barriers.

4 *What is the funding model for streetscape regeneration in an AV future? Are there financial opportunities?*

Many financial opportunities arise as we reconsider the ROW. In planning to repurpose streets, we need to consider not only physical design but also financial sustainability. Are there opportunities in treating streets as real estate assets? There may be new ways that cities can develop pricing models and capture revenue and financial opportunity based on the advent of AVs.

5 *How should we be thinking and planning beyond the car as robots, drones, and bio-hacking/implants become more prevalent?*

In discussing AVs, it is important to recognize that automation and innovation will involve more than just changes to cars. Our cities will likely grapple with issues related to delivery/service sector robots and drones. These technologies are equally complex and closely aligned with the autonomous vehicle and street design dialogue and warrant focus in this future. Furthermore, technological advances in bio-hacking and implantable technology need research and analysis, particularly since embeddable chips and wearable technology may offer autonomous system redundancy that ensures pedestrian and bicycle safety. As scary as it seems perhaps the transportation planning community should move from talking about requiring connected vehicles and infrastructure, to grappling with and advocating for national and international policy that requires connected people?

Conclusion

As a concluding thought it may be appropriate to think about sustainable transportation as an exercise in balance and equity. It prioritizes walking, biking, and transit as primary desired modes of travel for most trips within metropolitan areas. Sustainable transport modes are space-efficient, energy-efficient, or non-polluting, available to almost all members of society independent of age or economic situation. They may be time-efficient with the appropriate infrastructure and also enhance social interaction, health, and happiness.

These traits stand largely in contrast to the individually-owned car-based transportation system developed and built over the last seventy years in many countries. In our minds a truly sustainable transport system offers more choices to more people, and reduces the disparities in opportunity of access, speed, comfort, and dignity of travel for various socio-demographic groups.

And this type of radical vision is enabled by new mobility and disruptive transport.

References

Airbib, J. and T. Seba. 2017. "Rethinking Transportation 2020-2030: The Disruption of Transportation and the Collapse of the Internal-Combustion Vehicle and Oil Industries." RethinkTransportation. RethinkX.

Anderson, J. M., N. Kalra, K. D. Stanley, P. Sorensen, C. Samaras, and O. A. Oluwatola. 2014. *Autonomous Vehicle Technology: A Guide for Policymakers*. Rand Corporation. https://books.google.com/books?hl=en&lr=&id=y0WrAgAAQBAJ&oi=fnd&pg=PP1&dq=Autonomous+17+Vehicle+Technology:+A+Guide+for+Policymakers.&ots=-6K7e4NENQ&sig=ZeCAbm066Tpr_gG3A7q1CueUmb4.

Bahamonde, B., F. Jose, B. Kickhöfer, D. Heinrichs, and T. Kuhnimhof. 2016. "A Systemic View on Autonomous Vehicles: Policy Aspects for a Sustainable Transportation Planning." http://elib.dlr.de/108647/.

Brown, A., J. Gonder, and B. Repac. 2014. "An Analysis of Possible Energy Impacts of Automated Vehicle." In *Road Vehicle Automation*, 137–153. Springer.

Cervero, R., E. Guerra, and A. Stefan. 2017. *Beyond Mobility: Planning Cities for People and Places*. Island Press.

Clewlow, R. R., and G. S. Mishra. 2017. "Disruptive Transportation: The Adoption, Utilization, and Impacts of Ride-Hailing in the United States." Research Report UCD-ITS-RR-17-07. Davis, CA: University of California, Davis, Institute of Transportation Studies. https://itspubs.ucdavis.edu/wp-content/themes/ucdavis/pubs/download_pdf.php?id=2752.

Cohen, A. and S. Shaheen. 2017. "Planning for Shared Mobility." Planning Advisory Srvices 583. American Planning Association. https://www.planning.org/publications/report/9107556/.

Coles, C. 2016. "Automated Vehicles: A Guide for Planners and Policymakers."

Fagnant, D. J. and K. M. Kockelman. 2014. "The Travel and Environmental Implications of Shared Autonomous Vehicles, Using Agent-Based Model Scenarios." *Transportation Research Part C: Emerging Technologies* 40: 1–13.

Firnkorn, J. and M. Müller. 2012. "Selling Mobility Instead of Cars: New Business Strategies of Automakers and the Impact on Private Vehicle Holding." *Business Strategy and the Environment* 21(4): 264–280.

Fulton, L., J. Mason, and D. Meroux. 2017. "Three Revolutions in Urban Transportation." Davis, CA: Institute for Transportation & Development Policy. https://www.itdp.org/publication/3rs-in-urban-transport/.

Glaeser, E. 2011. *Triumph of the City: How Our Greatest Invention Makes Us Richer, Smarter, Greener, Healthier, and Happier*. Penguin.

Guerra, E. 2015. "Planning for Cars That Drive Themselves: Metropolitan Planning Organizations, Regional Transportation Plans, and Autonomous Vehicles." *Journal of Planning Education and Research* 1:15.

Harb, M., Y. Xiao, G. Circella, P. Mokhtarian, and J. Walker. 2018. "Projecting Travelers into a World of Self-Driving Cars: Naturalistic Experiment for Travel Behavior Implications." In *Proceedings of the 97th Transportation Research Board*. Washington, D.C.

Isaacs, L. 2016. "Driving Toward Driverless." New York: WSP | Parsons Brinckerhoff. http://www.wsp-pb.com/Globaln/USA/Transportation%20and%20Infrastructure/driving-towards-driverless-WBP-Fellow-monograph-lauren-isaac-feb-24-2016.pdf.

Larco, N. 2017. "When Are AVs Coming? (10 Car Companies Say Within the Next 5 Years…) | Urbanism Next." 2017. https://urbanismnext.uoregon.edu/2017/08/28/when-are-avs-coming-10-car-companies-say-within-the-next-5-years/.

Lipson, H. and M. Kurman. 2016. *Driverless: Intelligent Cars and the Road Ahead*. MIT Press.

Litman, T. 2014. "Autonomous Vehicle Implementation Predictions." *Victoria Transport Policy Institute* 28. http://sh.st/st/787f28ed3e745c14417e4aec27303038/http://www.vtpi.org/avip.pdf.

Meyer, G. and S. Shaheen. 2017. *Disrupting Mobility: Impacts of Sharing Economy and Innovative Transportation on Cities*. Springer. https://books.google.com/books?hl=en&lr=&id=3y_XDQAAQBAJ&oi=fnd&pg=PR5&dq=s+shaheen+sharing&ots=f5r1rfhSJi&sig=lM5GzDO8bNSt6I-Wm4oiSnVatpU.

Millard-Ball, A. 2016. "Pedestrians, Autonomous Vehicles, and Cities." *Journal of Planning Education and Research*, October, 0739456X16675674. https://doi.org/10.1177/0739456X16675674.

Riggs, W. 2018. "Technology, Civic Engagement and Street Science: Hacking the Future of Participatory Street Design in the Era of Self-Driving Cars." In *Proceedings of the 19th Annual International Conference on Digital Government Research: Governance in the Data Age*, 4:1–4:6. Dgo '18. New York, NY, USA: ACM. https://doi.org/10.1145/3209281.3209383.

Riggs, W., M. R. Boswell, and R. Ross. 2016. "Streetplan: Hacking Streetmix for Community-Based Outreach on the Future of Streets." *Focus: The Journal of Planning Practice and Education | Journal of the City and Regional Planning Department | Cal Poly, San Luis Obispo | Volume 13* 13: 59.

Riggs, W. and J. Gilderbloom. 2016. "Two-Way Street Conversion: Evidence of Increased Livability in Louisville." *Journal of Planning Education and Research* 36(1): 105–18. https://doi.org/10.1177/0739456X15593147.

Riggs, W. W. 2017. "Modeling Future Street Options in an AV Future Using Restreet." Selected Works University of San Francisco. Retrieved from: https://scholar.google.com/scholar?oi=bibs&cluster=11588135873009610852&btnI=1&hl=en.

Riggs, W. (2018). Technology, Civic Engagement and Street Science: Hacking the Future of Participatory Street Design in the Era of Self-driving Cars. *In Proceedings of the 19th Annual International Conference on Digital Government Research: Governance in the Data Age* (pp. 4:1–4:6). New York, NY, USA: ACM. https://doi.org/10.1145/3209281.3209383.

Riggs, W. W. and Michael R. Boswell. 2016a. "No Business as Usual in an Autonomous Vehicle Future." https://works.bepress.com/williamriggs/53/.

———. 2016b. "Why Autonomous Vehicles Probably Won't Induce Sprawl." https://works.bepress.com/williamriggs/60/.

———. 2016c. "Thinking Beyond the (Autonomous) Vehicle: The Promise of Saved Lives." https://works.bepress.com/williamriggs/71/.

Riggs, W. W., L. Seth, and M. R. Boswell. 2017. "Autonomous Vehicles: Turn On, Tune In, Drop Out?" *Planetizen*. https://works.bepress.com/williamriggs/88/.

Schlossberg, M., W. W. Riggs, A. Millard-Ball, and E. Shay. 2018. "Rethinking the Street in an Era of Driverless Cars." *UrbanismNext*. https://urbanismnext.uoregon.edu/files/2018/01/Rethinking_Streets_AVs_012618-27hcyr6.pdf.

Schlossberg, M., J. Rowell, D. Amos, and K. Sanford. 2013. "Rethinking Streets." *An Evidence-Based Guide To* 25. http://pdxscholar.library.pdx.edu/cgi/viewcontent.cgi?filename=0&article=1054&context=trec_reports&type=additional.

Shoup, D. C. 2005. The high cost of free parking. Planners Press, American Planning Association. Retrieved from http://www.connectnorwalk.com/wp-content/uploads/The-High-Cost-of-Free-Parking.pdf.

Talen, E. 2013. "Zoning For and Against Sprawl: The Case for Form-Based Codes." *Journal of Urban Design* 18(2): 175–200. https://doi.org/10.1080/13574809.2013.772883.

Willson, R. W. 2013. Parking reform made easy. Island Press. Retrieved from https://books.google.com/books?hl=en&lr=&id=E6o8-Me_FCAC&oi=fnd&pg=PR2&dq=willson+2013+parking&ots=w_MX5epvuj&sig=ZGXf4Fz1a4rQZtpNdpk00MctixY.

6 Real estate and new mobility

Deborah Stamm and William Riggs

Introduction

Global real estate is estimated to be $17 trillion, over 600 times larger than the combined $350 billion market capitalization of GM, Ford, Honda, and Toyota (Barnes & Tostevin 2016). This means that more wealth could be both lost and created by AV-impacted real estate than by manufacturing of the vehicles themselves. While the future of real estate in a new-mobility world will, to some extent, be influenced by factors that are as of yet hazy, what is certain is that there will be winners and losers created in the transition. For any policymaker, planner, developer, or citizen who hopes to create a just and sustainable future, this topic is perhaps the most important of our time.

Past transportation revolutions, like those precipitated by the steam engine and the automobile, dramatically changed where and how cities were built. Chicago's growth and success was originally a product of the railroads. Automobiles—and the highway systems that were created around them—spurred growth of disparate cities and, perhaps more dramatically, changed the land-use patterns within cities. LA would not sprawl over 4,850 square miles if not for the automobile. A rise in air travel has even led to the rise of new, airport-centric cities like Songdo, Korea. The impending revolution in vehicle automation will similarly impact which cities grow, how they grow, and what is built. When you consider that this revolution will include not only autonomous cars but also autonomous "flying cars" (i.e., small planes capable of vertical take-off and landing), it becomes clear that the impact could be even further-reaching. The question is, what will this future look like?

This chapter explores the implications of new mobility on real estate and how the rise of new mobility is likely to impact real estate values and growth patterns, building design, and streets themselves. While we focus primarily on some of the potential impacts of vehicle autonomy in the absence of policy interventions, we also discuss how policies will influence the outcomes and suggest potential solutions to new challenges presented by vehicle autonomy in an urban environment.

The effects of autonomous vehicles (AVs) on real estate can be broken down into impacts to land (where we build) and product (what we build). Both land and product will be affected through direct and secondary means. In addition, each building type (which we will refer to as "asset class") will be impacted differently, and we will explore the similarities and differences among them. Finally, we look beyond traditional real estate asset classes and consider streets themselves as a real estate asset, since, of all the changes to the built environment, changes to the streets themselves may be most dramatic.

Land: where we build

It is first very important to think about the key potential impacts on land, that are largely directed by where and how we choose to build. For example, there are very specific implications on urban land and real estate given traffic changes and tolerance for delay. We have tried to frame some of these questions in the Table 6.1, but even without knowing the precise answers to the questions, there are some likely outcomes that arise. These become particularly acute with self-driving cars and flying of autonomous vehicles.

The purpose of describing these impacts is not to predict the future, but rather to explore the types of dramatic influence that new mobility may have on real estate market forces. It is probable that dense urban areas will become even more dense, thanks to two key drivers.

First, developers will not need to build parking (because tenants, and eventually cities, will not demand it), which will reduce their total construction cost, which will in turn make more projects economically viable. This reduction in cost will be particularly impactful for certain projects in urban areas where costly, below-grade parking is required but where the investment in parking cannot be sufficiently returned—this is a particularly frequent case for residential development. Second, there will be an increase in demand for urban space as employees, residents, and customers no longer need to pay for parking; their total cost of living, working, or shopping in the urban core also goes down. An increase in density will be most prevalent in retail, office, and multifamily residential.

Ironically, while it is probably that the denser parts of already dense urban areas will become more so, it is also likely that cities will spread out. Again, there are multiple drivers at play, though in this case, the drivers are different for different asset types. One asset type that will be especially susceptible to suburbanization is residential—both single-family and low-density multi-family. As people are able to be more productive in their cars, they will be willing to spend more time in them. Additionally, once we get closer to 100 percent AV adoption, traffic should also decrease significantly, meaning that commute sheds based on commute times will grow. Those unable to afford cars and dependent on transportation may use shared AV for their last mile needs, which again will allow them to move further away from mass transit nodes; this will also depress land prices in those areas. Finally, people may be less concerned with being able to walk to amenities since it will be so inexpensive and easy to get into an AV and get dropped off at the nearest town center.

Table 6.1 Key questions and impacts on land use and real estate

Key Question	Critical Components	Urban Land Values Increase If...	Rural Land Values Increase If...	Best Guess
Traffic changes?	Passengerless car policy Carpool vs. individual Technology efficiency VMT changes, VMT taxes?	Traffic doesn't get much better.	Traffic gets better.	Long-run traffic could get better but VMT will not stay constant, so we will only have marginal improvement.
How pleasant will cities be?	Pedestrian friendliness Will existing car-dedicated land become green or public space? Urban speed limits	Cities are pedestrian- and bike-centric.	Cities are car-centric.	It will depend on local policymakers.
Zoning and density changes?	Will local governments limit density or will they use reduced parking and traffic needs to facilitate urban density?	More density in cities.	Additional density not allowed in cities.	It will depend on local policymakers.
Which roads experience most traffic reduction?	How good are AVs at increasing travel efficiency off-highway?	Urban street efficiency increases most.	Highway efficiency increases more than other roadways.	Studies point in different direction but likely similar impact to all roads.
What infrastructure is needed?	Will required infrastructure exist in suburban and rural areas?	Vehicle density is required for AVs.	AVs can function without external infrastructure.	Unlikely that infrastructure will be a constraint given existing technology.
Will people be willing to spend more time in the car?	Will commuters tolerate significantly longer commutes?	No, people are not willing.	Yes, people are willing.	Yes, but only to a point; the response to corporate bus programs provides insight.

Hospitality, and particularly the market for second homes, will also be affected. It is likely that there will be increased demand for more remote destinations, as travelers may be able to work or sleep in their cars en-route to vacations. Additionally, the dramatic increase in safety will make more remote destinations feel more accessible: a Friday night drive to a cabin deep in the woods on a dark, windy road feels less daunting if you're not the one driving the car. The lines between a vacation home and a full-time home may also become blurred, as the urban periphery grows and long commutes become the norm.

Finally, industrial real estate—especially warehouses and fulfillment centers—will expand further outside the urban core. There are several factors related to the rise of AI that will interact and produce this result. Much of the costs associated with logistics real estate is in the transport of the goods; as autonomous cars and trucks reduce these costs greatly, facilities will be able to move further outside of cities without drastically increasing their transportation costs. Also, logistics facilities currently need to stay close enough to urban areas to be able to attract the required labor force. As with residential, when AVs are introduced, labor will be willing to travel further to work. However, over time AI will probably reduce the number of employees needed in such jobs, since even those who argue that new jobs will be created as we lose existing ones to robots are unlikely to argue that the new jobs will be easily-mechanizable warehouse work. This will also be self-fulfilling: as warehouses stop representing jobs, municipalities will be less eager to allow their development and may reduce industrial zoning in many cities. One caveat to this is last-mile fulfillment, for which demand in urban core will likely remain strong. If municipalities start pushing industrial out of the city, companies may have to get more creative about their last-mile strategies in order to maintain urban locations.

As we have stated, it is likely that cities will become both more dense at their core and more spread out at their perimeters. But you may be wondering: how can this be? One answer is that these changes will not be constant across cities; one outcome or the other may be more pronounced based on existing infrastructure, geographic constraints, existing reliance on cars, and, of course, policy decision. However, we believe that some cities—specifically, megacities—will experience both changes, which means they will be able to continue exponential growth.

Real estate impacts among cities

One of the most likely outcomes of the rise of new mobility will be a continued growth of megacities and innovation hubs. Currently there is some level of downward pressure on large cities due to traffic and a high cost of living that often accompanies density. AVs will reduce both of those frictions. Although AVs may only marginally improve traffic in the short term, they are likely to drastically reduce it in the long term, and in either case, people's willingness to endure traffic will increase when they can be productive while driving. Similarly, in regions where urban growth is not bounded by an urban growth boundary or similar, there will be more potential residential land available within a manageable commute watershed, which should relieve pressure on housing prices and cost of living. Additionally, new land will become available within cities where land was previously dedicated to parking, which will likely be repurposed for commercial purposes or residential product to house the workers in the new commercial spaces.

The San Francisco Bay Area in California provides a great example of this. In the Bay Area, a commute of 2+ hours is not usual. In fact, the average commute is the second worst in the nation at 60 minutes (Craig 2017). Because affordability has become such a major issue, residents are forced to choose between housing they cannot afford or an unmanageable commute. Sometimes they chose neither, which is what is leading some to migrate out of SF (McCarriston 2018). The introduction of new mobility solutions, be they e-scooters or AVs, could add new infill housing supply and make commutes less onerous—increasing the overall population over time.

The streets as real estate

New mobility offers us a new opportunity to reimagine an incredibly large and valuable real estate. While the potential for rethinking their configuration is discussed in Chapter 5, we believe that cities can go further—that streets are not just real estate but an asset class. In saying this, we mean that they are a commodity that can be bought, sold, leveraged, and agglomerated, and that they have more value than simply for travel.

As urban land values have grown exponentially over the past several decades, the municipalities who govern streets have not always evolved policy and or usage-pricing to reflect this. Yes, street parking prices have increased, and in select pockets of the world congestion-pricing has been implemented, but for the most part, streets are operated the same way today that they were in 1950, when urban land prices were a mere 3.5% of what they were in 2017 (Barr, Smith, & Kulkarni 2015).

If dense urban areas were to value their streets, the results would be staggering. Using land values from a recent study, the average price per square foot of New York land is $119 (Albouy, Ehrlich, & Shin 2017). With a total land area of 305 square miles, and assuming 15 percent of all land is street, then there is approximately $23 billion of "street real estate" in New York City. While this is likely an overestimate, since roads are not shaped to allow for efficient building design, and a need for setbacks from existing off-street structures would further reduce the ability to build an efficient structure, this simple calculation still provides a powerful illustration of the order of magnitude of street value.

This idea is explored a bit further in Chapter 14 on livability, however as a primary exercise, rethinking the street as an asset class bolsters the case for appropriate usage-based pricing and illustrates the opportunity available to municipalities as new mobility potentially frees up public space currently dedicated to parking.

That said, we should not confuse public land that may become available with private land and market impacts. Many planners and urban dreamers eagerly eye parking lots and envision that the introduction of new mobility will allow them to convert these lots into public open space. The reality is, unless that land is publicly owned, that won't happen: private property will be redeveloped by the private market to its highest and best use.

Furthermore, it is worth recognizing the paradoxes in new mobility perspectives. For example, there have been many media reports about the positive and negative implications of personal transportation devices (e-scooters, Segways, skateboards, etc.) on cities. Most are based on select number of interviews, given the lack of research in this area, however, from the research that is out there, it is clear that these do provide improved services and equity in accessibility (Fang and Agrawal 2018; Fang and Handy 2017). Yet, the real estate (and city planning) response has been mixed. Many believe that things like scooters are fun, and appeal to new homebuyers who do not own cars, however, many do not like the visual impacts—for example, when they are left on the sidewalk (South 2018). These opinions have not only real estate relevance, but they have equity implications, assuming that cheap personal mobility can increase low-cost travel in places underserved by traditional transit.

Product: what we build

Certain features of our building are going to change in a consistent direction across asset classes. Buildings and homes will have less parking—or none at all. Instead, there will be demand for "drop-off" space, which may be public curbs or turn-arounds. Designers will also likely craft creative solutions to an explosion in package and food delivery: there may be robot-delivery rooms or even special robot-elevators. Less storage will be needed on site so space needs will be smaller as storage gets outsourced.

This is especially true for residential and is most applicable to urban residential. If a resident can easily store their skis and have them delivered cheaply, on-demand, they are more likely to prefer a smaller, less expensive unit. Finally, roof space will become a transit node as VTALs proliferate. More buildings will bring elevators up to the roof, and sky bridges and sky lobbies may become more common.

All building designs are going to change in some way, but in some cases, product types may go away altogether. From the lens of environmental and social impact, this is the more important shift in what we build. Driver-centric product like gas stations, commercial garages and parking lots, motels, dealerships, and truck stops will stop being built, and what exists of these products types will probably shrink, evolve, or go out of business. For example, low-end motels in rural areas, who depend on truckers and road-trippers who are simply looking for a pillow to sleep on, may lose business to cars or buses with beds built in. Assuming that electrification and automation happen in tandem, gas stations will be doubly devastated.

While some types of retail real estate will survive the introduction of vehicle autonomy, the total volume of traditional retail assets per capita will tend to shrink as AVs are employed for e-commerce. Experiential, destination-based retail and retail in especially densely populated areas will continue to thrive but convenience retail, especially in less dense areas, will be even more challenged than it is currently. Retail "real estate" may also go mobile. Beyond the model of replacing traditional brick-and-mortar retail with fulfillment centers and delivery vehicles, retailers may develop an autonomous "clothes truck" where they bring a dressing room full of products to you so you can avoid the hassle of returning packages.

Social and environmental impacts and potential policy solutions

Impacts

The outcomes of where we build and how we build have resounding environmental and social impacts, both positive and negative. Most significantly, a suburban renaissance could expand and worsen many of the ills that the first wave of suburbanization did. A low-density suburban landscape leads to increased energy use both in the home and in transportation, as houses are larger and commutes are longer (Glazier et al. 2014; Cervero and Kockelman 1997). Low-density suburbs also result in higher water use per capita for landscaping, increased impervious surface per capita, and a reducing of other key land uses including farmland or native landscapes that provide important ecosystem services (Birch and Wachter 2008; Newman and Jennings 2008). Finally, there are clear health benefits to an active commute (walking or biking), and while a car-centric, low-density suburban landscape may still have recreational exercise available, it does little to promote commute-related activity (Frank 2011; Frank et al. 2005; Forsyth et al. 2007).

To the extent that the suburbanization patterns of the twentieth century will repeat themselves, we may see wealthy, predominantly white, households move toward the suburbs. We may see a rerun of suburbanization with a hallowing out of urban infrastructure and an acceleration of socio-economic and racial inequality. As urban property prices fall, funding for urban school will fall in tandem. Instead, as the suburbs grow, we will start pouring funds into suburban infrastructure in the form of new roads, utilities, and schools. Urban cores in smaller cities may be particularly impacted by migration both to the suburbs and to megacities.

The reduction in demand for certain types of real estate will also have reverberating impacts. Most planners would agree that vibrant, walkable retail is a critical ingredient in urban design. As discussed, retail will struggle to survive, and it may become more difficult to cultivate an active public commons. In the case of vehicle-centric real estate, some buildings may be difficult to repurpose, and we could end up with abandoned properties. For example, is anyone going to redevelop four adjacent roadside motels in a small town in Nebraska on I-80? If not, who will pay for these assets to be demolished, or will they simply be abandoned? Even more problematic are gas stations, since the environmental cleanup required for reuse on such sites can be very costly. We may well see abandoned gas stations in locations where land values don't justify remediation and redevelopment costs.

Depending on how fast the transition to vehicle autonomy happens, there could be another key societal impact: a reduction in all real estate values. Currently, real estate prices in urban areas reflect a scarcity of land and buildable square footage (which is dictated by height and density restrictions). As we transition to vehicle autonomy and commute sheds expand, there will be more supply of appealing land, which will drive down prices. Layered onto that, there will likely be an additional supply of new land in the form of parking lots and parking garages that are no longer needed. In mega-cities that continue to grow due to reduced friction from new mobility, it is possible that there will not be a reduction in real estate values, but in smaller cities that are on the losing end of the continued shift to mega-cities, these impacts may be magnified. The scale, timing, and geography of such a shift in values is extremely difficult to predict, but such a shift could have meaningful impacts on everything from the home values of middle-class families to the returns on the real estate assets in pension funds.

The good news is that there is the potential for some environmentally and socially beneficial outcomes. First, increased density should be possible in urban areas. As traffic is alleviated through new mobility and parking needs are decreased, there may be reduced opposition to, and increased political will for, increasing density in urban areas. This means decreased per capita energy use, water use, and impervious surfaces, increased active commuting, and potentially increased revitalization of socially and racially diverse urban areas.

Also, two themes discussed above as potentially negative—suburbanization and a decrease in real estate values—do have a beneficial upside: affordability. As has been widely studied, in the past several years, housing affordability in certain urban areas has become a crisis. A glut of new land supply, especially if paired with new construction methods that would reduce construction costs, would result in more housing that lower- and middle-income households could afford.

Policy solutions

There are a few simple policies that would likely steer cities toward a more socially just and environmentally sustainable new mobility future.

First, governments should instate "Smart VMT" taxes. Such taxes could vary depending on time of day, location, and number of passengers. We now have the technology to make this economist's dream of dynamic pricing into a reality. Creating such a fee scheme would appropriately price urban expansion to reflect the infrastructure cost. There are significant hurdles to implementing a smart VMT tax, most notably challenges around privacy.

Second, local governments who wish to curtail sprawl should consider policies that enable smart growth within the existing urban core and discourage suburban growth. An Urban Growth Boundary is one such policy tool. Other policies that make dense urban development easier or more profitable represent a softer approach.

There is an opportunity to up-zone neighborhoods where density is currently constrained by tight parking or traffic congestion, as new mobility may ease both, especially if a Smart VMT tax is employed. To the extent that new public infrastructure is needed to fully realize the benefits of new mobility options (e.g., dynamic streetlights, etc.), a charge for up-zoning and additional floor-to-area-ratio could be employed as a way to fund those needs. Urban development would be further encouraged by decreasing or eliminating parking requirements, which would help project economics and increase supply.

In the short term, when parking may still be needed, governments could be more lenient in allowing above-grade structure parking if it is designed to be convertible to another use (e.g., retail) in the future. Currently many municipalities require parking to be below-grade, which is significantly more expensive to construct and will be more difficult to convert to another use when the parking is no longer needed.

Conclusion

In sum, real estate and asset classes are already being impacted by new mobility with increased attractiveness of curb space and increased accessibility by mobility on demand and new forms of travel like e-bikes and scooters. These impacts on land and real estate will only become more acute as AV technology becomes more pronounced. And to paraphrase the old Will Rogers quote, we should "invest" in these assets—as we certainly aren't making any more of them.

References

Albouy, D., G. Ehrlich, and M. Shin, M. 2017. Metropolitan Land Values. *Review of Economics and Statistics*.

Barnes, Y. and P. Tostevin. 2016, January. *Around the World in Dollars and Cents–2016: World Real Estate Accounts for 60% of all Mainstream Assets*. Retrieved from Savills: http://www.savills.co.uk/research_articles/229130/198667-0.

Barr, J., F. Smith, and S. Kulkarni, S. 2015. What's Manhattan Worth? A Land Values Index from 1950 to 2013. *Working Papers Rutgers University, Newark 2015-002*.

Birch, E. L. and S. M. Wachter. 2008. *Growing Greener Cities: Urban Sustainability in the Twenty-First Century*. Univ of Pennsylvania Pr.

Cervero, R. and K. Kockelman. 1997. "Travel Demand and the 3Ds: Density, Diversity, and Design." *Transportation Research Part D: Transport and Environment* 2(3): 199–219.

Craig, M. 2017, October. *Ahead of Halloween, Robert Half Reveals U.S. Cities with Spookiest and Most Stressful Commutes*. Retrieved from Robert Half: http://rh-us.mediaroom.com/2017-10-23-Ahead-Of-Halloween-Robert-Half-Reveals-U-S-Cities-With-Spook-iest-And-Most-Stressful-Commutes.

Fang, K. and A. Agrawal. 2018. "Electric Kick Scooters on Sidewalks in Virginia but Not in California? A Review of How States Regulate Personal Transportation Devices." Mineta Transportation Institute. http://transweb.sjsu.edu/research/1713-WP-Regulating-Scooters.

Fang, K. and S. Handy. 2017. "Skateboarding for Transportation: Exploring the Factors behind an Unconventional Mode Choice among University Skateboard Commuters." *Transportation*, July, 1–21. https://doi.org/10.1007/s11116-017-9796-9.

Forsyth, A., J. M. Oakes, K. H. Schmitz, and M. Hearst. 2007. "Does Residential Density Increase Walking and Other Physical Activity?" *Urban Studies* 44(4): 679–697.

Frank, L. D. 2011. "Carbonless Footprints: Promoting Health and Climate Stabilization through Active Transportation." UC Berkeley, April 18.

Frank, L. D., T. L. Schmid, J. F. Sallis, J. Chapman, and B. E. Saelens. 2005. "Linking Objectively Measured Physical Activity with Objectively Measured Urban Form: Findings from SMARTRAQ." *American Journal of Preventive Medicine* 28(2): 117–125.

Glazier, R. H., M. I. Creatore, J. T. Weyman, G. Fazli, F. I. Matheson, P. Gozdyra, R. Moineddin, V. K. Shriqui, and G. L. Booth. 2014. "Density, Destinations or Both? A Comparison of Measures of Walkability in Relation to Transportation Behaviors, Obesity and Diabetes in Toronto, Canada." *PLoS ONE* 9 (1): e85295. https://doi. org/10.1371/journal.pone.0085295.

McCarriston, G. 2018, February. *Affordable Inland Metros Drew People from San Francisco, New York and Los Angeles.* Retrieved from Redfin: https://www.redfin.com/blog/2018/02/ q4-migration-report.html.

Newman, P. and I. Jennings. 2008. *Cities as Sustainable Ecosystems: Principles and Practices.* Island Press.

South, G. 2018. "Real Estate Agents See Electric Scooter Boom as Mixed Blessing." *Inman.* May 18, 2018. Retrieved from: https://www.inman.com/2018/05/18/real-estate-agents-see-electric-scooter-boom-as-mixed-blessing/.

7 Future transport and city budgets

Getting bottom-line savvy in an uncertain future

Benjamin Y. Clark and Rebecca Lewis

Introduction

The changing nature of mobility is on the cusp of massive change. For example, Robert Spillar, Austin, Texas, Transportation Director has been quoted as saying, "Half my revenue for transportation capacity and operations improvements is based on a parking model that may be obsolete in a dozen years" (quoted in Maciag 2017). In line with this, cities are rightfully worried about the future will do to key revenue sources. And the changes experienced by cities will extend far beyond parking and traffic citation revenues. We can expect to see the finances of nearly everything a local government touched in some way by the future transportation. This chapter will broadly explore the challenges that cities are facing and provide some illustrative in-depth coverage in a couple of case studies that focus on local government revenues.

The exact nature of the impacts of new mobility and things like autonomous vehicles (AVs) is still largely unknown. As we work through issues surrounding AVs (both narrow and broad), we are speculating based on our best assumptions and current knowledge of these impacts. This chapter, like so many written today, may be out of date to some extent shortly after it is written. As KPMG notes, "If we anticipate an AV future today, we can avoid wasting taxpayers' money on investments that may soon prove obsolete, or worse, frustrate the realization of AV benefits" (Threlfall 2018, 6). This is precisely the aim of this chapter—so public managers and policymakers can anticipate what is to come.

The extent of saturation of AVs on the roadway is still quite limited, but their deployment is spreading rapidly. For example, as of June 1, 2018, there were fifty-five companies that had received permits from the California Department of Motor Vehicles to test autonomous vehicles up from thirty-one in June of 2017 (California Department of Motor Vehicles 2018). The players in this field include the traditional automakers (GM, Toyota, VW, Ford, Honda, Nissan, Mercedes, BMW), auto-parts makers (Delphi, Bosh, Continental), the tech industry (Google/Waymo, Qualcomm, Apple, Samsung, Intel, NVIDIA), transportation network companies (Lyft, Uber), and a host of others. The Alphabet/Google AV unit, known as Waymo, has "Since 2009.... self-driven more than 5 million miles, mostly on city streets" (Waymo 2018). While there are set-backs and tragedies associated with the testing of AV, such as the first pedestrian death in March 2018 in Tempe, Arizona (Bensinger and Higgins 2018), the progress toward more autonomy in mobility continues.

Advances in AVs mobility will affect several modes of passenger transportation, including single-occupancy vehicles and mass transportation. A driverless twelve-passenger shuttle bus is being tested by Deutsche Bahn, which is the largest train and bus operator in Germany (Scott 2017). This is accompanied by more than twenty other (pilot or existing) public transportation programs using AVs across Europe. In the United States, private shuttle bus operator Bauer's Intelligent Transportation has a permit to test on its AV buses in the state of California (California Department of Motor Vehicles 2018).

There remains uncertainty over how we will use AVs. Using UberPool or Lyft Line models as examples, the growth of shared-rides have seen these services garner more than 50 percent of all rides from the two companies (Steinmetz 2015). While transportation network companies (TNC) of today are not autonomous, the willingness of users of TNCs to ride with strangers adds to the viability of a shared mobility future. While many are still pessimistic that Americans in particular will ever give up their cars, there is increasing evidence that the number of cars we are buying is decreasing when TNCs become available—Ward et al. (2018) found this decline can be up to 4.6 percent in cities three years after TNC introduction.

We believe that we should accept AVs as the coming reality and as such we have to move toward understanding how they will impact our cities. The literature on the secondary impacts of AVs is rather sparse. Earlier works on the budgetary impacts are largely limited to Clark, Larco, and Mann's (2017) whitepaper. This chapter seeks to extend this earlier effort and further the discussion on how to plan from a budgetary and policy perspective for AVs. This work focuses on the impacts of AVs on city budgets because of changes in transportation. We focus on the city budget broadly and provide specific examples that primarily look at the transportation budget.

How are AVs going to affect local government budgets?

The impact of AVs, like many innovations today, is likely to be varied based on a range of factors. Three areas we see as driving the discussion for cities budgets include: revenue diversity, statutory limitations or constraints from state governments, and population and economic growth trajectory. Every state and region has the potential to create a range of scenarios that may play out differently for local governments in different places, thus the impact of AVs has the potential to differ. Growing and densifying urban cities like San Francisco or Portland are likely to experience an AV world different from the cities of the Rust Belt or Appalachia.

Table 7.1 Current transportation funding sources, 2017

	Portland	Tigard	Tualatin
General fund	5.7%	0.0%	0.0%
Parking	23.6%	0.0%	1.5%
Fees	15.8%	7.4%	0.0%
Bonds	12.2%	0.0%	0.0%
Gas tax (local)	5.2%	6.3%	0.0%
System development charges	0.0%	12.3%	0.0%
Utility fee	0.0%	22.5%	10.2%
Transportation development taxes	0.0%	18.4%	54.4%
Gas tax (pass through)	24.9%	30.7%	34.0%
Grants and donations	12.6%	0.0%	0.0%

As part of the Sustainable City Year Program at the University of Oregon (https://sci.uoregon.edu/), graduate students partnered with TriMet—Portland's public transit agency—and examined how AVs could impact transportation revenues in three different cities in the Portland region – Tigard, Tualatin, and Portland (Peterson and Lewis 2017). Table 7.1 shows the current transportation funding sources for each city. The researchers estimated that transportation revenues might decline 5.4 to 25 percent with the adoption of AVs.[1] Furthermore, the analysis found that the predominant sources impacted included motor fuel excise taxes, vehicle registration, traffic citations, vehicle impound fees, and parking revenue. Some transportation revenue sources will not be impacted or will be minimally impacted by AV adoption including system development charges, transportation development taxes, bonds, and utility fees. Across the three cities, the impact estimates ranged from 5.4 to 15 percent of the total transportation budget for groups that assumed a 50 percent adoption rate.

Including and beyond those changes, we see a range of potential changes to city budgets. Without analyzing the specific potential impact, these may include:

- Fuel excise taxes (Gasoline and Diesel taxes): Taxes on motor fuels are in peril with or without AVs. Vehicles have become more efficient, and rates have remained at the federal level since 1993. These taxes are applied on fuels at the federal, state, and at times the local level. With greater reliance upon electricity to power vehicles regardless of the shift to AVs, we expect these revenues as a source for transportation capital financing to continue their downward trajectory without intervention by elected leaders. "The replacement revenue could come from a variety of sources, including per mile charges, toll roads, additional excise taxes for electricity generation, geometry taxes, and others. The bottom line is that this is one of the important taxing issues that will have to be addressed in the very near future. (Clark, Larco, and Mann 2017).

- Vehicle registration and licensing: Fewer vehicles are expected to be needed to provide transportation if we shift toward a shared mobility model with AVs—car sharing or ride sharing. In these models, we will buy shares or time for transportation rather than actual vehicles themselves. This would likely result in large fleets of vehicles owned by private or public entities. As seen with many fleet vehicles with car rental and shipping companies, there may be states that offer substantial tax benefits for vehicles to be registered in those states. Without policy changes, this could result in many cars being registered in a state with the lowest registration and licensing fees. The effects of fleet vehicle purchasing will also be seen in sales taxes (discussed more below).

- Traffic and parking citations: AVs are expected to obey traffic laws in ways that human drivers do not. In fact, we examined the records of AV-involved accidents from 2015 to 2018 in the State of California. One of the most striking patterns is that the AVs already obey traffic laws to such an extent that it is frustrating to many drivers, which has led to human errors causing nearly every AV-involved auto accident. Thus, it is conceivable that the ultimate trajectory of traffic and parking citations will decline as humans get used to how these vehicles drive and as we have more vehicles that obey the law precisely. Fewer impaired drivers behind the wheel would also lower the number of driving-under-the-influence citations.

- Vehicle impound fees: Impound fees are assessed when vehicles are towed and stored by a local government if a vehicle was parked illegally, abandoned, or if the driver of the vehicle was no longer allowed to drive the vehicle. This often results in a driver's license being revoked for a period of time. With a potential decline in driver-owned vehicles because of shared-mobility becoming more popular, it is clear that we would expect fewer personally owned vehicles to be subject to impounding from abandonment. Corporate ownership of vehicles would likely ensure that vehicles are accounted for and not left in a state of abandonment. AVs would also have a low probability of illegal parking, as they would likely park in designated places by default.

- On and off-street parking revenue: The impact of parking revenue is going to hit both public and private revenue streams. On-street parking is largely the domain of local governments. Although impacts remain reasonably small thus far, sources of TNCs are already beginning to show an impact on parking demand in some cities. It is easy to imagine that once AVs become more common, the need to park on the street or in a off-street lot will dramatically decrease. Parking will not disappear altogether, since AVs will need to remain parked while not in use. With that said, AVs will be able to park much closer to each other thus using the parking lots much more efficiently and decreasing the square footage needed in lots.

- TNC/Taxi revenues: With the advent of TNCs in the last ten years, city revenue from taxis has been hit very hard. Cities and airport authorities have taken notice and adjusted rates and fee schedules to include charging TNCs to recapture lost revenue. These governments will continue to see robust growth from TNC revenue for the foreseeable future, and sense that AV mobility services are assessed similar fees. The complexity of vehicles driving with and without passengers has not gone unnoticed, and some scholars and policymakers are proposing that we charge for empty vehicles on the roadway to discourage fleets of zombie cars (vehicles without passengers) circling and congesting streets. These AVs might be circling while they wait for their owners to finish their business, and avoid paying for parking, or be fleet vehicles waiting to find someone that needs to be picked up.
- System development charges and transportation development taxes: System development charges (or impact fees) are assessed on new development to pay for the cost of infrastructure associated with new development. As development patterns shift, certain cities on the periphery may see an increase in development while central cities may see a decline in development.
- Road utility fee: These fees are often assessed on frontage along roads that will be improved. As the function and design of streets shift and e-commerce expands, tax assessments on commercial properties may decline.
- Bonds: Several cities use local option property taxes to finance street improvements through revenue backed bonds. These revenue sources may be negatively impacted by property tax valuation (this is discussed in more detail in the next section.)

There are other areas of municipal budgeting that we also expect to be impacted by the introduction of AVs. These budgetary impacts are wider ranging and have what we think are likely to be higher variability in their changes. These taxes and fees are likely to change because of the secondary impacts of AVs on cities. So, as we change how we work, live, and get around, our cities are likely to change as a result, thus change those budget categories. Some of the areas we expect to see changes in are:

- Property taxes: Much of the expected change in property tax revenue is tied to parking—the single largest land use in cities (Shoup 2005). Some estimates put the amount of land in cities being used for parking at somewhere between 14 and 25 percent and it has been projected that with AVs up to 90 percent fewer parking spaces will be needed (International Transport Forum 2015, Zhang 2015). As cities change parking minimums for commercial and residential properties, the land devoted for parking will go down while productive and higher value land uses will increase. This has the real potential to increase the value of these properties, which can in turn increase property tax revenues. In California, property tax limitations (Prop 13) have, for years, limited the growth of tax digests. This creates substantial gaps in the taxes neighbors pay in property taxes. As land used for parking lots, for example, is freed up—as AVs will need up to 90 percent less parking (International Transport Forum 2015, Zhang 2015)—the potential for new assessments of those new uses of land have the potential to positively benefit those California cities. If we look at cities that have seen long periods of decline in population, such as Youngstown or Cleveland, the declining demand for parking will add land available for development in places that already have excess or unused land in the urban core. This could potentially depress land valuation, leading to lower tax collections for cities.

- General sales taxes: With a shift toward shared or fleet ownership of AVs, the amount of sales taxes collected may be impacted. It is estimated that we may only need ten percent of the vehicles that are currently on the road with a full shift to AVs (Clark, Larco, and Mann 2017). This dramatic drop in number of sales will hit the bottom line of cities and states that collect these taxes. While an individual buying a car may not make a long voyage to purchase vehicles in a state or locality that does not charge a sales tax on vehicles, a corporate entity could be expected to make such an effort when buying their fleets. AVs will be used more efficiently than the human-driven vehicles of today and thus add more miles to each vehicle more quickly. This could lead to a short life span of AVs, "so the decline in revenue is not likely to be a full 90 percent" (Clark, Larco, and Mann 2017). Fleet owners "may also be able to take advantage of "Like-Kind Exchanges" replacement of vehicles to avoid paying federal taxes (Internal Revenue Service 2016). For example, a fleet owner might pay taxes on the purchase of the AV fleet, and we will say it has a fleet of fifty thousand AVs. As they replace each vehicle, federal tax laws allow the firm to avoid paying additional taxes on the replacement vehicle for the fleet since this capital good is simply maintaining the production capacity of the fleet owner. They would pay taxes on vehicles that add to the overall size of the fleet (in our case here, the stated fleet size of fifty thousand vehicles). States and localities would want to address these potential loopholes early on to hedge against a potentially large hit to sales tax revenues (Clark, Larco, and Mann 2017).

While this list of potential tax and fee revenue effects is not exhaustive of all potential areas of concern, it does provide a window into some of the key areas policymakers need to start thinking about as they prepare for the future with AV-enabled mobility.

What can TNCs as a form of transportation tell us about our future in the city budget office?

Currently, AVs are not on the road in any sort of meaningful volume to allow us to study how they impact cities today as technology. The transportation network companies (TNCs), such as Uber and Lyft, are serving essentially the same purpose of shared AVs because the passengers call for a ride and get in/get out without having to drive the vehicle. Consequently, TNCs give researchers an opportunity to explore what the impact of AVs might look like in the future. Learning from changes today and projecting the impacts into the future is a vital task for public managers today. Public managers need to start encouraging political leaders to widen their view of how to pay for government based on today by planning for tomorrow today. The following is not an exhaustive treatment of what the impacts of TNCs have already had on local government revenues, but rather provide an illustrative list of what local government leaders need to begin to think about.

Parking

Parking is one area in which there is growing evidence of behavioral change because of TNCs. While parking revenues (meters, garages, and enforcement) are on average less than 2 percent of local revenue (Clark, Larco, and Mann 2017), this share can be considerably larger for some cities as the quote from Robert Spiller at the start of this chapter indicates. Maciag (2017) found that "cities identified as most likely to incur the steepest revenue losses in our analysis were densely populated localities where parking comes at a premium." Although 2 percent may not seem like a huge share of overall revenue, it still cuts into a reliable source of revenue for governments and will have to be replaced with new sources. Perhaps a bigger threat to local government financial security comes from the potential decline in personally owned vehicles, some estimates place this figure as 90 percent fewer vehicles on the road in the future (Clark, Larco, and Mann 2017). To gauge the scope and size of parking as an American phenomenon, it has been estimated that there are "3.4 to 8 parking spaces for each car" in the United States—which would cover an area the size of West Virginia (Pitcher 2017).

The effects of AVs are not as far off as they might first seem. The effects of vehicles driven by someone other than the one seeking mobility in mass are beginning to manifest themselves on balance sheets today. Census data indicate that the number of car-free households is already increasing (Peterson 2016), though from this data it is unclear why they are car free. The disruption of TNCs to Austin, Texas have provided a natural experiment, which has allowed researchers to show that when the TNCs left Austin (due to city council ordinance) most TNC users were switching back to use of personal vehicles rather than using public transportation (Hampshire et al. 2017). The opposite effect has been seen as TNCs become more common in other cities though the magnitude is still small. The reason that lower rates of car ownership matters for cities is that parking and car-related revenue backed projects are threatened when fewer people drive because these projects become less in demand. The threat is strongly seen in revenue bonds for parking garages or parking excise taxes that support specific activities within a city (perhaps a sports stadium bond). If the revenue for these bonds goes away, the city is still going to want to find a way to continue to pay those debts owed or face credit downgrade on non-revenue bond issuances. The implications for bond default or fiscal stress initiated by these disappearing revenues is that their access to credit may be diminished and the borrowing costs could soar, even on projects beyond parking. As public managers plan for needed parking, they have to think of ways in which these projects can be repurposed for other uses to ensure financial sustainability.

Airports

Airport management and ownership varies from location to location, but for the most part they are owned and operated by city governments (Ibarcena 2017). Consequently, the relationship between TNCs and airport revenue is substantial. "Federal regulations prohibit airports from making a profit. But they are expected to raise enough money to cover their costs. And to do that, they collect revenue from a number of sources" (Bergal 2017). Airports rely upon two general types of revenues: aeronautical and non-aeronautical. Car rentals, parking, and ground transportation make up a substantial part of the non-aeronautical revenues—more than 40 percent (Ibarcena 2017). For some airports, car rental fees are the largest single source of revenue, making the shift to TNC use particularly troubling for those owners. TNCs have become a big piece of actual or potential revenue for these airports because in 2017, they made up about one quarter of all TNC trips taken (Ibarcena 2017). In Miami, Uber's "share of the business travelers segment increased from 17 to 67 percent in just two years" (Ibarcena 2017, 61) These trips accounted for revenues in excess of $2 million. In Dallas-Fort Worth International Airport's FY2018 budget, they state that non-airline "Revenues are essentially flat, recognizing the impact of Transportation Network Companies (TNCs) on parking and rental car revenues. This is occurring at all airports throughout the country" (Dallas Fort Worth International Airport 2017, 12).

Many of the taxes and fees collected by airports are designed to hit tourists or visitors rather than locals. When the tax revenues from the non-aeronautical sources dive, the sustainability of the airport becomes in question. As a consequence, airports have begun assessing pick-up and drop-off fees to the TNCs to cover the losses in revenue. The extent to which a single fee, of say $3 per trip, would replace the loss of a multi-day parking fee is quite clear. This means that TNC riders are now subsidizing the capital costs of parking garages and car rental facilities they are not using. There are also cases where TNC fees have been rejected by the elected bodies that control them (Bergal 2017). This will likely lead to higher parking rates, which could push more people into taking TNCs to the airport and lowering parking revenue further—ultimately creating a vicious cycle where the parking infrastructure lacks sufficient funding.

Some airports are working on plans to discount parking to compete with TNCs. Dallas-Fort Worth Airport (DFW) managers are typically seeing only 60 to 65 percent of their parking being used (Williamson 2018). Airport officials are seeking out ways in which a TNC user might be able to compare their costs using the airport parking lot versus the TNC cost and getting substantial discounts paying ahead of time to park at the airport instead (Williamson 2018). This may stem the flow of red ink temporarily for airports with declining parking demand, but the cost of mobility is expected to drop further with the advent of AVs as they no longer have to pay for a driver of the vehicle transporting people. Ultimately, the cost could drop by half or more.

Rental car alternatives "could become a threat to the rental car business" (Dallas Fort Worth International Airport 2017, 32). At the Dallas-Fort Worth airport alone, the risk of car rental revenue alone is putting "an estimated exposure of $1.0 million" in the next fiscal year (Dallas Fort Worth International Airport 2017, 14). This is not a Dallas-only phenomenon but a nationwide one.

Beyond the struggles airports are facing from TNC, some states are preempting airport authorities from charging fees on TNC trips or controlling their activities in other ways (Goodin and Moran 2017). TNCs were introduced more rapidly and without regulations applied to the taxi industry that has "traditionally been regulated at the local level" (Goodin and Moran 2017, 19). This has a lot to do with the economic and political power behind TNCs that is concentrated in a few companies, while taxis have long been highly localized and often sole-proprietors. These actions by states will hamper airports in those states from a range of options that would assist them in recovering revenues from TNCs that were lost in areas of airport operations (parking, rental car fees).

Public transportation

Seattle has recently made news as ridership in its public transportation system continued to increase (Beyer 2017)—while other cities have flat growth or declines in usage (Manville, Taylor, and Blumenberg 2018; Masabi 2018). TNCs have been blamed for some of this decline in other cities, but as a study of Southern California residents points out this explanation is far too simplistic. In the case of the greater Los Angeles area, purchases of cars have increased as people's incomes have gone up after the Great Recession, and with those increases, the number of cars purchased has also gone up (Manville, Taylor, and Blumenberg 2018). This creates more opportunities for new car owners to obtain access to the job market but puts a strain on public transit budgets. If we couple this shift in mobility from public transportation to private cars using the findings from Austin, Texas, the picture of private-vehicle preference becomes pretty clear. This could mean that TNCs, which offer private or semi-private and direct routes to destinations, will and are putting strains on public transit systems. Some public transit systems are taking TNCs on directly by partnering with those companies to get riders onto buses and trains by subsidizing the first/last mile of trips via TNCs taken in combination with public transit.

The directional impact of TNCs on public transit is complicated and mottled because little research has been done on the topic. In a recent survey of public transit riders, Masabi (2018) researchers found that users of TNCs were more likely than non-TNC users to feel that public transit systems were improving. This is coupled with an increasing likelihood of public transit-TNC joint trips (Masabi 2018). The same survey found that the key to getting an increase of joint trips might depend on the TNC providers and public transit systems using the same app or payment system in order to facilitate these types of trips. Furthermore, these researchers find that the "use of shared mobility services vastly increases the likelihood of riding public transit, pointing to a growing urban mobility ecosystem" (Masabi 2018, 7).

From a cost perspective, use of personal vehicles is estimated to be about $0.54/mile. Public transit operating and capital cost per mile is about twice that at $1.08/mile. Meanwhile the fares charged by TNC ranged from $0.65 to $2/mile (Polzin 2016). Due to a lower per-mile cost to the consumer in AVs, this is "expected to increase the competition with public transportation as some share of travelers choose automated vehicle services in lieu of public transportation" (Polzin 2016, 7). The effects of TNCs and eventually AVs on public transit is likely to "undermine transit ridership, particularly in markets in which transit services is not time-competitive, transit trip circuitry is greater, or the share of the transit travel time that could not be used productively" (Polzin 2016, 7). Thus, cost and convenience are intrinsically tied in efforts to plan for TNCs and the AV future (Masabi 2018; Polzin 2016).

While these examples of impacts of TNCs on local government revenues and services remain limited to date, these examples begin to shed light on how the TNC to AV transition in mobility is already happening and showing signs of impact. TNCs have given people new ways to move around their communities. The exponential growth of TNC use has not abated since their introduction and we should not expect that they are simply a fad. When AVs become widely available they are likely, at first, to be mostly used by the wealthier individuals—just as TNCs are. With this said, the high capital cost of AVs becomes less prominent as more people share vehicles and share rides, which will spread that cost across more people (Fehrenbacher 2018) just as public transportation can do. This has the real potential to get people out of their own vehicles and into a shared mobility option.

What are the equity concerns that AVs pose in relationship to city budgets?

Public transportation

Some of the biggest equity concerns that have come to the forefront in recent years are the potentially devastating effects that AVs could have on public transit systems. Some of these issues were broached in the previous section. Again, if we seek to learn from the experience of TNCs and apply those lessons to AVs we can see that the riders of TNCs may not be as diverse economically as public transit riders (City and County of San Francisco 2017). In essence, the opportunity to switch to a TNC or MaaS option is not equal within cities or across metropolitan areas. Further, beyond a pure dollars and cents perspective, the flight of wealthier riders may erode public support of public transportation systems as these individuals' political capital may stand behind TNC access over public transit access—though this is largely speculative at this point in time.

Motor fuel excise taxes

Motor fuel (gas and diesel) excise taxes have long been regressive in nature but will become more so in the future. The reason that motor fuel excise taxes pose a serious equity issue is that poorer populations are potentially the last adopters of AVs just as they are with TNCs (City and County of San Francisco 2017). Underlying this is the assumption that AVs will be largely powered by electricity rather than petroleum, thus fewer and fewer wealthy individuals will pay into these funds. Their use of roadways will likely increase rather than decrease. While the electric vehicle (EV) has a relatively small share of the market today, it is growing rapidly. EVs today do not pay a similar share of taxes to fund roadway infrastructure that petroleum-powered vehicles do. Since more people are transitioning to EVs, this places a large burden on those that maintain their use of petroleum-powered vehicles into the future. Some states are experimenting with vehicle mileage traveled (VMT) based taxes, yet their adoption has not been widespread or gone beyond pilot projects. We will talk more about VMT taxes later in the chapter.

Traffic citations

Given evidence of bias in ticket-issuance behavior by police—in that they are more likely to give speeding tickets to minorities (Goncalves and Mello 2017)— AVs provide an opportunity to reduce this bias (implicit or explicit) in government. This has the potential to diminish the regressivity of moving violation-related fines and fees. From the police perspective, a California Highway Patrol (CHP) captain spoke about how AVs are going to dramatically change norms in policing tactics (Davis 2016). The CHP captain noted that the "traditional traffic stop, a cornerstone of policing for decades, could be all but eliminated" (Davis 2016).

Given the myriad of examples of how these "traditional traffic stops" are often used, or at least seen as a way to introduce inequity in policy making, there is a potential that AVs could decrease bias in policing, as "an autonomous vehicle that does not commit traffic violations may never be subject to a traffic stop by a law enforcement officer" (Davis 2016). This, too, has the potential to reduce the disparate level of fines and fees that are charged to minorities, but in the minds of the police community this will "create the need for a more specialized law enforcement community" (Davis 2016).

Urban sprawl

A very substantial unknown with the introduction of AVs is whether or not people will move further away from the city center as the cost of mobility drops, if they will stay where they are, or move closer to the city center. AVs provide an opportunity for people to lose less productive time in transit between home and work because the occupant can potentially work while commuting. This creates a fear by planners and political leaders alike that this will create a push people further and further away from the city center, creating massive sprawl and congestion. Given the history of white-flight to the suburbs in past generations, creating inequality, AVs create that same fear that flight of those with resources further from the city center could exacerbate existing inequalities based on place and create new ones that are not yet fully understood.

Mitigating or leveraging the changes from AVs

Up until now we have proposed very little in the way of advice on how a local government might mitigate or leverage the effects of AVs. Some "fixes" in the era may be as easy as upping a tax rate, but the issues that we expect to see may require more than small or marginal adjustments. To set out on this investigation we had our graduate students work with the largest public transit agency in the State of Oregon, TriMet, the City of Portland, and a number of smaller metro area suburban communities to explore some of these questions. Seven student teams examined 24 different sources to fill revenue gaps that we expect to be created by the widespread adoption of AVs. Each team created three revenue packages. Variations in revenue packages evaluated included ways to incentivize transit means for varying fees for shared vehicles and private vehicles, varying fees by zone, and maintaining the status quo.

Traditional or existing revenue sources

Traditional revenue sources are expected to decline as a result of the implementation of AVs. As a result of the anticipated decline in traditional revenues, some teams suggested increasing and/or restructuring traditional revenue sources. The administrative structure already exists for these traditional revenue sources, but changes to rates or ways in which they are administered may need to be augmented. Table 7.2 represents an increase in the tax or fee on top of existing fees. Traditional transportation revenue sources include motor fuel excise

Table 7.2 Traditional transportation revenue options

Revenue Option	Fee	Multiplier	Implementation	Description
Motor fuel excise tax	$0.08 – $0.13 increase	Gallons	Local or state	Increase tax to offset improved fuel efficiency and increase in electric vehicles
Registration fees	$3 – $91 increase	Vehicles registered	State	Restructure fee to include AVs or increase fee generally or add additional rideshare registration fee
Heavy use vehicle taxes	1% increase	Heavy vehicles	State	General fee increase
Rideshare fees	$0.5 – $4 per ride, and 5%	Rideshare trips	Local	Increase or create a per-ride rideshare fee
Parking fees	$35 per fleet parking space, $195 per commercial business	Number of parked cars, monthly fee or daily fee	Local	Restructure or add parking fees or add AV fleet parking fee or add a commercial parking fee
Development charges	Varied based on development	AV fixture development	City	Add development charge for AV development fixtures

taxes, registration fees, maintenance fees, heavy use vehicle taxes, fees/taxes on ridesharing, parking fees, and development charges.

- Motor fuel excise taxes (gas tax): These taxes are the predominant source of revenue for transportation financing. As vehicles become more efficient and the fleet becomes increasingly electrified, cities could increase motor fuel taxes to offset the decline from fuel efficiency and electrification.
- Registration fees: Registration fees are an existing revenue source and registration fee increases could apply at the local level or disparately to autonomous vehicles or ridesharing vehicles.
- Heavy use vehicle taxes: Increase the existing heavy use vehicle taxes. Heavy use vehicle taxes are assessed on large trucks and other vehicles that are heavier and put a greater strain on city streets. The level of these taxes varies widely from city to city.
- Rideshare fees: Charge ridesharing through TNCs a per-trip fee or through licensing or franchising fees. Instituting licensing fees for firms (namely, on-demand ride-sharing firms such as Uber and Lyft) who wish to operate

autonomous vehicles in their jurisdiction could be a way to reclaim lost revenues that will result from shifts toward autonomous vehicles—a shift these ride-sharing firms will benefit from.

- Franchise fees: Franchise fees for rideshare companies and AV fleets would give access to dedicated pick-up zones and rideshare lanes on major thoroughfares as well as access to city transportation data. Using existing electricity franchise fees as a basis to structure this new fee, a rideshare franchise fee would be based on revenues from rides originating in the city.
- Parking fees: As traditional parking revenue declines, cities could turn to different types of parking fees targeting fleets or ridesharing to recoup lost revenue. A fleet parking fee is an annual permit for the use of storage and parking of fleet vehicles in public parking garages. A fee like this would be necessary if rideshare companies to used parking garages as fleet storage facilities. This agreement would help maintain existing buildings and their uses in the short term as cities adjusts to AV adoption.
- Development charges: Charge development fees on infrastructure for autonomous vehicles which may include charging infrastructure and parking facilities. The implementation of autonomous vehicles will change the way we shape our streets. Many ride-share and private autonomous vehicles will need space to pick up passengers. The impact fee would charge shared autonomous vehicle companies to reallocate street space to pick-up and drop-off zones.

New revenue sources

The researchers suggested that the Portland region can look to new revenue sources that have been implemented in other cities. New options included, vehicle miles traveled (VMT) fees, cordon pricing, and on/off ramp fees. Currently, OReGO program, a VMT fee, is being tested by the State of Oregon (Table 7.3).

- VMT: A VMT tax is a road usage charge (pay per mile) that transportation departments can use to overcome the limitations of the fuel tax and address potential future operations and funding concerns. In Oregon's pilot program OReGO, drivers plug a device in to their vehicle, which tracks their mileage. At the end of each month, the driver receives a road usage charge invoice in lieu of paying the fuel tax at the pump. There are multiple other ways to administer VMT that provide user- and government-friendly options at a low administrative cost. There are some privacy concerns with tracking mileage and particularly location. Third-party data collection may be necessary and include data privacy restrictions that limit governments' access to these data will likely be necessary before wide-spread adoption.

Table 7.3 New transportation revenue options

Fund Name	Fee	Multiplier	Implementation	Description
Vehicle miles traveled (VMT)	$0.00706–$0.57	Per mile	State	Per mile fee to replace gasoline tax
Cordon pricing	$0.25–$2.5	Per crossing or per day	State	Automatic license plate recognition to charge use of certain roads at certain times
On/off ramp fees	$2	Per on/off ramp use	State	Charge on use of on/off ramps

- Cordon pricing: Cordons are one-time charges to drive within or into a congested area within a city. These are easily adopted through the vehicle-to-infrastructure communications network, which will be available with Coordinated Autonomous Vehicle (CAV) technology (Liu et al. 2017). London and Singapore are two cities that have been using these fees for years, linked to vehicle license plate numbers rather than more high-tech solutions enabled by CAV—though it is clear the CAV will make these easier to administer.
- Ramp fees: A ramp fee is similar to a cordon price but charges a one-time fee for each vehicle entering or existing an on-ramp to a limited access highway. These are widely used on highways around the United States and could be adopted for wider use.

Innovative AV-focused revenue sources

Innovative revenue options that focus on AV technology are potential revenue options for the future. Local and state governments can capitalize on the AV technology structure and create new revenue sources. Innovative revenue sources discussed included pick up and drop off zones, empty seat taxes, fleet parking fees, use of curb access, GPS and data fees, a mobile business tax, electricity fees, charging station fees, and advertisement taxes (Table 7.4):

- Pick-up/drop-off zones: Assuming that rideshare companies provide autonomous options for travelers, cities can establish various drop-off and pick-up zones for automated rideshare vehicles. The rideshare vehicles would have specifically designated zones where they would be allowed to interact with customers and would be required to pay to use the space. In order to preserve space, these zones should be located near existing parking areas and the city should expect compensation similar to what it receives in parking for expected revenue losses.
- Empty seat tax: To disincentivize traveling with empty seats in their vehicle and to encourage a more economically efficient mode of transportation.

Table 7.4 Innovative transportation revenue options

Fund Name	Fee	Multiplier	Implementation	Description
Pick-up and drop-off zones	$10,000, $1,000, or $1	Per space, per zone, or per ride	Local	Charge AV companies to use pick-up and drop-off zones. Offset lost revenue from lost parking.
Empty seat tax	$0.0966 – $0.50	Empty seats	State	Charge fleet AVs or all vehicles for empty seats.
GPS and data fees	$1,500 per AV	Number of AVs	State	Partnerships with technology industry to access AV data.
Mobile business tax	6%	Corporate income	State	Collection of corporate income tax revenue from mobile businesses.
Electricity fees	$0.003 per kWh	kWh used	Local	Energy consumption tax.
Advertisement tax	5% per advertisement	Number of advertisements	State	Companies have discussed displaying advertisements in AVs. Charges taxes on advertising in AVs.
Charging station fees	$10 or 5% per month	Number of charging stations	Local	Fee on charging stations (private and public) may encourage a shared fleet model.

To assess the tax, user's vehicle would have a remote seat occupancy "smart sensor" that could be installed and/or required in vehicles. Then the device would communicate with toll-reading sensors or traffic monitors placed throughout the city to calculate the variable rate (rate dependent on the number of occupants) for payment. Similar to OReGO's VMT, drivers would receive invoice statements at the end of each month linked to an Easy Pass transponder. Much like utility services, riders will be charged consuming space that is not being used efficiently. These "smart meters" will require strict regulations similar to those enforcing odometers.

- GPS and data fees: Strides must be made in the ways we approach data storage and sharing before we can adapt to the needs of CAVs, however, data companies stand to make a lot of money in providing this service to the CAV market. As such, charging data corporation partners a monthly fee per CAV would generate sizeable revenue to the city in ways that will still be agreeable to the corporations.

- Mobile business tax: It will be important to consider permit and licensing procedures for mobile businesses, especially those serving food, which will require periodic health and safety inspections. Cities may want to consider coordinating the rules and administrative procedures for the food-based mobile business with those used for food trucks and other similar vendors currently in operation. Jurisdictions may also want to reconsider what constitutes zoning and building codes for mobile businesses, and ways in which revenue might be collected from the fees associated with each.

- Advertising tax: This is a tax to be collected for the city on the revenue that fleet operators make from selling ads displayed within the vehicle. It will be collected at the same time as business income tax. Shared fleet vehicles are likely to display ads inside the vehicles as an additional revenue stream. The revenue calculated is based on assumptions about average ad length and price.

- Charging station fees: Fees for charging stations are a pay-for-use system. Vehicles parked at charging stations are often assessed as a parking fee in addition to the charging station fee. Cities can incentivize electric CAV's by developing electric-friendly infrastructure with charging stations in cities, rural areas, and along highways and interstates. Smart, connected AV networks can guide cars to the most efficient charging station locations and prevent charging station queue congestion. Electric charging station fees could set a leasing framework with a wide variety of private companies at a set rate of payment to the city. This would require a consistent payment structure for citizens.

Conclusions

It is clear that AVs are likely to exacerbate transportation funding issues facing governments at all levels. State and local governments should examine existing transportation funding sources and project the potential declines in existing transportation sources. Transportation revenue declines will vary between cities based on current funding sources and the rate and pace of adoption. Some innovative revenue sources explored could be implemented at the local or state level. It is important that cities and states start to consider the issues in the short run and adapt new structures that anticipate the shift in technology. Further analysis is needed to determine political feasibility of many of the options proposed.

The fears of empty cars creating congestion are real and should be addressed proactively. It appears that TNCs are already creating congestion in our cities from a similar phenomenon that we could expect to see with AVs as they circle the city looking for riders (Clewlow and Mishra 2017). Consequently, as Clewlow and Mishra (2017, 29) note, "substantial policy action may be required to ensure that ridehailing can effectively be woven into the transportation network while reducing congestion and the emissions of transportation services. Absent of these efforts, congestion and emissions appear likely to grow." Congestion and empty miles will cost cities in more wear and tear on the roadways, costing the city more money in the long-run, but also create economic disincentives for people to work, play, and live in these areas.

Additionally, city leaders from around the country are already seeing congestion issues popping up from the pick-up and drop-off of TNC riders. With the advent of AVs and the demise of parking as we know it is only peaking those concerns of city leaders. As we have already mentioned, as cities seek out ways to transform parking areas to pick-up/drop-off areas they should think about ways in which to monetize them. The right-of-way allocated to parking has a price, so should the pick-up and drop-off allocations. San Francisco and Seattle are already piloting projects to push TNCs off main thoroughfares onto side streets to reduce the TNC-generated congestion of the pick-up and drop-off. The technology to know that this is happening in practice also allows cities to set fee or price for using high-demand areas for the pick-up and drop-off more broadly. Parking in high-demand areas costs more, so too should the curb use for TNCs in these areas.

We know that capital funding for road building and maintenance has been under constant threat for years because of a lack of a political willingness to modify excise tax rates on motor fuels. While some of the political unwillingness is driven by a public that is not aware of what taxes they are already paying (Duncan et al. 2017), a great deal of the opposition is imbedded in an unwillingness to be taxed/charged in any way for public goods. The funding for roadways is going to be a bigger challenge as vehicle power sources transition from internal combustion to electric, though today "Plug-in cars are responsible for a very small percentage of declining tax revenue" (Dumortier et al. 2016, 187). Consequently, in the short- and medium-term, tax and funding solutions should not be designed around the fuel source (Dumortier et al. 2016, 187), but rather around the use of the roads or curbs. This means that the fix may not be as simple as raising the rate at which we tax each gallon of fuel sold but rethinking the whole process of collecting funds to enable mobility.

The political realities of raising sufficient revenue to replace the fuel taxes are challenging (Duncan et al. 2017; Duncan and Graham 2013), but evidence suggests that an VMT tax of "$0.01 per VMT ($30 per 3,000 miles driven) would be sufficient to generate the same amount of revenue that was deposited into the [Federal Highway Trust Fund] in 2010" (Duncan and Graham 2013, 422). Surveys of the general population suggest that even fees that are that low are going to be hard to pass political muster. The average number of miles driven each year is about 13,500—meaning each VMT would cost about $135/year. It would still face tremendous headwinds. Tolls have been shown to be more politically palatable today (Duncan et al. 2017), so the task may be to introduce VMTs as a toll and transition how we talk about them over time. This may point to a lack of general understanding of VMT-based taxes or a weariness of a "new" kind of tax.

The budgetary and financial stress that AVs may create over time are not entirely pessimistic. Our own analysis is showing that transitioning municipal trash and recycling collection from human operated to at least partially AV-operated—with the truck being AV-driven—could save cities 26 to 53 percent on their cost to collect residential refuse. Similar automation of street sweeping and other maintenance tasks also provides local governments with an opportunity to lower operating expenses. The budgetary requirements of first responders is also likely to be pushed downward as more AVs are introduced onto the road-ways. Nearly all accidents on the roadway are human error. These accidents create high demand for fire and EMS response. Fewer crashes are expected, thus the size of those crews could be decreased dramatically, saving cities money in the process.

Overall, the future is going to bring a tremendous amount of change to how we get around and how government works. It is important that local leaders begin to plan for what this future will bring even with the level of uncertainty it brings. Starting massive infrastructure projects that are centered around how we get around today is becoming more and more risky. The public financial markets are already starting to become aware of the risks associated with issuing credit to these projects (Connery 2016; Clark, Larco, and Mann 2017). The flexibility and modifiability of infrastructure in the future may be what allows these projects to go forward without putting the bottom line at risk.

Note

1. Some student teams assumed revenues would decrease by 50 percent based on a mid-range adoption of AVs as suggested by Fagnant and Kockelman (2015). However, this simple assumption did not consider the specific sources of revenue and thus we do not discuss these estimates in this report.

References

Bensinger, G. and T. Higgins. 2018. "Uber Suspends Driverless-Car Program After Pedestrian Is Killed." *Wall Street Journal*, March 20, 2018, sec. Tech. https://www.wsj.com/articles/uber-suspends-driverless-car-program-after-pedestrian-is-killed-1521551002.

Bergal, J. 2017. "Airport Parking Takes Hit From Uber, Lyft." 2017. http://pew. org/2t98Rmr.

Beyer, S. 2017. "The Right Kind of Transit for 'In-Between' Cities." Governing Magazine. September 2017. http://www.governing.com/columns/urban-notebook/gov-transit-growing-cities.html.

California Department of Motor Vehicles. 2018. "Testing of Autonomous Vehicles." June 15, 2018. https://www.dmv.ca.gov/portal/dmv/detail/vr/autonomous/testing.

City and County of San Francisco. 2017. "2017 San Francisco City Survey." San Francisco, CA. http://openbook.sfgov.org/webreports/details3.aspx?id=2446.

Clark, B. Y., N. Larco, and R. F. Mann. 2017. "The Impacts of Autonomous Vehicles on Local Government Budgeting and Finance." SSRN Scholarly Paper ID 3009840. Rochester, NY: Social Science Research Network. https://papers.ssrn.com/abstract=3009840.

Clewlow, R. and G. Mishra. 2017. "Disruptive Transportation: The Adoption, Utilization, and Impacts of Ride-Hailing in the United States. Institute of Transportation Studies, University of California." Davis, Research Report UCD-ITS-RR-17-07. https://itspubs.ucdavis.edu/wp-content/themes/ucdavis/pubs/download_pdf.php?id=2752.

Connery, B. 2016. "Autonomous Vehicles and Municipal Bonds." New York, NY: Morgan Stanley.

Dallas Fort Worth International Airport. 2017. "FY 2018 Adopted Budget." Dallas Fort Worth International Airport. https://www.dfwairport.com/cs/groups/webcontent/documents/webasset/p2_905540.pdf.

Davis, K. 2016. "Preparing for a Future with Autonomous Vehicles." *Police Chief Magazine* (blog). July 1, 2016. http://www.policechiefmagazine.org/preparing-for-a-future-with-autonomous-vehicles/.

Dumortier, J., M. W. Kent, and S. B. Payton. 2016. "Plug-in Vehicles and the Future of Road Infrastructure Funding in the United States." *Energy Policy* 95 (August): 187–95. https://doi.org/10.1016/j.enpol.2016.05.005.

Duncan, D., and J. Graham. 2013. "Road User Fees Instead of Fuel Taxes: The Quest for Political Acceptability." *Public Administration Review* 73(3): 415–26. https://doi.org/10.1111/puar.12045.

Duncan, D., V. Nadella, A. Clark, S. Giroux, and J. Graham. 2017. "Searching for a Tolerable Tax: Public Attitudes toward Roadway Financing Alternatives." *Public Finance Review* 45(5): 678–700. https://doi.org/ 10.1177/1091142116653818.

Fagnant, D. J., and K. Kockelman. 2015. "Preparing a Nation for Autonomous Vehicles: Opportunities, Barriers and Policy Recommendations." *Transportation Research Part A: Policy and Practice* 77 (July): 167–81. https://doi.org/10.1016/j.tra.2015.04.003.

Fehrenbacher, K. 2018. "The future of sustainable transportation is—Uber Pool?" Text. GreenBiz. March 22, 2018. https://www.greenbiz.com/article/future-sustainable-transportation-isuber-pool.

Goncalves, F., and S. Mello. 2017. "A Few Bad Apples? Racial Bias in Policing." Working Paper. http://dataspace.princeton.edu/jspui/handle/88435/dsp01z890rw746.

Goodin, G., and M. Moran. 2017. "Transportation Network Companies." College Station, TX: Texas A&M Transportation Institute. https://policy.tti.tamu.edu/wp-content/uploads/2017/03/TTI-PRC-TNCs-SBC-031417.pdf.

Hampshire, R. C., C. Simek, T. Fabusuyi, X. Di, and X. Chen. 2017. "Measuring the Impact of an Unanticipated Disruption of Uber/Lyft in Austin, TX." http://dx.doi.org/10.2139/ssrn.2977969.

Ibarcena, C. 2017. "Going under the Hood: The Winners and Losers of Florida's Transportation Network Companies Law Notes and Comments." *Nova Law Review* 42: 45–68.

Internal Revenue Service. 2016. "Publication 544: Sales and Other Dispositions of Assets." https://www.irs.gov/publications/p544/ch01.html#en_US_2016_publink100072371.

International Transport Forum. 2015. Urban Mobility System Upgrade. International Transport Forum.

Liu, Z., Y. Zhang, S. Wang, and L. Zhibin. 2017. "A Trial-and-Error Method with Autonomous Vehicle-to-Infrastructure Traffic Counts for Cordon-Based Congestion Pricing," Journal of Advanced Transportation, Vol. 2017.

Maciag, M. 2017. "How Driverless Cars Could Be a Big Problem for Cities." Governing Magazine. August 1, 2017. http://www.governing.com/topics/finance/gov-cities-traffic-parking-revenue-driverless-cars.html.

Manville, M., B. D. Taylor, and E. Blumenberg. 2018. "Falling Transit Ridership: California and Southern California." Southern California Association of Governments. https://trid.trb.org/view/1500403.

Masabi. 2018. "Key Factors Influencing Ridership in North America." Masabi. https://info.masabi.com/hubfs/Masabi%20Transit%20Survey%20Report%20-%2008-1.pdf?utm_campaign=Mass%20Transit%20Rider%20Research%20Report&utm_medium=email&_hsenc=p2ANqtz-9S6Wct4XfEsWisycdodWdudaI-YNFb1tHPZCMwDQ1hNCjHGZ0NuB9XMLDpFSgKFGYQ1EXxmURMv66cag-iM6hZRr_aupJw&_hsmi=62675183&utm_content=62675183&utm_source=hs_automation&hsCtaTracking=f5353a22-69a6-402c-8c8e-c96e677ad82b%7Cb23a8cef-9a85-4433-8161-e8cf08edc25d.

Peterson, J., and R. Lewis. 2017. "Autonomous Vehicle Revenue Implications Portland, Tigard, and Tualatin." Sustainable City Year Program (SCYP) Final Project Reports. Eugene, Oregon: School of Planning, Public Policy, and Management, University of Oregon.

Peterson, S. J. 2016. "Car-Free Living in the United States: What the Data Says." *Medium* (blog). December 14, 2016. https://medium.com/@sjpeterson/car-free-living-in-the-united-states-what-the-data-says-bc5bd396f52e#.3s6jkv8cp.

Pitcher, P. (Paige Marie). 2017. "Hit the Deck: Impacts of Autonomous Vehicle Technology on Parking and Commercial Real Estate." Thesis, Massachusetts Institute of Technology. http://dspace.mit.edu/handle/1721.1/113471.

Polzin, S. E. 2016. "Implications to Public Transportation of Emerging Technologies." National Center for Transit Research. https://www.nctr.usf.edu/wp-content/uploads/2016/11/Implications-for-Public-Transit-of-Emerging-Technologies-11-1-16.pdf.

Scott, M. 2017. "The Future of European Transit: Driverless and Utilitarian." *New York Times*, May 28, 2017. https://www.nytimes.com/2017/05/28/technology/the-future-of-european-transit-driverless-and-utilitarian.html.

Steinmetz, K. 2015. "How Uber and Lyft Are Trying to Solve America's Carpooling Problem." Time. 2015. http://time.com/3923031/uber-lyft-carpooling/.

Threlfall, R. 2018. "2018 Autonomous Vehicles Readiness Index | KPMG | GLOBAL." KPMG. January 16, 2018. https://home.kpmg.com/xx/en/home/insights/2018/01/2018-autonomous-vehicles-readiness-index.html.

Ward, J. W., J. J. Michalek, I. L. Azevedo, C. Samaras, and P. Ferreira. 2018. "On-Demand Ridesourcing Has Reduced Per-Capita Vehicle Registrations and Gasoline Use in U.S. States." In https://trid.trb.org/view/1496632.

Waymo. 2018. "On the Road." Waymo. 2018. https://waymo.com/ontheroad/.

Williamson, R. 2018. "Airports, Facing Competition Enhance Parking Technology for Competition with Uber, Lyft." Bond Buyer. 2018. https://www.bondbuyer.com/news/airports-guard-parking-revenues-against-ride-hailing-services.

Zhang, W., S. Guhathakurta, J. Fang, and G. Zhang. 2015. "Exploring the impact of shared autonomous vehicles on urban parking demand: An agent-based simulation approach." *Sustainable Cities and Society*:12. doi: 10.1016/j.scs.2015.07.006.

8   Policy and program innovation in anticipation of the new mobility future

Joshua Karlin-Resnick, Jeff Tumlin, and Meg Merritt

Introduction

In the early twentieth century, cities across North America were caught off-guard by the emergence of personal motorized transportation. At the time, streets were filled with things like vehicles crossing in front of horse-drawn carriages—slowing to make way for pedestrians crossing wherever they could. At the urging of auto companies and the growing class of drivers, however, those in government quickly saw this arrangement as chaos.

As part of an effort to convince the public and therefore local planners and engineers, to solve these problems by putting cars at the center of the public realm, those developing the technology produced alluring visions like the General Motors Futurama exhibit (as shown in Figure 8.1) at the 1939 World's Fair in New York. Over the next several decades, cities made a series of policy choices that together overhauled the way we use public rights of way in the interest of making things more orderly and aligned with this vision of "the future." Almost universally, North American cities (and in more recent years, cities around the world) designed streets to make vehicular movement as fast and easy as possible, shunting other users to the margins and ignoring other policy goals.

In their efforts to catch up with the demands of new technology, these cities failed to think about the unintended consequences of this radical re-prioritization of public space: Uncomfortable and unsafe conditions for pedestrians and cyclists, a poor public realm that erodes the unique and interesting character of neighborhood commercial centers, and an ever-growing expectation of fast vehicular movement that cities can never achieve in light of the congestion that is endemic to areas in which autos have essentially been made the only mobility choice. Most major roadways, continent-wide, now look more like multi-lane concrete expanses with little accommodation for anything but vehicles.

In more recent decades, some cities have been using a range of policy tools to begin to reverse the worst excesses of auto-oriented right-of-way planning. Through streetscape redesigns that reflect complete streets and vision zero policies, cities have slowly but surely started to reprioritize non-motorized travelers, making certain areas safer, more comfortable, and more inviting for lingering, shopping, and other pro-social behaviors. However, after decades of auto-oriented

Figure 8.1 Futurama vision for streets, 1939 World's fair

planning and street design, it will take decades more for these policies to have their full effect and truly return people to the center of the public realm.

A new set of visions of the future

In recent years, we have begun to see the emergence of a new set of visions for the future, again often created and promoted by those developing an exciting new technology. The companies spending billions of dollars developing autonomous vehicle technology, have proclaimed that there will be a range of potential benefits in quickly adopting this technology, from eliminating traffic-related fatalities to reducing congestion by increasing the carrying capacity of roadways to freeing drivers to sleep, work, or relax during commutes instead of nervously gripping the steering wheel. Some analysts have pointed out that achieving all of these benefits will likely require further marginalizing non-motorized travelers, in a replay of the history reviewed above. As autonomous vehicles begin to proliferate in the coming years and as their needs come into conflict with other modes, there will surely be calls to manage rights of way such that minimizes potential conflicts as much as possible. One way or another, cities will need to make new policies or adjust existing ones to incorporate autonomous vehicles in urban life.

Other potential byproducts

In addition to marginalizing people in public rights of way, unfettered autonomous vehicle travel could change how we live in a range of other ways, with major consequences for life in cities. The allure of autonomous vehicles is centered on the ways in which they may greatly expand personal convenience by making door-to-door travel more available and less burdensome than it is today. That could reduce or eliminate disincentives to living on the urban fringe, encouraging people to move further and further from their jobs and triggering a dramatic reshuffling of our built environment. Of course, such a reshuffling would greatly exacerbate congestion and increase vehicle miles traveled. In the absence of a massive increase in the share of energy generated from renewable sources, this would also supercharge the warming of our planet. A range of indicators show that we might already be on a disastrous trajectory—researchers have found that the emergence of ride-hail services is associated with increased VMT per capita and travel behavior that makes less efficient of the transportation system (Clewlow and Mishra 2017; Schaller 2017).

The worst of these effects are only likely to happen if autonomous vehicles are adopted as private mobility resources, in much the same way cars were adopted a century ago. An alternative model—shared mobility—has emerged in recent years, such as market entrants like ride-hail companies (e.g., Uber and Lyft in North America, Didi in China, and MyTaxi in Europe), car-share companies (e.g., round-trip versions like Zipcar and Getaround and point-to-point versions like Car2Go), bike-share companies (e.g., docked bike-share by companies like Motivate and dockless versions by companies like Jump and Spin), and scooter-share companies (e.g., those that emerged on the streets of American cities in the spring of 2018 like Lime and Bird). Some companies and governments envision a world in which all of these mobility choices are organized in a simple, user-friendly platform that allows people to choose from a variety of mobility services to find the one that meets their need for a specific trip. This idea is sometimes called "mobility-as-a-service," and it is a model that looks a lot like the one that has taken over the music, television, and movie industries in recent years.

If autonomous vehicles are incorporated as part of this quickly growing ecosystem of shared mobility services, there might be a significant number of opportunities to *improve* the public realm and other important aspects of urban life. To start, a reduced need for parking and more efficient use of right-of-way space could make much more room for the social interaction and commerce that draw people to cities in the first place.

Proactive people-centered policies

Cities have a range of policy tools at their disposal that can help them shape the autonomous vehicles' operating environment—public rights of way—and help ensure that the technology is adopted and accommodated in ways that align with the public good. What exactly does "the public good" mean? In modern democracies, including the United States, local jurisdictions often have a great deal of room to define that for themselves, through planning documents and local policies.

A number of cities are already beginning to lay out the framework and develop policies that aim to manage the public rights of way for the public good, both in response to the emergence of new mobility technologies in recent years and in anticipation of more dramatic changes in the future. Revising mistakes of the past, these cities are focused on the movement of people through streets rather than the prioritized movement of vehicles. The following sections review some of the areas in which cities (and, in some cases, full regions, states, and countries) are proactively working to make policy.

Forward-thinking cities have begun to establish policies and frameworks in the following key areas:

- Establishing proactive policies to address new mobility options as they emerge
- Using grant funding to pilot new mobility options or to expand access to existing transportation infrastructure
- Pricing mobility to reward travelers in higher-capacity modes with faster travel times and disincentivize travelers in inefficient, network congesting single occupant or low-occupancy vehicles
- Managing curb space and modal conflicts around it
- Increasing developers' flexibility through parking and transportation demand-management requirements
- Testing autonomous transit
- Establishing data-sharing requirements and protocols
- Reorganizing government for the future of mobility

This chapter shares examples of policies made in each of these areas and concludes by discussing a set of policies or design approaches cities should consider implementing today, to ensure that incentive structures encourage behavior that is consistent with the things that make our most treasured urban places special.

Early policy moves

It is difficult to make policy that addresses an uncertain future. However, we already have a sense of the types of changes that may be coming. Car- and bike-share services have added brand new ways of using modes that previously required personal ownership. Ride-hail services (also known as transportation network companies, or TNCs) have made it easier to use for-hire vehicle services by making it simple to hail a car and pay for a ride with a smartphone. Cities that are leading the way use experiences grappling with regulating these new modes to establish frameworks that will guide engagements with future additions to the mobility ecosystem. Others are adjusting the way they regulate elements of the existing system to accommodate changes in travel behavior they are already seeing.

An attempt to highlight best practices in the quickly changing world of mobility can necessarily only be a snapshot in time, not a comprehensive or exhaustive list. As such, the sections that follow highlight some of the cities that have taken action in key areas as of spring 2018.

Mobility playbooks

Mobility playbooks are clear statements of values, policies, and/or strategies for dealing with emerging modes of transportation. The cities which have developed these playbooks have done so after realizing existing approaches to regulating the transportation system—and, in some cases, the time those approaches require—are not responsive enough to a fast-changing world. While many cities are eager to be seen as giving an open embrace to the future, the more thoughtful ones have taken the time to consider how new technologies might align with existing long-term policies and plans before throwing open their doors.

Mobility playbooks developed to date have come in different forms, and three cities offer examples of these different approaches: Seattle, Minneapolis/St. Paul, and Austin.

Seattle, Washington: leading with values

Seattle released its *New Mobility Playbook* in September 2017 (Seattle Department of Transportation 2017); the document is to guide the efforts of the city's New Mobility Program. The Playbook lays out the city's values as they relate to emerging mobility services, while framing the whole initiative in the context of past transformations in mobility technology and Seattle's broader values.

Specifically, the document lays out five "principles for new mobility" that are to drive decisions about how to accommodate, regulate, and/or support new modes in the coming years:

- "Put people and safety first": Focus on pedestrian, bicycle, and transit rider safety and comfort, especially in decisions about how to allocate street space.
- "Design for customer dignity and happiness": Simplify the experience of using individual transportation services while promoting the proliferation of new ones.
- "Advance race and social justice": Actively "roll back systemic racial and social injustices" caused by the transportation system in earlier generations.

- "Forge a clean mobility future": Address the city's ambitious climate goals in deciding how to handle new modes.
- "Keep an even playing field": Establish a "fair and flexible" regulatory environment.

The document also transparently addresses both the potential upsides and downsides of new technologies, at least as they stood when the document was authored in 2017. Specially, it discusses the potential of new technologies to either help the city accommodate growth without additional congestion or cause vast increases in congestion if or when the cost of motorized travel falls. It points to the potential positives and negatives of new technologies from equity and environmental perspectives. Other potential upsides it calls out are the potential to create more options for getting around while making the system more responsive to people's needs in real time. Potential downsides include eroding the user base and, in turn, the long-term finances of transit, disrupting the economy by causing significant job losses, and creating a cacophony of different mobility equipment and services in the public realm.

Finally, the document lays out a set of initial "plays," along with a set of strategies associated with each one, to guide the Seattle Department of Transportation's actions over the short term. These plays include ensuring that new mobility options are fair, accessible for all populations, actively supporting "safer, more active, and people-first uses" of streets, reorganizing the department to "manage innovation and data" more efficiently, create a useful new "data infrastructure," and more actively anticipating and responding to new transportation options as they emerge.

The city used an in-progress draft of the Playbook to guide its first-in-the-country approach to regulating free-floating bike share. As of spring 2018, SDOT also had an active initiative to bring electric-vehicle charging to public rights of way.

Twin Cities, Minnesota: A Strategic Framework for Policymakers

The Twin Cities' *Shared Mobility Action Plan* (Shared Use Mobility Center 2017) is a performance-oriented, rather than values-centered, action plan. It lays out two key objectives:

- Removing fifty thousand private cars from roads in the region over the next ten years
- Ensuring that the user bases of shared-mobility programs in the region reflect that of public transit in the region

To reach these two goals, the action plan lays out ten strategies:

- Growing shared mobility to support the use of transit
- Piloting flexible or on-demand transit

- Build on an existing local transit app to create a "data clearinghouse"
- Stabilizing car share and returning it to a growth trajectory in the region
- Evolve the region's successful bike share program and expand it to other parts of the region
- Elevating the role of vanpooling in commutes
- Encouraging the availability and use of carpooling and of fare-splitting versions of transportation network companies (e.g., Uber Pool and Lyft Line)
- Creating "mobility hubs," and concentrating the growing range of mobility options around these new hubs
- Improving transportation demand management in the region
- Optimizing parking and the use of street space to further encourage the use of shared mobility services

The document follows a more traditional planning-report format than Seattle's *Playbook*, starting with detailed discussion of existing conditions that reviews the region's growth plans, existing transportation options, and usage patterns. It then looks at existing travel behavior and assesses which parts of the region might be most primed for increased use of shared mobility options, based on drive-alone rates, population density, vehicle ownership, and other factors. After a detailed discussion of the ten strategies, the document concludes with an implementation timeline and prioritized list of next steps laying out specific actions for three two-year periods through 2021.

With its organization around performance goals and strategies, the Twin Cities' *Action Plan* seems to be aimed more at agency staff and policymakers than the general public. It provides specific recommendations on the roles of different agencies and jurisdictions, as well as those of key stakeholders like community-based organizations, employers, and developers.

Austin, Texas: A hybrid approach

The approach taken by Austin falls somewhere in between the values-based approach taken by Seattle and the strategy-based one taken in the Twin Cities. Austin's draft *Smart Mobility Roadmap* (City of Austin 2017) includes some discussion of local policy and planning goals, but much of the document is devoted to describing existing transportation conditions in the region, reviewing the status of and projections for different technologies, and laying out a series of recommended actions in each of a few basic categories:

- Shared-use mobility services
- Autonomous vehicles
- Electric vehicles and infrastructure
- Data and technology
- Land use and infrastructure

Like the Twin Cities document, Austin's seems to be aimed more at policy-makers and transportation professionals than the general public, with its lengthy review of existing conditions, policy actions to date, and detailed implementation tables for each policy and category. However, like the Seattle document, Austin's seems to have an eye toward the more distant future, and a much more specific one at that. It includes a detailed discussion of the trajectory of autonomous vehicle technology, and it calls for policymakers to actively plan for and encourage the integration of driverless vehicles into the local mobility ecosystem.

Pilot programs

Some cities are already actively supporting the proliferation of new transportation technologies, creating grant funding engines to fund new-mobility pilot programs that have particularly strong potential to meet public policy goals. Los Angeles and Pittsburgh are two cities highlighted in this section, but many more cities, counties, and metropolitan planning organizations (MPOs), as well as the federal government, have made grant funding available for studies of how to integrate new modes into the larger transportation system and for pilot programs that test approaches to partnering with new mobility providers and/or aim to expand access to new services.

Los Angeles, CA: Seeking "extraordinary innovation"

Los Angeles Metro, a county-level transit agency that runs one of the most extensive bus networks in the country, created a new division in 2015 that explicitly focuses on spurring innovations in the way mobility services are provided within its service area. The Office of Extraordinary Innovation (OEI) seeks to find "new ways of thinking and innovative new methods and approaches for bringing convenient, affordable, and effective mobility solutions to Los Angeles" (Los Angeles Metro 2018a).

OEI aims to deliver innovation through pilots that make direct use of emerging mobility technologies, public-private partnerships, and pitches from those with innovative ideas that "jump-start" the "traditional public procurement process." The division is also tasked with developing a new strategic plan for the agency and modernizing agency processes through internal consulting.

As of May 2018, the division was pursuing two major public projects. The first, a microtransit pilot that was scheduled to launch in mid-2018, aims to plan, design, implement, and evaluate a new transit-like service that allows for real-time requests and route generation within a defined set of service zones (Los Angeles Metro 2018b). The new service is to be "intuitive, user-friendly, and designed to encourage multiple modes of public transportation."

A second pilot, funded in part through the federal Department of Transportation's Mobility on Demand Sandbox grant program, would provide first- and last-mile connections to and from three major Metro transit stations.

Rides would use on-demand technology from Via. The pilot (which is also slated to start in mid-2018) aims to have them be:

- Shared, with multiple customers traveling in the same direction in the same car
- Affordable, with Metro covering some of the cost of the rides
- Accessible, with full accommodation of customers with disabilities
- On-demand, via either a smartphone app and a call center

Unlike the microtransit pilot, which would involve the use of a fleet of larger vans and shuttles, the mobility on demand pilot would be centered on the use of drivers' own vehicles.

Other projects the division is pursuing include: exploring new project-delivery methods, improving train and traffic signal systems through recently developed technologies, and understanding the potential utility of "internet of things" technologies to improve the upkeep and operation of the transit system.

Pittsburgh, Pennsylvania: Smart cities participant

The City of Pittsburgh has developed a range of "smart cities" programs, many in partnership with local universities, that were, together, part of its successful bid to join the Smart Cities Collaborative in 2018. The project is led by the think tank Transportation for America.

The effort was led by the city's Department of Mobility and Infrastructure, which was created in 2016 to bring together a range of transportation-related functions that had previously been spread across a number of city and regional agencies. A few of the projects included under the banner of the city's "smart cities" initiative (City of Pittsburgh 2018):

- An autonomous shuttle pilot that would connect a new development in the Hazelwood neighborhood, southeast of the city's downtown, with downtown and the research and technology research and employment hubs in the Oakland neighborhood.
- The development of a "data utility" that would be a "platform and process framework" for making decisions across city departments and in collaboration with the private sector. The utility would create data-format standards and make rich datasets available to the general public.
- An effort to create a "clean-energy transportation corridor" extending from downtown into Hazelwood that would include converting some of the municipal fleet to electric vehicles and installing vehicle-charging facilities, which would be publicly accessible during the day, in a city-owned parking lot along the corridor.
- Technology-based pilots targeted at improving mobility services for homeless people and for those trying to access healthcare facilities in parts of the city.
- The deployment of a signal-optimization technology developed at CMU along a wide range of key corridors.

The city was also an early epicenter of autonomous vehicle testing, with Uber launching a self-driving fleet in the city in 2016. Some of the technology included in early autonomous vehicles was developed in the robotics and artificial intelligence research programs at Carnegie Mellon University and other local universities.

Pricing

If the time and financial costs of motorized mobility fall significantly, as experts believe they will with a variety of technological developments in the coming years, the densest cities and most crowded travel corridors could see vast increases in demand for motorized travel that would, in turn, lead to crippling congestion. The most effective way to mediate travel demand is the most effective way to mediate demand for many limited commodities: To put a price tag on it.

Well before the recent explosion of technology-enabled mobility services, a few leading global cities had already developed robust programs for charging the least space-efficient travel behavior in their most crowded areas. These efforts, as well as emerging efforts to mitigate congestion caused in particular by TNCs, offer early models of efforts to encourage high-occupancy or non-motorized travel where it is most important. Mobility pricing efforts may become both more important and easier to implement as more and more travel is made in vehicles that are connected to data networks and whose functionality is rooted in global positioning systems (GPS).

London, Swedish cities, and Vancouver, British Columbia: Congestion pricing

Several cities have established or are in the process of exploring congestion pricing schemes, which establishes a cordon around congested districts or on congested pieces of transportation infrastructure and charge vehicles a fee that can vary by time of day, vehicle occupancy, or vehicle type.

London first established a congestion pricing zone in 2003 and it has evolved and expanded in several stages since (Transport for London 2008). The program charges 11.50 British pounds for private-vehicle travel into the zone between 7:00 a.m. and 6:00 p.m. on weekdays. Modes that tend to have higher occupancies (e.g., buses and taxis) or that take up less space (e.g., motorcycles) are exempt from the charge. Over time, the program has reduced vehicle volumes within the zone by 10 to 20 percent, with some reductions in private vehicle volumes offset by increases in high-occupancy vehicle volumes.

More recently, the Swedish national government established a "congestion tax" for travel into core zones in the country's two biggest cities, Stockholm and Gothenburg (Transport Styrelsen 2018). Charges are in effect between 6:00 a.m. and 6:29 p.m. on weekdays and prices vary by time of day, ranging from as low as 9 Swedish kroner (SEK) to as high as 22 SEK in Gothenburg and from 11 to 35 SEK in downtown Stockholm. A third charging zone covers a key highway through central Stockholm, the Essingeleden, and ranges from 15 to 30 SEK during the same hours. Drivers are charged automatically through a license plate reader (LPR)–based system.

With a failed effort to establish congestion pricing in lower Manhattan in early 2018, the region around Vancouver, Canada may be the first one in North America to establish a congestion pricing. Through the "It's Time" project, the region is currently engaging in a very public process to explore what policymakers call "decongestion charging" (Mobility Pricing Independent Commission 2018). The program is explicitly aimed at reducing congestion, promoting fairness, and generating funding for key infrastructure needs. In January 2018, the project completed an initial phase of research, public outreach, and analysis that laid out a limited set of viable decongestion charging alternatives. The next phase will further develop the details of a potential program and lay out what implementation might require.

Oregon: VMT-based charges

The State of Oregon has been piloting a VMT-based mobility fee program over the last several years in an effort to pioneer an alternative to gas taxes that are rapidly declining in buying power (Oregon Department of Transportation 2017). The program, known as OReGO, could provide an early model for efforts to scale charges for motorized travel to the level of impact on the transportation system.

Working with existing technologies, the program provides those who opt into the program with a device that, once installed in a standard car data port, tracks the number of miles traveled by the car. Participants are charged 1.5 cents per mile driven. Because drivers still pay gas taxes when they fill up, taxes paid are treated as a "pre-payment of road charges." Users can choose between devices that include or do not include GPS. The device also offers some bells and whistles, including engine diagnostics, a "find my car" vehicle location service, and "driving badges" to reward fuel-efficient driving behavior.

The pilot has shown that it is possible to manage a VMT charging program using existing technologies. Though program administrators have concluded "a system that relies exclusively on devices installed in vehicles will create challenges for a mandatory program." (Connected vehicles will likely offer a more scalable way to implement VMT charging for the reasons described earlier in this section.) Through surveys, the program also found that a plurality of Oregonians feels that "a mileage-based system for transportation funding is more fair than other options presented." Researchers also examined the potential equity implications of the program and found that urban users would likely pay more than rural users (because of greater use of fuel-efficient vehicles in urban areas) and the rich would likely pay more than the poor (because they drive more).

A coalition of states has joined Oregon in exploring the concept. While a bill has been introduced in the Oregon legislature to make the program mandatory, the legislature has yet to act.

Chicago: TNC fees

Establishing fees for travel by TNCs is another approach some cities have taken. The rationale for such fees has ranged from charging TNCs for impacts on the local transportation network like increased VMT to leveling the playing field between TNCs and traditional taxis to recouping some transit revenue lost due to declining ridership attributed to TNCs.

Chicago established a flat fifty-two-cent fee on all ride hail trips, no matter the distance, in 2015. The city recently raised the fee by fifteen cents for 2018 and by an additional five cents for 2019. The fee increases were explicitly tied to a need to raise revenue to support transit, and the additional revenues from the 2018 and 2019 fee increases are to go to the Chicago Transit Authority (CTA) (Spielman 2017). San Francisco, Portland, and New York City also levy per-ride charges on TNCs.

To truly align fees to the local impacts of TNC operations, fees might best scale to the length of trips and/or the combined revenue- and non-revenue travel distance of the vehicle used for a given trip or set of trips. Doing so would directly align the price signal to the externalities caused by the travel behavior. Sao Paulo explored per-mile fees in 2014 but ultimately did not implement them (Darido 2016). Fees could also range based on the number of passengers in a vehicle, with lower per-passenger fees for higher occupancy vehicles.

Curb space and modal-conflict management

Curb space is quickly becoming the epicenter of a wide range of pressures caused by new transportation options and evolving travel behavior. Increased passenger=loading demand (caused by TNCs) and commercial delivery activity (caused by the increase in e-commerce) have already begun having important effects on other users of the transportation system. In areas without available curbside loading space, double-parked passenger and commercial delivery vehicles can block unreinforced bicycle facilities (Brinklow 2017) and delay transit. Competition for curb space is likely only to increase as autonomous vehicles proliferate and as people continue to shop online in greater and greater numbers.

The National Association of City Transportation Officials (NACTO) recommends that cities take concrete steps to protect bicycle facilities and address transit delay challenges (NACTO 2017a). Specifically, the organization recommends prioritizing curb space for transit stops as well as dedicated lanes in commercial districts, where pressure on curbs from all modes tends to be highest and "it is usually impossible to accommodate all potential curbside uses immediately in front of their destinations."

Creating ample loading and delivery activity down the block or around the corner, and pricing or otherwise managing the use of loading spaces to ensure that vehicles stay in them only as long as needed, can help significantly reduce double-parking, when accompanied by robust enforcement. Creating "flex zones," in which use of curb space vary by time of day based on demand and/or policy goals, is another potential approach. When curb space is allocated to bikeways and nearby uses could create demand for curbside loading activity, NACTO recommends using both horizontal separation (buffer zones) and vertical separation (safe-hit posts, raised curbs, or other physical reinforcement) (NACTO 2017b).

A few cities provide examples of using these types of approaches to proactively address increased pressure on curb space. In the examples below, cities have established frameworks for prioritizing curbside uses, worked with TNCs to direct drivers to specific zones, or created large designated loading zones and lots (mostly at sites with intense demand like airports and professional sports facilities).

Seattle: A prioritization framework for curb space

Seattle has created a prioritization framework for the use of curb space throughout the city. The city treats streets' edge lanes—used almost exclusively for private vehicle parking in most cities—as flex zones, with the function of the zone varying based on a clear hierarchy of uses that varies by context (Seattle Department of Transportation 2018).

In residential zones, the framework prioritizes "access for people" (e.g., for transit stops, bike parking, or passenger loading) while in the industrial and commercial/mixed-use areas prioritizes "access for commerce" (e.g., commercial vehicle loading zones). In all areas, the city prioritizes "support for modal plan priorities," which can include transit lanes, bicycle facilities, and other facilities for active mobility.

Reallocating curbside lanes from their traditional function as space for parked private vehicles can be controversial. A clear framework for thoughtfully allocating curb space based on the context can "give project managers assurances of policy support in making the case for localized curbside changes that support transit," according to NACTO.

San Francisco: Coordination with TNCs for curb management pilots

As of spring 2018, San Francisco was in the process of developing a curb loading zone pilot with the two main TNCs, Uber and Lyft. The pilot would transition some space currently used for parking to passenger loading zones in busy commercial areas like Hayes Valley and the Marina. The TNCs would "geo-fence" certain blocks, or create restricted zones in their apps, and direct drivers and passengers to specific loading zone locations (Fitzgerald Rodriguez 2017).

The companies would also agree to give the city data for trips to and from the pilot areas, which the city would use in turn to assess the extent to which the new loading zones reduced double-parking activity and associated transit delay or bicycle lane blockages. The city could expand the pilot citywide if it is found to be successful.

Lyft is already geo-fencing a multi-block zone along a bustling section of Valencia Street, in the Mission district, as well as several other areas in the city

(Fitzgerald Rodriguez 2018). Valencia Street currently has bicycle lanes that are mostly unreinforced by horizontal or vertical separation, and it has been an epicenter of concerns cyclists about TNC double parking. Passengers who request to be picked up or dropped off on specific blocks in the area are directed to passenger loading zones on side streets. The San Francisco Bicycle Coalition praised the effort.

Las Vegas, Charlotte, and Atlanta: Airport and sports facility pick-up and drop-off zones

Dealing with increased passenger loading traffic, it is particularly urgent for land uses that attract large numbers of people and/or have extreme peaks in demand at specific times. Airports and sports facilities are two prominent examples of such land uses, and a number of facilities are providing leading-edge examples of how to deal with these kinds of pressures.

Some airports across the country have created dedicated areas for TNC loading and worked with the TNC companies to direct passengers and drivers to those areas for active loading and unloading using geo-fencing. Airports also have extensive experience dealing with for-hire passenger vehicles, and they have employed some strategies that have long been used to handle taxi and other vehicles. One common strategy is to create "hold lots" where for-hire vehicles wait in line to be called for a pick-up (LeighFisher, Inc. 2015).

Las Vegas's McCarran International Airport is an airport that uses both of these strategies (Uber 2018). TNCs must check-in within the geo-fenced zone at the airport and are directed to a "staging lot" near the airport to wait to be called for a pickup. Passenger loading occurs in designated areas of parking facilities immediately adjacent to each of the airport's two terminals.

Sports facilities in Charlotte and the Atlanta area have used similar approaches. At PNC Arena in Charlotte, the facility management team has established an Uber loading area just outside the arena's south entrance that "offers fans a convenient pregame drop-off point and a one-stop location to request Uber rides and their drivers after games" (Carolina Hurricanes 2018). SunTrust Park in Cobb County, Georgia (where the Atlanta Braves baseball team plays) has two identified loading areas for Uber in stadium-adjacent parking lots (Atlanta Braves 2018). Uber uses a process for matching drivers and riders dynamically based on the order of requests.

Parking, transportation demand management, and developer flexibility

If autonomous vehicles are mainly adopted as part of shared fleets, some believe parking demand could decline by as much as 80 to 90 percent (International Transport Forum and Corporate Partnership Board 2015). There is already some evidence of declining parking demand in the places like downtown San Francisco, where both transit and TNC use are highest (Barba 2017).

If these initial trends and projections bear out over the long term, they would dramatically reshape the way people interface with buildings, potentially moving the main access point from the garage or off-street parking lot to the curb and front door. They would also beg for a change in the way we think about how to provide access to private developments. In most of North America today, cities presume that most people will arrive to each and every land use by car, no matter the land use or transportation system context. They build this presumption into zoning codes in the form of minimum parking requirements, which by some estimates, require that for every square foot of active space, one must provide more than half a square foot more for car storage. Should parking demand decline significantly, all of those square feet dedicated to parking would essentially be wasted space.

Many U.S. transportation departments are beginning to recognize the drawbacks of standard Transportation Impact Assessment (TIA) policies that focus on measuring intersection level of service for vehicles only. A few cities are leading the way to head off this potential waste by making their parking regulations more flexible and requiring that, to encourage people to begin traveling in more space-efficient ways today, developers build transportation demand management into their projects.

Buffalo, New York and Sacramento, California:
A flexible approach to parking

Buffalo became the largest city in North American to completely eliminate minimum parking requirements when it enacted its new "Green Code" in 2017 (Camiros 2012). The form-based code also added requirements for the design and environmental performance of parking.

Parking minimums were eliminated in an explicit effort to allow "the market to respond to changing lifestyle preferences and a range of transportation choices." The code also updated bicycle parking minimums and integrated them in the code. The code also included some explicit prohibitions of new surface parking in the city's downtown.

Design requirements regulate how parking should look from the public realm and where it can be located if it is provided. Environmental performance requirements, which establish standards for paving design and materials, attempt to address the heat-island effects and water runoff challenges associated with asphalt-covered expanses.

Sacramento eliminated minimum parking requirements in certain central districts when it updated its zoning code in 2012 (City of Sacramento City Council 2012). Rationale for the elimination of minimums was focused on reducing the effect of "onerous or inflexible parking requirements" and to enable infill projects where they would have been difficult with a requirement to provide significant on-site parking. The Sacramento code also encouraged increased sharing of off-street parking resources, to make more efficient use of any parking that might be built.

Cambridge, Massachusetts and San Francisco, California: Building demand management into the DNA of new developments

TDM ordinances require that developers build vehicle-trip-reduction into the DNA of their projects, supporting reduced-parking approaches. While these ordinances have not been established to explicitly "future-proof" developments, they do offer ways to help projects bridge the gap between a system in which private vehicles dominate and a future in which motorized transportation could look much different.

Cambridge established the most robust TDM requirements in the United States in 1998 and made them permanent in 2006. The city's TDM ordinance requires that projects that are planning to build between five and nineteen parking spaces develop and implement a "small project PTDM plan," which must include three approved TDM measures and a small-project form submittal. Projects providing twenty or more parking space must commit to keep single-occupancy-vehicle mode-shares below an agreed-upon level (typically 10 percent below levels shown in 1990 census data), must implement a "comprehensive set" of TDM measures, and must submit annual reports documenting employee single-occupancy-vehicle mode shares, car and bike parking occupancy, and the implementation status of TDM measures.

In the city's Kendall Square area, home to a number of large biotechnology firms and research and academic institutions, more than 4.6 million square feet of commercial and institutional development have been built over the past 10 years, but automobile traffic has decreased on major streets by as much as 14 percent (Moskowitz 2012).

San Francisco took a similar approach when it established a TDM ordinance in 2017. San Francisco's ordinance is more directly scaled to the number of parking spaces a development provides: Projects that provide more parking are required to invest more in TDM. The city developed a list of more than twenty potential TDM measures projects could implement, with each measure worth a certain number of points based on its documented effectiveness. Projects are required to report regularly on the implementation status of TDM measures to which they commit in their entitlement application.

Autonomous transit

Autonomous vehicles have the potential to change the cost structure of providing mobility services, be they in small vehicles like traditional automobiles or large ones like shuttles and buses. For existing public transit services, this would only come with a dramatic restructuring of the labor force—eliminating or repurposing the large number of drivers currently required to operate buses. The societal implications of this kind of transition cannot be understated. Any discussion of delivering existing fixed-route transit more cost-efficiently must also include a robust consideration of the human impact of such a transition.

However, there are areas in which the combination of driverless vehicles and transit could deliver better and more cost-effective service without costing existing jobs. Many transit agencies today struggle to serve low-density areas in which demand is sporadic and dispersed, if they serve these areas at all. With a combination of real-time demand aggregation and small driverless shuttles, it might be possible to provide these areas with quality connections, in a fiscally prudent way, to parts of the system that are more sustainable even with today's cost structure: high-capacity transit spines. Driverless technology is not yet developed enough to comfortably operate in mixed traffic on public streets, but a few communities are testing small driverless shuttles in ways that could provide proof-of-concept for broader use of these vehicles in areas traditional public transit struggles to serve.

Pleasanton, California, Las Vegas, Nevada, and Ann Arbor,
Michigan: Getting users ready for driverless transit

Driverless shuttles are being piloted in several places in the United States as of spring 2018.

The Bishop Ranc office park in San Ramon, CA began testing an EasyMile shuttle on private roads within the park in March 2017 (Ruggiero 2017). The pilot uses vehicles with a capacity of twelve people that travel at twelve miles per hour along a fixed route between buildings. The trial will help EasyMile improve the technology, but it also aims to get people (both riders and pedestrians outside the vehicles) used to driverless shuttles as a concept.

The shuttles were purchased by the manager of the office park, and the contract with EasyMile includes two years of service from EasyMile's engineers to address any challenges as they came up. The program is also receiving financial support from the Contra Costa Transportation Authority and the Bay Area Air Quality Management District. The shuttles were initially tested at a former Navy base that is now being used as a technology testing ground.

In Las Vegas, eight-passenger Navya driverless shuttles have been the subject of a twelve-month trial in the city's downtown. The vehicles run in a 0.6-mile loop around the area in what the sponsors call the "largest self-driving pilot project in the U.S" (Hawkins 2017). Organizers are aiming for a total ridership of 250,000 people over the course of the pilot.

One shuttle was part of a minor collision with a delivery truck on the first day of operation. Officials responded to the incident by saying that "had the truck had the same sensing equipment that the shuttle has, the accident would have been avoided."

The University of Michigan has been a key testing ground for driverless vehicles. In spring 2018, the university is aiming to launch a public pilot, also with Navya shuttles, to provide connections between its engineering center and its North Campus Research Complex. The route would be two miles long, and the vehicles would each have a capacity for fifteen people.

Data-Sharing Protocols

New mobility services are already generating reams of data, and the torrent promises to get only stronger as a greater share of travel is done via connected vehicles. However, today most mobility service providers' data are in different formats, and many providers have been reluctant to share data given concerns about data anonymity and fear of sharing too much about their business models with competitors. Giving governments and the public access to these datasets, in a standard format, could provide powerful new input to transportation planning, and user-facing data aggregators which could make the vast array of services more understandable and manageable for users.

NACTO has already seen the potential power in harnessing this growing base of mobility data. The organization released a set of data sharing principles in 2017. The document asserts that, because those providing mobility services do so on publicly owned and maintained streets, "data created on city streets must be available to cities in an accessible format in order to support sustainable, accessible, and affordable transportation" (NACTO 2017c).

Better data can support transportation planning, efforts to ensure that mobility services are inclusive and equitable, and efforts to improve safety on streets.

- For transportation planning: Information that providers are already generating on speeds, travel times, and volumes can help with street management. Information on pick-up and drop-off locations can help inform more strategic curb management and minimize behaviors like double-parking that cause safety challenges. To help ensure the whole system moves more people, information on vehicle occupancies, non-revenue VMT, and dwell times can inform system pricing and management decisions.
- For equity: Information on denied, declined, or cancelled rides, as well as demand for wheelchair vehicles, can help public entities target resources in ways that might compensate for service that might inequitable if left exclusively to the private market.
- For safety: Information on incidents of "rapid acceleration and deceleration," disengagement of autonomous operation, and collisions could all inform engineering decisions.

To achieve these goals, NACTO is aiming to use the World Bank's Open Traffic standards to harmonize data across cities in the short term, and then "work with its member cities and private mobility providers toward secure and standardized exchange of anonymized data" over the long term.

While service providers have refused to provide data to many municipalities to date, a few cities offer examples of how to get data flowing.

*Portland, Oregon, and New York City: Requiring data disclosures
in exchange for permission to operate*

Lyft and Uber began operating in Portland without sanction in 2014, but the city ordered them to cease operations while it sorted out how to regulate TNCs in relation to other for-hire vehicle services. The 2015 deal that ultimately allowed Lyft and Uber to operate in the city included some important provisions on data sharing.

City code requires that permitted TNC services furnish the city with anonymized data on the number, date, and time of "fulfilled requests," the number of unfulfilled requests, wait times, trips declined by the driver, cancelled rides, and origin and destination zip codes (City of Portland 2017). The city initially used data gathered during a trial period for the new permit system to better understand usage patterns and finalize the regulations.

New York City collects and publishes monthly usage data for all for-hire passenger vehicles for which the city's Taxi and Limousine Commission has issued permits (New York City Taxi and Limousine Commission 2018). The robust datasets have enabled some of the most detailed analyses of how TNCs are affecting travel behavior, including a 2017 report by local transportation planning firm Schaller Consulting (Schaller Consulting 2017).

Reorganizing government for mobility-as-a-service

Most governments are currently organized in ways that reflect the structure of the transportation system in 1950.

At the state and county levels, there are agencies that focus on building transportation infrastructure, with a focus on building and maintaining highways and arterial roadways that reflects the auto-oriented era in which they were chartered. While some such agencies have begun to fund and build transit infrastructure as well, the vast majority of their budgets tend to be directed toward roadways.

At the regional and local levels, there are public transit service providers. Providing transit is widely accepted as a role for local government, in recognition of the collapse of private transit service in the middle of the twentieth century. Their missions are often centered on providing benefits that are as widespread and equitable as possible within their service areas, though many of them fail on the latter point. The value of the benefits they provide is usually limited by costly political mandates and a lack of control over their operating environments.

In between, there is a mix of planning and funding agencies that support both types of activities and, sometimes, attempt to fill in the gaps by regulating modes like taxis.

These structures have proven brittle in the face of new mobility services that either do not fit cleanly in existing portfolios or that could offer greater benefit if coordinated with major public investments or services. They also fail to take advantage of one of the most powerful opportunities computing technology might offer the mobility world—the ability to maximize user flexibility and utility by aggregating and coordinating a range of mobility services in a simple user interface. Some governments are exploring ways of reshaping their activities to better take advantage of these opportunities and to better safeguard the public good in the face of new services that government agencies were simply not designed to regulate.

Finland: Organizing activities around mobility-as-a-service

In early 2018, the Finnish national government embarked on a major restructuring of the way it interacts with mobility service providers through the Act on Transport Services. The act calls for all service providers to make key pieces of data available in a central clearinghouse and to provide access to ticket and payment interfaces, to enable the user-friendly aggregation of services across modes (Finnish Transport Agency 2018).

This is the first effort by a national government to require mobility service providers to make their services interoperable. This, which is an essential step in enabling effective MaaS platforms to emerge. An explicit goal of the act is to link different transport services, such as taxis and train journeys, into a system of trip chains. The act essentially transforms the Finnish Transport Agency (one part of a larger Ministry on Transport and Communications) into a regulatory body that is tasked with managing data, making it accessible to all manner of mobility companies, monitoring the supply of transportation services and their relationship to transportation demand, and facilitating the creation of new services. It does not call on the agency to manage new services itself.

The Finnish reforms have taken place at the national-government level, and no state or region in North America has yet attempted something as ambitious. However, health care offers a precedent for regulating and aggregating a key service at the sub-national level.

Conclusions: A recommended approach to policymaking for the driverless age

The case studies throughout the previous section all provide examples of ways cities are responding a rapidly changing mobility ecosystem in real time. These types of policymaking efforts will only get more important as autonomous vehicle technology improves enough to handle widespread deployment. This final section brings these different strands of policy together in a comprehensive framework that responds the changes we have seen to date and anticipates an increasingly rapid pace of change as we move forward.

Clarify values and develop frameworks for responding to new technologies

It is easy to get caught up in the promise of new technologies without thinking critically enough about potential byproducts or ways in which certain technologies may fly in the face of strongly held local values. It is also easy to forget that all new mobility technologies will need to run on a publicly owned platform—the public right-of-way. Cities are responsible for ensuring that public rights-of-way are managed for the public good.

Definitions of the "public good" may vary across cities, but it is important to develop a clear articulation of local values in a format that can guide decisions on how to manage the public right-of-way and incorporate new technologies as they emerge. Local values are often embedded in a range of legislative actions like vision zero and complete streets policies and in planning documents like general plans.

Following Seattle's lead, cities should:

1   Clarify values: Identify which policies are likely to be most relevant to regulating and/or actively supporting new mobility services.
2   Transparently discuss opportunities and challenges in understandable ways: Help policymakers, stakeholders, and the general public understand the mobility ecosystem as it exists today and the potential effects of new services on the system as a whole in the future.
3   Establish a policy framework for new mobility: Lay out an action plan to holistically manage and, where needed, expand access to the range of travel options that already exist.

Double down on efforts to prioritize bikes, pedestrians, and transit in dense areas and high-traffic corridors

After decades of auto-oriented planning, many North American cities have made efforts in recent years to re-prioritize pedestrians, cyclists, and transit vehicles, especially in their downtowns and crowded commercial districts. These efforts will only get more important as driverless vehicles proliferate, as the cost equation encourages more motorized travel and as technology enthusiasts call for street design changes that allow unfettered movement by private vehicles.

Simple geometry means that movement on foot, by bike, and on transit vehicles will continue to be the most space-efficient way to get around, no matter who or what is operating private cars. If cities are to retain the vibrancy that makes them interesting places to live and play, they will need to redouble efforts to prioritize space efficient modes, in the short and long term.

Cities should:

1   Price congestion: Send a clearer signal to transportation network users about the externalities of certain travel behaviors.
2   Price wasted space and pilot urban HOV lanes: Use price and travel-time savings to incentivize the use of high-occupancy vehicles, both public and private.

3 Move toward autonomous feeder transit networks and BRT: Begin exploring the ways in which driverless technology might allow for cost-efficient service expansions to areas that have heretofore been prohibitively costly and consider ways to reallocate the time of workers displaced by technology to other activities that add value to the rider experience or make transit service more accessible to sensitive populations.

Think critically about the curb

Competition for curb space has increased dramatically in recent years, and autonomous vehicles may vastly increase that completion, especially if they are widely adopted as part of mobility service provider fleets. Starting one hundred years ago, most curb space was given over to private vehicle storage. The already-in-progress transformation in mobility technology makes it imperative that cities rethink how they manage curb space. It offers the opportunity to vastly decrease the inefficiencies and safety issues that are byproducts of the way curb space is currently managed in most places.

Cities should:

1 Develop clear design standards for curbside loading: Eliminate or vastly reduce conflicts with bicycles and transit vehicles through designs, reinforcement materials, and location.
2 Establish fees for curbside access in the highest-traffic areas: Establish a clear price signal that encourages vehicles to use loading zones only as long as they absolutely need to and promotes higher occupancy trips.
3 Promote flexible use of curb space to meet different needs in different contexts and/or at different times of day: Create nuanced but easily understood regulations that prioritize different users at different times, and ensure such regulations are effective through enforcement.

Modernize parking regulations and elevate demand management efforts

Parking requirements bake our existing mobility system and people's often misinformed assumptions about how people get around into buildings with useful lives that should carry them into the next century. By reforming parking regulations, cities can enable the built environment to evolve as travel behavior evolves. By actively incentivizing the use of non-auto modes, they can also help people move toward a more multimodal future that takes pressure off private development to allocate vast amounts of money and space toward mobility needs.

Cities should:

1 Eliminate minimums, establish maximums, unbundle, and share: Modernize parking regulations to enable developers to size parking facilities to true market demands and to make more efficient use of the parking spaces they do ultimately build.

2 Price parking and employ other demand-management techniques in the short term: Use price signals to create parking availability for those who need it and to encourage the use of more space-efficient modes.
3 Promote adaptability: Encourage developers to design parking facilities they do decide to build so they can be adapted to other uses should parking demand drop dramatically.

Put equity front and center

Over the past century, numerous transportation investments have either created or reinforced inequities along racial and class lines. New mobility services offer the opportunity to address some of these age-old challenges, but private mobility providers have an imperfect track record on ensuring that their services are equally accessible to everyone. In addition, the profit motive often leads private-sector service providers to ignore those with the greatest need.

Cities will need to work to ensure they can take advantage of the opportunities in this area and mitigate the potential that new technologies (especially ones like autonomous vehicles that are likely to be expensive in early days) will exacerbate age-old problems.

Cities should:

1 Examine all policy proposals to determine how they can advance equity: Given our history, equity should be an important criterion in understanding the value of new mobility services and in identifying how the public sector might help expand access to these services. In evaluating policy proposals, they should focus on how outcomes related to health, employment access, and the share of income and time spent on mobility are expected to vary across different population groups.
2 Involve community leaders and the private sector in developing performance standards and monitoring progress on this important topic: To understand the extent to which new mobility options address equity challenges, cities need a clear and cost-efficient way of measuring performance.
3 Use pricing to make the system more equitable: By establishing fees for using the least-efficient modes (whose user bases are often skewed toward those with higher incomes), cities can generate funds to subsidize mobility for those with the fewest choices.

Establish data protocols for the public good

Many new mobility technologies run on data; they offer the opportunity to understand travel behavior and monitor changing preferences in real time. They will only do so, however, if datasets from private mobility providers can be integrated and analyzed in a meaningful and cost-efficient way. Cities will need to establish data protocols and reporting requirements to ensure that is the case.

Cities should:

1 Mandate reporting in exchange for the use of city streets: In one way or another, mobility technologies all use public rights of way and streets that are maintained by tax dollars; in exchange for this privilege, it must be seen as reasonable to ask for anonymized data that can help inform better and faster public investment decisions.
2 Develop easy-to-use data depositories for analysis and reporting: Because of the potential volume of data from technology-enabled mobility providers, it is critical that cities develop systems to efficiently pull in, process, and generate useful insights from a wide range of potential data sources.
3 Validate the data: To ensure that data submitted by mobility service providers truly reflects actual travel activity, a third-party regulatory body should be established to validate the accuracy of data submitted.

Reorganize government around mobility

Government needs to be nimbler and more responsive to rapid changes in technology and travel behavior. They can do so by ensuring that administrators and regulators have clear but flexible policy frameworks that enable them to respond to new entrants to the mobility ecosystem quickly but in ways that are consistent with community values. Funding mechanisms and decision-making structures will likely also need to be realigned to reflect the new ways in which mobility services are provided.

Cities should:

1 Realign taxation: Gas and parking taxes are the main ways in which North American governments raise money to fund transportation infrastructure and services. Those taxes are premised on a transportation system in which gas-powered privately-owned vehicles are predominant, as they have been for decades. As vehicle fleet electrifies, taxes will need to adjust to reflect the impact of vehicle travel on public roads. A combination of VMT-based fees and congestion pricing can work together to encourage more efficient use of the vehicle fleet.
2 Consider regional mobility authorities: With a growing range of private-service providers and rapidly evolving user behavior, the world of transportation is beginning to look a lot like the world of broadcasting, in which the government defers to private service providers to determine the substance of programming but regulates the use of air waves for the public good. Regionally, it might be possible to reshape transportation system management to look similar to that age-old model. Following the Finnish model, such an arrangement should include data-sharing requirements and support for services that aggregate different transportation services to encourage trip-chaining.

Proactively prepare for the future of work

The labor-market implications of new transportation technologies are massive. The elimination of professional driving jobs would affect millions of low-skill workers and could dramatically increase the structural inequalities that have taken root in the United States over the last several decades. Transit agencies are potentially at the center of this transition. Cities will need to begin working with them today to plan for the future of their labor forces and support their efforts to migrate workers to new jobs or other industries. Future jobs in the mobility sector will likely require technology and customer service skills, and both cities and transit agencies can start to help the mobility labor force make the transition today.

Cities should:

1   Work with transit agencies to develop a thoughtful long-term labor strategy: Transit agencies will need help to consider the potential future role of autonomous vehicles in providing transit service and to identify areas in which workers might be able to help enhance the quality of transit service or increase access to the system.
2   Enhance local job-training programs and partnerships with new industries to help workers re-skill: In the end, it might be best for society for technology to phase out certain jobs; cities have an important role to play to ensure that those with obsolete skills are not left behind.

References

Atlanta B. 2018. Ride with Uber (https://www.mlb.com/braves/ballpark/transportation/uber), Accessed 1 May 2018.

Barba, M. 2017. Declining Union Square parking revenue puts Rec and Park in a tight space, San Francisco Examiner (http://www.sfexaminer.com/declining-union-square-parking-revenue-puts-rec-park-tight-space/), Accessed 1 May 2018.

Brinklow, A. 2017. Lyft, Uber commit 64 percent of downtown SF traffic violations, *Curbed San Francisco* (https://sf.curbed.com/2017/9/26/16367440/lyft-uber-traffic-citations-sfpd-board-supervisors), Accessed 1 May 2018.

Camiros. 2012. A New Zoning Direction for Buffalo: Technical Report, City of Buffalo (http://www.buffalogreencode.com/documents/New_Directions_Tech_Report.pdf), Accessed 1 May 2018.

Carolina Hurricanes. 2018. Uber Zone at PNC Arena (https://www.nhl.com/hurricanes/arena/uber), Accessed 1 May 2018.

City of Austin. 2017. Smart Mobility Roadmap (http://austintexas.gov/sites/default/files/files/Smart_Mobility_Roadmap_-_Final.pdf), Accessed 1 May 2018.

City of Pittsburgh. 2018. SmartPGH Programs (http://smartpittsburgh.org/programs), Accessed 1 May 2018.

City of Portland. 2017. Portland City Code 16.40.240, part J (https://www.portlandoregon.gov/citycode/28593), Accessed 1 May 2018.

City of Sacramento City Council. 2012. Zoning Code Parking Update (https://www.cityofsacramento.org/-/media/Corporate/Files/CDD/Planning/Zoning/Council_Report_1031121.pdf?la=en), Accessed 1 May 2018.

Clewlow, R. R., and G. S. Mishra. 2017. "Disruptive Transportation: The Adoption, Utilization, and Impacts of Ride-Hailing in the United States." Institute of Transportation Studies, University of California, Davis, Research Report UCD-ITS-RR-17-07.

Darido, G. 2016. Sao Paulo's Innovative Proposal to Regulate Shared Mobility by Pricing Vehicle Use, The World Bank Transport for Development Blog (http://blogs.worldbank.org/transport/sao-paulo-s-innovative-proposal-regulate-shared-mobility-pricing-vehicle-use), Accessed 1 May 2018.

Finnish Transport Agency. 2018. The Act on Transport Services enables flexible travel chains (https://www.liikennevirasto.fi/web/en/transport-system/the-act-on-transport-services#.WvtVXogvxaQ), Accessed 15 May 2018.

Fitzgerald Rodriguez, J. 2017. "Documents reveal which streets SF is considering for Uber, Lyft curb pilot," *San Francisco Examiner* (http://www.sfexaminer.com/documents-reveal-streets-sf-considering-uber-lyft-curb-pilot/), Accessed 1 May 2018.

Fitzgerald Rodriguez, J. 2018. "Lyft pilots program to curb Valencia Street double parking," *San Francisco Examiner* (http://www.sfexaminer.com/lyft-pilots-program-curb-valencia-street-double-parking/), Accessed 1 May 2018.

Hawkins, A. J. 2017. "Las Vegas is expanding its self-driving shuttle experiment," *The Verge* (https://www.theverge.com/2017/11/6/16614388/las-vegas-self-driving-shuttle-navya-keolis-aaa), Accessed 1 May 2018.

International Transport Forum and Corporate Partnership Board (2015). Urban Mobility System Upgrade: How shared self-driving cars could change city traffic, Organization of Economic Co-operation and Development (OECD) (http://www.itf-oecd.org/sites/default/files/docs/15cpb_self-drivingcars.pdf), Accessed 1 May 2018.

LeighFisher, Inc. 2015. ACRP Report 146: Commercial Ground Transportation at Airports: Best Practices. Transportation Research Board.

Los Angeles Metro. 2018a. Office of Extraordinary Information (https://www.metro.net/projects/oei/), Accessed 1 May 2018.

Los Angeles Metro. 2018b. MicroTransit Pilot Project (https://www.metro.net/projects/microtransit/), Accessed 1 May 2018.

Mobility Pricing Independent Commission. 2018. It's Time Metro Vancouver (https://www.itstimemv.ca/), Accessed 1 May 2018.

Moskowitz, E. 2012. "Car-free commuting push pays off in Kendall Square," *The Boston Globe* (https://www.bostonglobe.com/metro/2012/07/24/kendall-square-car-traffic-falls-even-workforce-soars/C4Fio7iKZnwEMAw7y4cJgN/story.html) Accessed 1 May 2018.

New York City Taxi & Limousine Commission. 2018. TLC Trip Record Data (http://www.nyc.gov/html/tlc/html/about/trip_record_data.shtml), Accessed 1 May 2018.

NACTO. 2017a. Curb Appeal: Curbside Management Strategies for Improving Transit Reliability (https://nacto.org/wp-content/uploads/2017/11/NACTO-Curb-Appeal-Curbside-Management.pdf), Accessed 1 May 2018.

NACTO. 2017b. Designing for All Ages & Abilities: Contextual Guidance for High-Comfort Bicycle Facilities (https://nacto.org/wp-content/uploads/2017/12/NACTO_Designing-for-All-Ages-Abilities.pdf), Accessed 1 May 2018.

NACTO. 2017c. City Data Sharing Principles: Integrating New Technologies into City Streets (https://nacto.org/wp-content/uploads/2017/01/NACTO-Policy-Data-Sharing-Principles.pdf), Accessed 1 May 2018.

Oregon Department of Transportation. 2017. Oregon's Road Usage Charge: The OReGO Program, Final Report (http://www.oregon.gov/ODOT/Programs/RUF/IP-Road%20 Usage%20Evaluation%20Book%20WEB_4-26.pdf), Accessed 1 May 2018.

Ruggiero, A. 2017. "San Ramon: Driverless shuttles make their debut," *East Bay Times* (https://www.eastbaytimes.com/2017/03/06/san-ramon-driverless-shuttles-make-their-debut/), Accessed 1 May 2018.

Schaller Consulting. 2017. Unsustainable? The Growth of App-Based Ride Services and Traffic, Travel and the Future of New York City (http://schallerconsult.com/rideservices/ unsustainable.htm), Accessed 1 May 2018.

Seattle Department of Transportation. 2017. New Mobility Playbook, Version 1.0 (http://www.seattle.gov/Documents/Departments/SDOT/NewMobilityProgram/ NewMobility_Playbook_9.2017.pdf), Accessed 1 May 2018.

Seattle Department of Transportation. 2018. Flex Zone/Curb Use Priorities in Seattle (https:// www.seattle.gov/transportation/projects-and-programs/programs/parking-program/ parking-regulations/flex-zone/curb-use-priorities-in-seattle), Accessed 1 May 2018.

Shared Use Mobility Center. 2017. Twin Cities Shared Mobility Action Plan (http:// sharedusemobilitycenter.org/wp-content/uploads/2017/10/SUMC_TWINCITIES_ Web_Final.pdf), Accessed 1 May 2018.

Spielman, F. 2017. Emanuel's 2018 budget passes with only three dissenting votes, Chicago Sun Times (https://chicago.suntimes.com/news/city-council-poised-to-approve-emanuels-8-6-billion-budget/), Accessed 1 May 2018.

Transport for London. 2008. Central London Congestion Changing: Impacts Monitoring (http://content.tfl.gov.uk/central-london-congestion-charging-impacts-monitoring-sixth-annual-report.pdf), Accessed 1 May 2018.

Transport Styrelsen. 2018. Congestion taxes in Stockholm and Gothenburg (https:// transportstyrelsen.se/en/road/Congestion-taxes-in-Stockholm-and-Goteborg/), Accessed 1 May 2018.

Uber. 2018. McCarran International Airport: Information for driver-partners (https:// www.uber.com/drive/las-vegas/airports/mccarran-international/), Accessed 1 May 2018.

9 Think different

Reframing jobs and economy

Shivani Shukla and William Riggs

Introduction

When do the machines take over? As the quote from *Terminator* below suggests, technology and digital revolution are the primary sources of growth in economies today, and even if they will not fight us like they did in the movie—they will reshape employment and jobs.

> "The Skynet Funding Bill is passed. The system goes on-line August 4th, 1997. Human decisions are removed from strategic defense. Skynet begins to learn at a geometric rate. It becomes self-aware at 2:14 a.m. Eastern time, August 29th. In a panic, they try to pull the plug. Skynet fights back."

While somewhat comical, this suggests technology and digital revolution are the primary sources of growth in economies today, and even if they will not fight us like they did in the movie—they will reshape employment and jobs. We take a look at these jobs because of the way that jobs can have both positive and negative impacts on society. For example, there are differing views on the way employment gets looked at. There are the pessimistic views ("destruction" of jobs and stagnation) and optimistic ones to economic growth (value creation by moving above the "mundane" functions). Thus, while not being pessimistic, we argue that the profile of these jobs that will change in the new mobility future. Disruptive transport and autonomous vehicles (AVs) will bring about substitutions in human skills and the need for them, rather than replace humans altogether (as Skynet tried to do in *Terminator*).

We can use Silicon Valley as the prime example where technology is likely evolving faster than anywhere else. The median income reached $94,000 in 2013, much above the national median of around $53,000. Yet an estimated 31 percent of jobs pay only $16 per hour or less, quite below what is required to sustain a family in an area known for its expensive housing and high standard of living.

This growth in inequality may be contributed by technological changes that eliminate the need for many lower-middle or middle-class jobs (Rotman 2014). There is an overall exponential growth in productivity and GDP, yet not everyone seems to benefit due to a weak growth in jobs. This is commonly referred to as the "great decoupling" (Bernstein and Raman 2015).

The effect of technological adoption on labor and national income has been studied extensively (see Elsby et al. 2013; Piketty 2014; and Karabarbounis and Neiman 2014). It has also been highlighted that the contributions of labor to national income has fallen in many nations since decades due to the increased adoption of technology across many sectors. The trend is expected to continue given that technological development is moving at a fast pace. However, there is little to indicate exactly when and how much will labor be affected.

A massive technological change normally leads to movements among populations—that is—rural to urban migrations in search for jobs. Low-skilled jobs get replaced with technology or certain occupations just do not remain viable. For instance, since the early 2000s, India's economy changed from an agricultural to a service one. As more and more rural populations move to urban areas that create competition in skills and resources in urban agglomerations, a transition in them is observed. A vigorous urban to urban migrations takes place as people move around in search for what we call "individual equilibriums."

These equilibriums are induced by exogenous factors of an economy but also have endogenous influencers of societal and living preferences, skills, and financial considerations that differ from individual to individual. It is noteworthy that all of the exogenous and endogenous factors, further explained as micro and macroeconomic factors are transient in nature. An individual goes through an evolution of financial requirements as she moves from a single household to a family. On the same lines, skills would also go through an advancement with time (at different rates for different individuals). This has a direct effect on the job migration rates over time. In this chapter, we try to explore the short- and long-term effects technological advancements have on labor markets.

Interestingly, economic theories suggest that the role of financial constraints in the poorest countries is limited and skill composition and macroeconomic drivers that do not change in the short-run are key to labor migration. Low-skilled workers have a lower migration rate since microeconomic drivers (food, commodities, wages to buy them) matter more to them (Dao et al. 2017).

Further if the average skill evolution of a country is too high and does not match the industrial/economic development, there is high migration observed within and among countries. Higher-skilled workers are more responsive to these macroeconomic changes, while lower-skilled workers are susceptible to microeconomic changes—again large global changes versus the price of things in your daily life.

The technological revolution impacting the mobility sector (particularly AVs) will likely begin at a microeconomic level, but then quickly influence the macroeconomic factors of an economy. Hence, the beginning of the change will create emigration among low-skilled jobs, only to eventually reach a point of stabilization—something that economists (see Nordhaus 2015) talk about as an "economic singularity." Economists explain that "rapid growth in computational abilities and artificial intelligence will cross a threshold, namely, Singularity, after which economic growth will increase sharply." (Nordhaus 2015).

While we may be far from such a drastic event, it is easy to fall into the media-induced belief that machines will be suited for every task that a human performs. While AVs attempt to take on tasks that are only tacitly understood by humans—judgment, sensitivity, adaptability, and complex decision-making with too many moving pieces on a road, they will from time to time require human intervention as humans begin to explicitly start defining the tasks to be performed. Currently, machines are not as flexible and adaptable, and they will never completely replace humans. This could be true in other industrial sectors, however, with AVs, they are likely very well suited since the entire purpose is to replace drivers who can only engage in a handful of tasks at one time.

It is critical to note that a lot depends on the technology under scrutiny, the way organizations and individuals accept and adopt it, and the policy frameworks that control the adoption and growth. Polarization is on the rise, but the value of human skills is mounting as well, especially given that the more mechanical and laborious jobs are the ones under threat. The future emphasis on jobs will be on value creation. Organizational business models and societal and individual operative models will need to change to adapt to the exponential growth that disruptive technologies like AVs can bring about.

Arntz et al. (2016) argue that effect on employment of new technology depends on the ability of workplaces to adjust to the new division of labor. They also state that new technologies may exert positive effect on labor demand if there is an increase in the product demand owing to competition which could lead to a positive effect on wage rates. However, this is more in the context of manufacturing and other mechanical industry related technology. Automation aims to replace human labor completely at the low- and middle-skill levels. The analysis is indicative but not useful to AVs since they cater more to services than product development.

Multiple studies have looked at susceptibility of jobs to computerization, and the effects of technology on wage inequality and employment polarization. While some have empirically shown promising results, we observe empirical results with a certain degree of skepticism, especially since they are based on data that do not directly apply to the technological advancements today and the ones that are anticipated.

In this chapter, we present the results of a generalized model that creates a framework for testing the effects of policy decisions in the realm of AVs and disruptive transport onto employment. To the best of our knowledge, a direct analysis of this kind of technological advancement on jobs and employment in developed and developing economies from economic and policy standpoints is rare in the current literature. This chapter is organized as follows. In the first part, we discuss the structure of a competitive labor market equilibrium model that maximizes the aggregate output of the transportation sector highlighted by new mobility options in the backdrop of consumers' propensity to spend, labor and wages, and costs of supply of vehicles (cost of capital). We present the applicability of the model, existence of its results, and the impact it can have in the decision-making process of policymakers in this space. The section continues the discussion to policy initiatives required on various fronts to handle inclusion of AVs into economies and societies. These discussions pave way to altering the model to include these changes and analyze the impact on the equilibrium. We conclude with a brief note on our key observations and discuss the course for future research.

Labor market equilibrium model for automation in transportation

How will labor markets respond to the AV transition? We propose a model and generalized framework of how a competitive labor market will attain equilibrium in the context of autonomous vehicles. This goal is based around some of the following questions:

- What is the contribution of AVs on the GDP? This will provide an estimate of the impact of AVs on productivity.
- Under specified conditions, what will be the labor market equilibrium? The conditions can be modified as per the policy effects that are to be analyzed. The model can also be tested on the stability of the equilibrium to show the type of policy interventions that will be required to sustain the said equilibrium.
- To what extent will AVs replace jobs?
- What are the benefits that other industrial sectors in an economy will reap given the adoption of AVs in the surface transportation sector?

Methodology

We refer to framework from Acemoglu and Restrepo (2017) that formalizes the changes in employment and wages vis-à-vis robotic automation in the realm of production, and builds on Burstein et al. (2017), Caliendo and Parro (2015), and Acemoglu and Autor (2011).

We utilize the generalized form of the Cobb-Douglas aggregation function to model the output, in other words, contribution of vehicular movements to the GDP. Local labor markets are bifurcated in zones, and to initiate the model, these markets can be differentiated by regions or industry. Due to possible wage differentials, there could be interactions/migrations between markets to attain higher levels of utility. We focus on a single market at this time in the model. However, it can certainly be extended to quantify interactions between markets. In this model we do allow for market specific output functions, costs, and wages which are vital inclusions.

The output for each option and choice in each market is asymmetric, that is the output of say autonomous cars depend on the output of non-autonomous cars as well. This is pragmatic as the various mobility alternatives will have implications on the outputs of their counterparts in a competitive economy. The model includes efficiency parameters that affect the productivity of the various transportation options and labor/automation choices.

Autor and Salomons (2018) discuss the notion of technological change in the face of automation and labor. The model assumes that human labor and automated machines are perfect substitutes even though their relative productivity/costs may differ. Furthermore, the model assumes that the supply of human labor and machines are inelastic. Our model relaxes both.

A Nash equilibrium is achieved when no entity can unilaterally improve upon the output by choosing a different strategic consumption quantity. We also assume that the feasible set is closed and convex to ensure existence of the equilibrium. This model can be extended to include various endogenous and exogenous phenomena. Will AVs create as many jobs as replace? The question regarding maintaining the labor market equilibrium can get answered by the model above.

Specific output functions for each option and choice can be included. More importantly, the model also allows for nonsymmetric functions. For example, output from an autonomous rail would have varied degrees of implications on the output of all the other comparable transportation options available, making the equilibrium more realistically indicative. These are the kind of important policy related inferences that can be drawn from an equilibrium analysis of this sort. Additionally, this model can also be applied to a specific industry with the goals of profit maximization and/or cost minimization.

Estimates of elasticity of mode parameters affecting the aggregate output, efficiency parameters that affect the productivity of the various transportation options and labor/automation choices, income allocation to transportation by consumers, price of the mode option, and prevailing wage rates in the market were partly derived from the Nielsen global survey of Automotive Demand 2014 and were partly simulated.

Results

What were the results? We ran an initial (simplified) simulation for 5 years, that considered three mode choices, two industrial sectors, and two markets within the United States characterized by skills, wage rates, prices of the modes, and labor efficiencies.

- We employ the income approach of calculating the GDP[1] rather than the expenditure approach[2] as it is more indicative of productivity in our context. Equilibriums are achieved every year in a five-year time span showing an increase in the average wage rates. This indicates that more medium- to high-skilled labor was being employed.
- Labor gains/losses are strongly connected with consumption quantity. The more AVs are used, the lesser drivers are employed. This causes an eventual increase in the overall salaries of workers in the transportation sector, however, there are fewer people employed. Corporate profits and incomes show benefits.
- Labor surplus was constantly observed through the years. If the other sector modeled required and was able to absorb all of the labor, there was an overall increase in the GDP through the years. However, if it could absorb only a part, then the wage rate in the sector absorbing the surplus determined the GDP.

Discussion

These findings offer vast potential for policy intervention and practice, particularly in the areas of: development phasing; supporting market equilibrium through eased international labor flows and strengthened wage standards; skill evolution; and providing subsidy and/or benefit. We discuss these in the paragraphs that follow to show the implications government agencies or even the private sector can have on labor growth and stability in an AV future.

Phased deployment

The common methods of moving from an existing system to a new one are: (1) Phased implementation—change takes place in stages; (2) Direct changeover—"Big Bang adoption"—instant changeover; and (3) Parallel running—old and new systems operate side by side. By applying these commonly known changeover techniques onto disruptive transport and AVs, one can provide an operational framework. For example, using the parallel running approach, the new system (AVs) can gradually replace the older system (vehicles that require humans) until AVs. That said, we argue that phased implementation/deployment may be more pragmatic given that there are anticipated negative impacts of the deployment of new mobility options for urban sustainability and society.

To achieve a sustainable system of new mobility, the focus will eventually shift from the fancy technological capabilities of these vehicles to their illustrated feasibility and management of stakeholders that are on the deployment, usage, and governance sides. Deployment of AVs is expected in multiple forms through controlled pilots starting with urban areas for passenger transport and the more rural areas for freight transport (long hauls). These beta projects will then be fully expanded to cover more regional ground and ultimately merge. There will expectedly be significant attempts toward intermodal passenger and freight movements and intercity mobility. This process will require continuous intervention of governance, policymakers, technology and telecom players, and academic institutions. Consistent feedback from users will drive the deployment phases from one to the next. The quality of regulations, dedicated departments within departments of transportation, government funded testing scenarios, and possibility to invest in infrastructure are the key policy related avenues that will drive the implementation of AVs into societies. This is more of a structured adoption planning.

The capabilities of governments differ across countries, in addition to their economic growth, the value proposition of AVs, requirements, growth possibilities for labor markets, existing infrastructure and ability to invest, private-sector participation and so on. The more developing countries will likely adopt these technologies in a much different manner and scale than the developed ones that have set structures to exercise. For example, the energy reforms in Mexico are expected to help oil and gas production. This is in contrast to the electric or hybrid electric AVs that are set to transform mobility and improve the environment. There are several countries with significant dearth of infrastructure and ability for governance. For these markets, we expect that the deployment will be rather unstructured. Private sectors can drive the adoption, however without addressing safety, accessibility, regulations, and proper policies to control, there will be limitations. Besides, the objective of profit maximization will be more pronounced than that of maximizing social welfare.

Competitive equilibrium across labor markets

An industrialized and technologically driven economy is continually subjected to many shocks that can cause shifts in the labor markets inside and outside an industry. Transportation is no different. It is, hence, unlikely that the labor market even reaches a stable equilibrium. The purpose of models like ours is to understand the changes that employment and wage can cause in a market which is technologically highly productive. As factors like efficiency, elasticity, wage rate, and cost change, a new equilibrium is reached. There is a significant connection between the effects that economic output can create on the more conventional forms of mobility and vice versa.

Under the concept of "efficient allocation," any excess in labor that is caused by more technologically advanced mobility alternatives that depend less on human labor would lead to a worker surplus (and wage rate reduction) wherein the labor market does not completely absorb them and they are monetarily better off working in a different market. If the supply of human labor is inelastic, it is theorized that wage differentials between labor markets can cause migration of human labor between markets and/or migration in the form of the mobility itself. In addition to wage differentials, it is critical to note that in the case of automation in the transportation sector, there will be likely "skill differentials" as well, further exacerbating the wage differentials between markets. Every geographic region in the United States (or the world for that matter) will adopt automation in transportation differently and to varied extents. Long hauls in freight movements will more likely be automated while the last-mile deliveries (urban and suburban areas) will continue to require human labor due to the higher cognitive responses required for the job like traffic navigation for a longer time period. Similarly, industries might be varyingly receptive to alternative mobility options.

Such migration flows will cause a shift in the supply of labor, especially if there were free entry and exits of workers in the markets. While possible to achieve a higher utility in a different market, labor migration might be severely limited due to sociological factors. In economics, as the wage differentials disappear, the incentives for shifts in demand and supply disappear. We argue, that in order for the wage differentials, caused by AVs, to disappear, the adoption of similar technology across labor markets (industry/geographical) around the same time will have to take place. This is unlikely as disruptive technologies are more organically deployed than in a planned manner (at least not along all markets).

Considerable emphasis should also be given to human capital, in other words, the investment propensities of the enablers (agencies of AVs and other mobility options) and spending propensities of the consumers in markets. These differences could fundamentally place various markets on non-similar growth paths with regards to their economies and their productivity. Passenger transportation and last-mile deliveries might be visibly different across markets. On the other hand, international transportation, and intermodal passenger or freight movement across boundaries and industries can help markets to converge in the sense that there will need to be linearization in terms of vehicles for smoother operations. Nevertheless, that need might be limited given that uniformity may or may not be required at the points of transfer in the supply chain.

Reduction in human error, constant and consistent operations, and higher productivity are among the various benefits of AVs. In the favor of open markets for adoption of automation in transportation, one can argue that policies that influence free trade can eventually lead to economic efficiency. Jobs that are highly substitutable will be the ones that will be affected. However, from our analysis above, that notion is to be looked at with a certain degree of skepticism. Jobs substituted by AVs or semi-automated vehicles might lead to: (1) Labor migration—this may only temporarily lead to higher utilities for low- to mid-level skill workers/drivers since organic adoption of automation may phase them out eventually, and (2) migration of the type of mobility itself—tasks earlier performed by expensive machines could get replaced by more affordable human labor in a different market, thereby, absorbing the freed labor in the transportation sector of a certain region. Semi-automated tasks might move to a market with freed labor to utilize the manpower for their human component at a lower wage rate.

Evolution of constitution of skills and job creation

With the augment of artificial intelligence, robots, and AVs, the productivity is expected to increase, which normally translates to cascading benefits for the economy and jobs that are broad and deep. However, based on the discussions above, we argue that low to mid-level skilled jobs will suffer and the wage rate for those will decline. Our model will help assess the new equilibrium in various markets. We also provided a discussion as to the implications of market related competition.

Given this information, we state that it is the job profile and the constitution of skills that will change. Due to a rise in productivity and, as a result, higher economic activity, increase in aggregate income and rise in final demand, new jobs will be created that span sectoral demands. The skills required from humans will govern the rules of the game. Human perception and pattern matching are hard to replicate through automated vehicles. Complex traffic maneuver, for instance, is not possible for the planned AVs to emulate yet. There are limitations to their scope. One can argue that advances in artificial intelligence (AI) might meet this challenge to an extent, yet they are confined due to the prevalent safety and security concerns. *Higher-level cognitive skills will complement the mid and low-level skills that AVs will substitute.* The displaced blue-collar workers in a certain market could also provide complementary skills for another market that may lead to their temporary or permanent absorption.

Consequent development of organizational and even individual business models will eventually be required to handle the changes that AVs and AI will cause. The key may well be to constantly complement AVs rather than compete. The benefits of technology will not be seen across the board in the economy or the societies as we know them. Awareness and training, education, and skill development programs are ways to invest into more skilled labor that can work with simple to sophisticated technology in transportation. Educational policies, policies around phased deployment if AVs undergo planned adoption, and, more importantly, the extent and willingness of industrial and customer adoption are the principle influencers in the structured adoption of AVs. In the cases where the adoption is unstructured, a more likely scenario, policies will need to be more responsive than preventative; much to the chagrin of the society yet opportunistic for the elements of the social fabric that are more adaptive in terms of their operative model.

Mandated benefits and subsidies

As seen so far, AVs have impact on public policy within and outside of the transportation sector. Much of the anticipated job loss will be a natural consequence of the adoption of this technology. There are definite economic growth opportunities attached to AVs, yet there are revenue-related concerns as well for governments. Government incentives for plug-in hybrid vehicles were established by many national and local governments globally to financially incentivize their usage. These incentives included tax exemptions and tax credits, more access to bus lines, waivers on parking and tolls, and so on. Some of these benefits were extended to fuel cell vehicles and electric version of hybrid electric vehicles. In the current AVs, hybrid and electric are two major areas of development. For example, Cruise Automation, a subsidiary of General Motors, that runs its test vehicles on the streets of San Francisco is autonomous and electric. On the other hand, Alphabet's Waymo is also plug-in hybrid electric, and Ford has ventured in hybrid-electric technology as well for its AV efforts (DeBord 2018).

The planned or unplanned advent of AVs into regional and national markets might vary but the common denominator, given the subsidy above, would be loss of revenue for governments that are subsidizing these vehicles. More consumption of AVs will lead to more vehicles on the roads and, hence, lesser collection of taxes. Increased productivity might offset this loss, however, policy-wise, governments will have to think of other ways to compensate.

Loss of jobs might further pressurize governments to respond in terms of policies. Encouraging human labor, at least temporarily, until skill progression takes place that changes the anticipated lull in employment, will be the prime expected response of governments. Mandated benefits, a commonly used method to affect labor market outcomes in wages and employment could be a response. There is a spectrum of possible benefits that can be provided. A specific example could be that of health insurance, which is considered to be one of the major cost benefits in replacing humans with machines. Governments can ensure that human labor receive particular benefits by mandating so through employers. If a typical worker values benefits in terms of health insurance and perceptively they make them better off, this affects the supply and demand ends of the equation. A new equilibrium is achieved indicating the new wage rate and the employment point.

In contrast to the competitive equilibrium, employers face higher costs, and employees receive lower compensation. If, however, the mandated benefits are valued at the same rate as the costs to provide the benefits, the equilibrium remains unchanged which means inclusion of AVs temporarily did not majorly affect employment. Workers are expected to value health insurance more in a situation wherein their jobs are under threat. There is empirical and evidentiary support to prove that health insurance mandates can easily have significant repercussions on the labor market (Baicker and Chandra 2006). Health insurance is one of the many mandates possible. Many of the changes are possible depending on the elasticities of the demand and supply. Also, it is difficult to trace the benefits across all markets. Yet, policies on the lines of the discussion above will be essential and attempt worthy.

Conclusions

The impact of AVs may currently either exaggerated or underestimated—and it's time to think different about how they will connect with labor and economic trends. With replacement of professional human drivers there is a need to address how jobs will be replaced in a fair and equitable manner. Job loss and replacement will not be limited to ridesharing jobs but result in far reaching impacts that affect everyone from traditional taxi drivers, mail carriers, and freight and cargo drivers, to name a few. We offer a model that can be immediately actionable with a policy response.

Policymakers and planners can make decisions to facilitate skill evolution and/or skill migration. They can offer wage standards to counterbalance limited labor absorption. Governments can mandate that ridesharing companies may need to retain workers to supervise vehicles while they are in use so while there may no longer be a need for a human driver. Agencies can establish roles for individuals to troubleshoot vehicles and supervise cars while in use, or to help those with a disability enter and exit the vehicle.

As we show AVs are certainly a step in the direction of a large technological evolution or shock, and there are clear labor and wage implications. The time for policy action, to maximize economic stability through this transition, is now. The time to "think different" about our autonomous future is now. And through our work here, we provide a framework for pivotal and predictive policy-making over time—so that we can co-evolve our labor policies in parallel with the AV revolution.

Notes

1. Wages, Salaries, and Supplementary income, Corporate profits and investments, Income from all businesses. For the sake of simplicity, we do not include the adjustments – Taxes and Depreciation.
2. Consumption + Investment + Government Spending + Export-Import

References

Acemoglu, D. and D. Autor. 2011. Skills, Tasks, and Technologies: Implications for Employment and Earnings. In *Handbook of Labor Economics, Vol. 4* (1043–1171). Elsevier.

Acemoglu, D. and P. Restrepo. 2017. *Robots and Jobs: Evidence from US Labor Markets.* MIT Department of Economics Working Paper No. 17-04.

Arntz, M., T. Gregory, and U. Zierahn. 2016. *The Risk of Automation for Jobs in OECD Countries: A Comparative Analysis.* OECD Social, Employment and Migration Working Papers, No. 189.

Autor, D. 2014. *Polanyi's Paradox and the Shape of Employment Growth.* NBER Working Paper No. 20485.

Autor, D. and A. Salomons. 2018. Is Automation Labor-Displacing? Productivity Growth, Employment, and the Labor Share. *Brookings Papers on Economic Activity.*

Baicker, K. and A. Chandra, 2006. The Labor Market Effects of Rising Health Insurance Premiums. *Journal of Labor Economics*, 24(3), 609–634.

Bartel, A., C. Ichniowski, C., and K. Shaw. 2007. How Does Information Technology affect Productivity? Plant-Level Comparisons of Product Innovation, Process Improvement, and Worker Skills, 122(4). *The Quarterly Journal of Economics*, 1721–1758.

Bernstein, A., and A. Raman. 2015, June. The Great Decoupling: An Interview with Erik Brynjolfsson and Andrew McAfee. *Harvard Business Review.*

Burstein, A., G. Hanson, L. Tian, and J. Vogel. 2017. *Tradability and the Labor-Market Impact of Immigration: Theory and Evidence from the US.* NBER Working Paper No. w23330.

Caliendo, L. and F. Parro. 2015. Estimates of the Trade and Welfare Effects of NAFTA. *The Review of Economic Studies*, 82(1), 1–44.

DeBord, M. 2018, April. *Waymo and GM are both Developing Self-Driving Tech that Could Change How We Travel—But There's One Big Difference Between the Two.* Retrieved from Business Insider: http://www.businessinsider.com/how-waymo-and-cruise-self-driving-car-strategy-differs-2018-4.

Elsby, M., B. Hobjin, and A. Sahin. 2013. *The Decline of the U.S. Labor Share.* Brookings Papers on Economic Activity.

Karabarbounis, L. and B. Neiman. 2014. The Global Decline of the Labor Share. *Quarterly Journal of Economics*, 129(1), 61–103.

Nordhaus, W. 2015. *Are We Approaching an Economic Singularity? Information Technology and the Future of Economic Growth.* NBER Working Paper No. 21547.

Piketty, T. 2014. *Capital in the Twenty-First Century (English edition).* Cambridge: Harvard University Press.

Rotman, D. 2014, October. *Technology and Inequality.* Retrieved from MIT Technology Review: https://www.technologyreview.com/s/531726/technology-and-inequality/.

Part III

Going big: Changes at the regional scale

10 Co-producing mobility

Lessons from ridesharing for a more just and sustainable autonomous future

Greg P. Griffin

Introduction

How can we go big and make changes to mobility at the regional scale? One way is getting more people in cars, and carpooling. This has become much of the dialogue in the "revolutionary" predictions planners, policymakers, and industry analysts have heard about sharing. However, there are many skeptics. The rate of carpooling has declined every decade since 1980 in the United States, yet more than one out of every seven American adults have used a ride-hailing app (McKenzie 2015; Pew Research Center 2016).

At the same time, growth in the use of smartphones as a platform for mobility presents an opportunity to promote individual and societal benefits of carpooling through savings in congestion, collisions, emissions, time, and money (Abrahamse & Keall 2012; Chen et al. 2000; Shaheen et al. 2016). These challenges create an opportunity for transport policies that manage the demand on roadway capacity (Abrahamse & Keall 2012; Currie et al. 2014; Gärling et al. 2002; Meyer 1999). Co-production of services traditionally offered by government returns agency to the public while offering flexibility for top-down and bottom-up approaches (Clark et al. 2013; Griffin & Jiao 2018); in this case, for mobility management. Early adopters of ridesharing platforms offer a glimpse into how carpooling might, or might not, support co-production of more sustainable use of our current transportation system (Rogers 1995; Siddiqi & Buliung 2013).

Recent studies demonstrate a conflict of views on ridesharing platforms—they provide the means for a flexible, inexpensive, efficient travel option, yet are plagued by limited availability and inconsistent perceptions of safety and other social challenges (Nielsen et al. 2015).

The purpose of this chapter is to provide a clear illustration of the potential for carpooling; evaluating a pilot carpooling app through the perspective of the critical mass theory of interactive media (Markus 1987). As a study, I hope to provide case details about the interaction of ridesharing technologies with transportation policy to support future policy development for ridesharing (Shirole 2017). Understanding of the functions of ridesharing affordances and transportation policies may support more efficient utilization of the roadway systems already in place—that could help mitigate many of the environmental, economic, and equity challenges faced in the global South and North.

As you may have inferred from elsewhere in this book, terms surrounding new mobility are in a state of flux, particularly when context changes the impact of laws and policies. Uber and Lyft happen to be the most extensive examples of convenient services performing similar functions to taxis—which are not really "ridesharing," but rather "ridehailing" since the driver was not likely already taking a given trip (Associated Press 2015). Following the definition in U.S. transportation-funding authorization, the term *ridesharing* refers to sharing of vehicle trips through an electronic platform, that allows reimbursement of costs from the rider(s) to a driver up to, but not exceeding the cost of the trip (One Hundred Twelfth Congress of the United States of America, 2012, p. 156).

The term *affordance* of ridesharing refers to include the communicative and financial interactions between the mobile ridesharing platform, its users, and the transportation network provider. *Critical mass* refers to whether an interactive media increases or decreases in the rate of use over time (Markus 1987). Since the critical mass theory of interactive media is foundational for this chapter, its application for ridesharing is described in the literature review.

To dive into this material, this chapter starts with a review of the literature concerning ridesharing affordances and critical mass, before introducing the empirical ridesharing pilot. I then describe the pilot methodology including recruitment for the pilot, and how the actual carpool trips worked. A discussion section addresses how this pilot test affected transportation in the region, and what the findings may mean for other transportation changes and technological advancements. I conclude with the limitations of the pilot study and directions for future research.

Ridesharing affordances and critical mass theory

Carpooling is as old as the car; no pun intended. However, concerted efforts to create lists of drivers and riders that could logically share trips came to being during WWII resource conservation, and again during the 1970's energy crises (Chan & Shaheen 2012). More recently, mobile technology has merged the formerly different challenges to facilitate ridesharing via the Internet through the combination of accurate and inexpensive GPS location, messaging, and instant payment on a widespread, though not ubiquitous level in developed countries (Pearce & Rice 2013; Perrin & Duggan 2015). Though mobile phones may have reached a critical mass of users some time ago (Leung & Wei 1999), analyzing the potential for widespread and regular use of ridesharing systems requires a full description of the critical mass of interactive media, and of ridesharing affordances.

Critical mass theory is an intuitive concept at face value, with wide-ranging potential impacts for interactive media (Markus 1987). The idea in social science stems from the difficulty of organizing groups to work together in the interest of the larger organization, especially when there is little direct benefit to an individual participant (Olson 1965). Critical mass theory suggests that the start-up time for a group is especially critical, when substantial efforts may be needed to get an idea for collective action in motion by a group (Oliver et al. 1985). The production function relates individual contributions toward a level of collective action. "In a decelerating production function, the first few units of resources contributed have the biggest effect on achieving the public good, and subsequent contributions progressively less. In an accelerating production function, successive contributions generate progressively larger payoffs, thus making additional contributions more likely" (Markus 1987, p. 496). Theoretical and empirical evaluations have confirmed the role of motivated early adopters with a supportive community (Markus 1987; Patterson & Kavanaugh 2001), high-level endorsement of use of the new ICT platform (Evans-Cowley & Griffin 2012), and the benefits of spatial proximity and friendships with ridesharers (Wang et al. 2017).

Travel demand management studies tend to show reduced personal costs, emissions reductions, and other benefits, but the pace of technological change complicates the transferability of results. Gamification, even when used with financial incentives, may be insufficient to impact travel behavior unless the incentives amount to significant savings in cost or time (Castellanos 2016; Zhu et al. 2015). Public events and encouragement programs show promise for immediate changes toward alternatives to driving alone, but short-duration events may not change travel over the long term (Wall et al. 2017). Transportation policies that impact both convenience and direct cost to the driver, such as the availability of parking, may be more effective over time (Riggs 2014; Shoup 2005). Early evaluation of variable parking pricing shows promise for effectively managing demand (Maternini et al. 2017). Recent approaches to managing demand leverage information collected by users, often through smartphones and other wearable devices.

Ridesharing platforms are enabled by the communicative affordances of mobile media (Casas & Delmelle 2017; Schrock 2015), enabling an entire dynamic database of drivers and riders in a ridesharing system to be carried anywhere, while providing direct communication with participants on their schedules. Further, ridesharing platforms can support payments (as in commercial vendors), and incentives (rewards for sustainable choices), providing new ways to provide carrot or stick behavioral cues (Castellanos 2016). Locational identity given by the GPS reduces the burden of individuals to identify their location correctly, confirmed through a digital photograph and text that confirms the identity of the users. So what does this mean to Schrock's general typology of mobile media affordances toward any who might consider ridesharing? My goal is (and was) for us to consider a new "socio-technical perspective" so that mobility is co-produced by participants and the technology (Bijker 1995; Mitlin 2008), using an example of ridesharing in Central Texas.

Ridesharing in Central Texas

The year 2014 was pivotal for ridesharing in Central Texas. The Federal Highway Administration (FHWA)-sponsored carpooling policy pilot launched in partnership with the region's transportation agencies and a private company in February 2014, with Uber and Lyft beginning a ride-hailing market just three months later (Ross 2014; Wear 2015). The carpooling pilot was a naturalistic research project, measuring the impacts of carpooling via a smartphone app, but with a critical distinction—carpools with one rider could take tollways at half the cost, while two or more riders with a driver were fully refunded their tolls in the pilot system (Griffin 2014). The app used in the pilot allowed reimbursement of the driver only up to the cost of the trip—limited to $0.56 per mile in 2014—so trips made sense for drivers when they already were headed that way, but would not enable profit in the form of a taxi service (Harding et al. 2016).

This policy approach is consistent with a peer-to-peer sharing model described as helping offset the cost of driving trips through micropayments, such that drivers can offer carpools they "intended to make any way, but below amounts that would incentivize additional journeys" (McLaren & Agyeman 2015, p. 301). Drivers could also use the app without charging a rider—so there was no cost barrier to families or regular carpools to use it continually. In theory, the more this type of carpooling is encouraged, the more single-occupant vehicle trips are avoided—mitigating congestion and emissions while sharing the cost of travel (Abrahamse & Keall 2012; Shaheen et al. 2016).

Ride-hailing platforms are different. Since the drivers are paid a market rate for trips, they drive with no passengers to pick up riders, effectively increasing the miles driven for the same mobility benefit. Considered as convenient or more so than traditional taxis, ride-hailing offered Central Texas, and other communities in 2014 a new set of options to get around (Wear 2015). Ride-hailing and carpooling platforms are considered under a broader envelope of providing mobility-as-a-service, instead of a product—a harbinger of options that focus on offering transportation solutions independent of a particular mode.

As I will show, the toll discount carpooling pilot program failed to reach a critical mass of drivers, and, therefore, riders taking the service. Meanwhile, Austin regulations defined ride-hailing services like Uber and Lyft as ground transportation services, requiring registration with the city. These regulations were later superseded by state law (Batheja 2014). Following documented sexual assaults of several riders, Austin citizens voted in December 2015 to require ride-hailing drivers to be fingerprinted similar to taxi drivers (O'Brien & Wattles 2016). Rather than conforming to the new regulations, leading providers Uber and Lyft ended service in Austin, before state legislation overturned the city's authority to require fingerprinting, and the services returned in 2017 (Samuels 2017).

Methods

Given this, I chose to look at a post-assessment of the ridesharing pilot in the Austin region, providing a framework for the analysis of future services, and discussions about how to make the technology (and transport) more efficient. I focused on four key questions:

- What are the affordances of ridesharing platforms associated with successful critical mass?

- Absent a profit motive, which communication channels are associated with increased registration for carpooling?
- How are registering for a carpooling system and taking a trip related?
- What challenges with the carpooling system did participants report that could lead to not reaching a critical mass of users?

I used several sources of data to examine these research questions in depth. The primary information was from the Carma (the private partner) carpooling app which was used in Central Texas during 2014, enhanced by information from Uber in the market and time for context. The first dataset was derived from the examination of the ridesharing platforms themselves, as evidenced online and through the mobile apps. Driver data from the vendor was provided directly through the research pilot, and comparison data for Uber is adapted from published submarket data (Hall & Krueger 2015).

Uber data was available only for May through October 2014, but it was sufficient for estimating trends in the production function. Second, the number of drivers per month was a determinant of the scale of availability of the service in the region—drivers are critical for all other ridesharing affordances to be accessed (Lee & Savelsbergh 2015; O'Brien & Wattles 2016).

Next, the analysis used a database of recruitment actions taken by the private partner pilot team, which includes advertising, events, digital media, and outreach to neighborhoods and targeted major employers. Data from the ridesharing platform included the number of new registrants and trip actions that were taken throughout 2014—this was summary data only, rather than personally identifiable information. Finally, text responses to a single-question, post-pilot email were used to bolster these findings.

These datasets support a QUANT→qual mixed-methods approach to the analysis of the case study data (Creswell 2003; Stake 1995). QUANT→qual is used to indicate both the sequential order of data gathering and analysis and that the quantitative approach provides the primary theoretical drive for this empirical study on the critical mass theory of interactive media (Creswell 2010).

For the first research question, the study adapts previous research on the analysis of production functions as indicators to identify critical mass success. The number of drivers is considered a primary "production" of a ridesharing app, which enables the core mobility functions of the service. A second-order polynomial trend line of the number of drivers in each service with slope equations provide a comparison between each service, and the literature describing production functions associated with critical mass.

To analyze recruitment methods, deployment of various tactics by the ridesharing pilot team used on a daily basis throughout 2014 were coded under seven categories: employer, residential, event promotion, paid ads, media coverage, and driver-focused methods. The pilot recruitment team had first worked with a major employer located along a tollway to host breakfast and an information table about the pilot project; then undertook activities such as leaving door hangers at residences in target neighborhoods, hosting coffee events, and mailing postcards. Occasionally, they conducted major events, such as holding a free breakfast for people downloading the app or offering gift certificates for signing up in December.

Advertisement methods included ads on newspaper, radio, and billboards. Local news media also ran chapters describing the pilot, in addition to selected coverage by television news and radio. Recruitment targeted drivers through inserts in toll bills and temporary banners on transportation agency's online newsletters. Perhaps ironically, digital recruitment techniques were the most durable, since website development and social media posts remained discoverable throughout the project. Coding these activities resulted in a binary database (1 on a day with a given category of action, and 0 on days without). Least squares regression associated these explanatory variables with the number of registrations for the carpooling pilot.

The third research question applies a bivariate least squares regression to examine the relationship between the number of program registrations, and actual trips taken during a given day, throughout the pilot. A direct correlation between registration for the pilot and trips taken during the same day would suggest few technical barriers to use—that is, people interested would be able to use the system. This regression technique will not uncover reasons why the program did not work for people, however. The final research question leverages actual reports from participants to describe issues that could challenge the program's potential to achieve a critical mass of users.

Results

What are the affordances of ridesharing platforms associated with successful critical mass?

Ridesharing platforms provide affordances for trip planning, during the journey, and after completion of the trip. Table 10.1 provides a descriptive contrast between platform affordances of the carpooling pilot, and the better-known Uber X ride-hailing service that was offered in the Austin region at the same time. Though they both enable the coordination of trips, there are several key differences to point out that may play a role in achieving critical mass. First, the pilot required matching of drivers and riders based on both the origin, and destination, of a given trip. The probability of riders and drivers sharing both an origin and destination within reasonable proximity is a persistent challenge to rideshare matching (Xia et al. 2015), which is addressed by profit-oriented models that are more akin to taxi services than true ridesharing.

Uber dynamically adjusts prices to manage both the supply of drivers willing to take trips and the demand by riders in specific markets over time, fostering both availabilities of the service and acceptability of the pricing (Harding et al. 2016). A minor difference is that Uber did not allow pre-trip scheduling in 2014—it was assumed that a driver in the service area will get to the rider quickly—whereas

Table 10.1 Platform affordances of a carpooling and ride-hailing app in 2014

Trip Phase	Platform Affordances	Carpooling Pilot	Uber X ride-hailing
Trip planning	Matching of drivers and riders based on *starting location* and time	•	•
	Matching of drivers and riders based on *entire route* and time	•	-
	Picture, contact info, and messaging	•	•
	Dynamic pricing to manage supply and demand	-	•
	Pre-trip pickup scheduling	•	-
	Real-time pickup	-	•
During trip	Cost estimate available for trip	•	•
	Trip map for driver and rider(s)	•	•
	Time and distance recorded for driver and rider(s)	•	•
	Discount on toll roads during pilot	•	-
	Driver payment can exceed cost of trip (profit potential)	-	•
After trip	Rating of drivers by riders	•	•
	Rating of riders by drivers	•	•

a match must be planned and scheduled using the app. The pilot afforded the ability to provide discounts on toll roads, which benefit longer trips from rural or suburban areas in Central Texas but would not be applicable for urban trips within the downtown area, where there were not toll roads. The key difference between the platforms is that Uber drivers can receive payment above the cost of the trip—the distinguishing affordance of a ride-hailing app.

These differentiating affordances are enabled by Uber's high level of capital investment to support the rapid start-up. Plotting of the number of drivers in each system during 2014 in Figure 10.1 shows that despite the toll road discounts offered to participants in the pilot, the suite of affordances was insufficient to support an accelerating production function. The number of drivers using the system peaked at 45 active drivers in June 2014, and subsequent recruitment efforts did not support enough participants to achieve critical mass. A total of 314 individuals had registered as drivers, suggesting people tried the service but did not continue. However, Uber achieved an active pool of more than 71 times the number of drivers in the pilot, with a trend line suggesting an increasing production function, and an intentional leveling-off of new-driver enrollment in July, 2014.

Two of the five differences in ridesharing affordances between the systems relate to profit motive for drivers, enabled by a massive influx of start-up capital. Recognizing that not all ridesharing systems begin with either a profit motive or venture capital, a closer look at the effectiveness of recruitment communication techniques is needed.

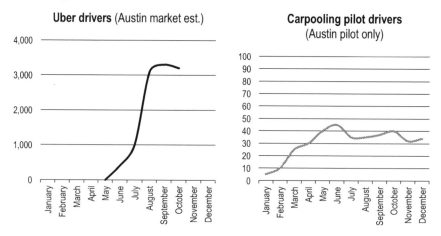

Figure 10.1 Ridesharing drivers in the austin market, 2014

Source: Drawn by the author using data from Hall & Krueger, 2015; Wood & Jones-Meyer, 2016. **Note:** Y-axis scales are different.

Absent a profit motive, which communication channels are associated with increased registration for carpooling?

Analysis of the recruitment actions coded by every day in the pilot suggests some methods may be more efficient than others. Event promotion, media coverage, and driver-focused messages have a positive impact on registration for the ridesharing program, as shown by least squares regression. Paid ads on billboards, newspapers, and radio were significantly associated with pilot registrations on the same day. Each of these methods has the potential for hundreds of thousands of visual impressions in a day, so there is a clear role for paid advertisement to disseminate information about such a ridesharing program. Event promotion, in this case, included several face-to-face events, including tangible incentives such as breakfast or small gift cards for participation.

This method couples the channel with the richest media available, face-to-face (Stephens & Mandhana 2017), with the social norms (social reciprocity norms) of offering an incentive for participation (Riggs 2017; Zhu et al. 2015). Driver-focused techniques like toll road bill inserts provided access to the target audience—tollway drivers, at precisely the moment they might be most interested in potential cost-saving measures. Residential-focused strategies, including small ads hung on front doorknobs, and employer-focused special events like employee breakfasts with information about the ridesharing pilot did not have a significant effect on daily ridesharing registration.

How are registering for a carpooling system and taking a trip related?

This pilot showed that if people are willing to register for a system, they will likely take a trip the same day. The first two research questions addressed the rate of registration, and which recruitment methods were associated with that rate. The third research question addresses whether enrollment in the program is likely to lead to an actual carpool taken with the system. A bivariate least squares regression between registrations and trips taken on every day in the pilot showed that registrations highly predicted carpool trips using the app, explaining 97 percent of the daily variance in taking carpool trips. Programs similar to this pilot may also find that focusing energy on getting new people to register for the system is more important than the next steps of using the system. Getting the word out about the approach may be a challenge, but platforms should be designed so that using the system is not a barrier.

What challenges with the carpooling system did participants report that could lead to not reaching a critical mass of users?

To uncover issues with using the carpooling pilot system not present in registration and use statistics, 341 driver participants in the pilot were emailed a single question: *Could you tell me about your experience using the carpooling system with the toll reimbursement program, and whether you feel it changed your travel choices?* Thirteen responses ranged from minimal experiences with the program to rich descriptions of how the program affected their travel. Nine respondents reported using the system to complete a trip, and all cited the toll road discount affordance as the reason. Four of the respondents did not use the app to complete a journey. The non-users either did not take toll roads on their commutes or could not find a carpool match. This response succinctly describes the problem of a lack of critical mass for the carpooling pilot:

> "I never used the service. There were no people in my part of town that traveled to my work area…." (female)

Others experienced more nuanced challenges with the system, such as this respondent concerned with the dependability of the system, showing the importance of fully testing the sociotechnical assemblage of communication, mobility, and fiscal policy affordances:

> "It seemed cool. My wife and I both installed it and started using it. We stopped using it when I found a big disconnect between how much the app said I 'had' and how much the toll was going to bill us. The tollways charge a lot of money if you don't pay, and seeing a different balance made me too nervous to use the app. We ride the tolls every day, so if things have changed, and there are other incentives to using it, then I would be willing to try again." (male)

Others provided full support of the system and described how the toll discounts encouraged carpooling while saving commute costs.

"Yes it was great—there are a few of us that live within a couple miles of each other and all work at the same place. Normally we took surface roads since it would cost us four dollars a day to take the tolls, but with the program we took the tolls each day and carpooled—instead of 4 cars on the road it was just 1." (unknown gender)

This carpool group was then able to leverage the toll exemption policy for a 3+ carpool to drive faster, and likely safer, using the tollway, rather than finding parallel routes. The richest explanation of their carpooling experience also incorporated the role of an individual's place in his life course and the use of different travel modes over time. Carpooling played a role in getting more out of a required commute, but eventually, the complexities of other family members place a higher demand on the driver:

"We originally shared a Cap Metro van for saving money. That got too expensive, and the members were not regular enough, so it disbanded. We then set up personal carpools. We used the app to save money on tolls. The app didn't cause the creation of the group, but it prolonged it. We did completely stop carpooling before the discounts ended. Our families have grown and our transportation needs have required greater flexibility in terms of departure times, so we each now drive our own vehicles. The flexibility need now outweighs the monetary savings need. [...] If I take the toll road, I get home about 13 minutes sooner, but it costs me $2.04. Those 260 extra evening minutes cost me $40.80 a month. When your family is growing, you need both time and money." (male)

Lessons for new mobility and disruptive transport

As you have seen, this naturalistic pilot showed that a carpooling program requires more than a nominal incentive to change transportation behavior. This suggests that users of new mobility, whether it be shared or autonomous vehicle services, require greater incentives to share trips with others. We should all be skeptical of the shared assumption. Though limited in generalizability, this study offers four lessons for developing policies to support just, sustainable, autonomous mobility—critical mass, planning for affordances, marketing, and the role of public policy during rapid technological advancement.

Convenience, cost, and critical mass

The carpooling pilot platform requires pre-planning to find and coordinate a match for a given route, making non-regular trips difficult, if not impossible. Since drivers can only be reimbursed up to the cost of the trip, the added time to coordinate a trip was more than the benefits derived from the carpooling pilot, with notable exceptions documented in the qualitative responses. The example of Uber shows a system where the benefits for drivers are immediate and financial—the difficulties in coordination are overcome by the capital investment of the company. Critical mass theory of interactive media suggests the overall interest and resources of an interactive media are supported by adoption by community leaders or incentives (Markus 1987). Carma was a relative unknown in the 2014 pilot community, while early adopters of Uber were portrayed in the media as leveraging cutting-edge technology to solve mobility problems. The pilot lacked both a recognizable champion and adequate incentives to create bottom-up leaders in local communities. The company continued to offer service following the conclusion of the toll road discount pilot in 2015, but use trickled to near zero, which also confirms Markus' first proposition: an interactive media will either achieve near-universal access or eventually completely fall off. Analysis of both the carpooling and ride-hailing systems during a period of early adoption suggests the critical mass theory of interactive media is both durable and relevant to ICT use for solving mobility challenges.

Plan for affordances, rather than features

The affordances approach to human-computer interaction is less than two decades old (Resnick 2001), and this study contributes a new understanding of how the trip planning, taking, and post-trip affordances of ridesharing platforms contribute to their tendency to reach critical mass. This is both a theoretical and practical contribution. The typology of ridesharing affordances can be evaluated and changed as sociotechnical advancements occur in the field. As automated vehicles enter the marketplace, many of my ridesharing affordances may become irrelevant, but the emphasis on affordances, rather than features, is likely to offer more generalizable knowledge (Faraj & Azad 2012; Treem & Leonardi 2012). Ridesharing affordances are also described in sufficient detail for app designers and transportation technologists to consider their role in widespread adoption.

Marketing matters

This research also provides practical implications for the future promotion of ICT-enabled mobility services. First, this evidence suggests that recruitment efforts targeted to residences and employers may be overemphasized. Rather than refuting previous research supporting these tactics (Neoh et al. 2015; Riggs 2015), this study provides evidence that paid media advertisements, organic media coverage, face-to-face events, and driver-oriented messages are all moderately related to enrollment in the carpool pilot program. Analysis of the registration and trip-making activity on the same day shows that the pilot implementation did not create systemic barriers to participation, yet qualitative responses show at least isolated examples of dissatisfaction with the system. Since a private-app vendor and a public-tolling agency were both pivotal for the toll-waiving system to function, this area of concern would need further research. Future travel-demand management programs should consider broad marketing approaches to capture users of an automated vehicle market.

Transportation policies remain in the driver's seat

Policymaking in Austin, Texas, showed that despite the rapid advancement in available mobility technologies, local and regional authorities could direct implementation toward, or against, just and sustainable mobility. Policies on transportation network companies caused them to leave the market, if temporarily, as governments wrestled to find a balance between supporting private-sector innovation and setting policies to protect users. The discount and removal of tolls for registered carpools with an emerging platform showed regional authorities' willingness to innovate, but the relatively low transaction value may have prevented reaching a critical mass of carpoolers.

Cities, metropolitan planning organizations, and states have the opportunity to direct policymaking for autonomous vehicles to encourage carpooling, rather than promoting single-occupant trips. This study showed potential for technology-delivered policies—through dynamic carpool registration—yet more partnership with the private sector may be needed to provide mobility options for lower-income communities in the autonomous future. A strong policy role can support just, sustainable transportation under a wide variety of future technologies, but only if transportation officials take leadership to support individuals' co-production of mobility.

Conclusion

Though this study provides naturalistic, mixed methods data on "how people *actually* use ICTs, not just how they *say* they use them" (Stephens & Sætre 2008, p. 34), the context of the pilot test imposes limitations. The Austin, Texas region lacks several conditions that are known to facilitate transportation mode choices other than driving alone. First is the lack of high-occupancy vehicle lanes, which previous research in the Dallas-Fort Worth and Houston areas in Texas shows is "the most important factor in their decision to form a carpool" (Li et al. 2007, p. 10) because they provide a speed advantage to avoid highway congestion. Second, increased automobile parking rates are associated with higher use of transportation modes other than driving alone (Christiansen et al. 2017; Hamre & Buehler 2014; Shoup 2005; Whitfield et al. 2016). Parking in Austin is largely free, with a $1/ hour charge for most on-street spaces in downtown (The Downtown Austin Alliance, 2016), which was the median rate for low-density United States cities in 2009 (Auchincloss et al. 2014). Travel demand management research shows parking is a vital part of travel mode choice (Riggs 2014). Finally, the price of gasoline dropped $1.42 per gallon during the pilot study—about the same cost as tolls on a suburban commute in the region, but more than the average reimbursement of tolls for the average trip in this study ($1.08) (Central Texas Regional Mobility Authority, 2015; U.S. Energy Information Administration, 2015). The decreasing cost of fuel during this pilot nullified the financial advantages of toll reimbursement, suggesting a similar pilot in different contexts could achieve different results.

In addition to conducting similar studies in different contexts, future research should examine the role of the sequencing of communication methods with potential carpoolers. Previous research on organizations suggests the order of different messages and channels could play a part expanding cues for behavior changes (Stephens 2007; Stephens et al. 2008). Future evaluations of ridesharing should also consider the role of access to mobile media through an equity perspective (Martens et al. 2012; Pearce & Rice 2013; Schwanen et al. 2015), which have ramifications to ladders of opportunity (Blumenberg & Pierce 2014).

At the same time, it is worth reinforcing a critical theme that arises from this work. Policy matters and sharing is not automatic. Citizens, policymakers, planners and engineers should be skeptical of overly optimistic assumptions, but they should also "lean-in" and shape travel incentives and marketing efforts that encourage more sustainable travel decisions in the disruptive, new mobility transportation future.

Acknowledgments

Preliminary work for this study was supported in part by the Federal Highway Administration through the Value Pricing Pilot Program, through the "Real-time Ridesharing Technology to Support Differential Tolling by Occupancy" research project with the Texas A&M Transportation Institute (TTI). TTI researchers Gretchen Stoeltje, Nathan Jones, Nicholas S. Wood, and Chris Simek each contributed to the original research on which this study is based. Keri Stephens at The University of Texas at Austin provided insights on the theoretical framing and valuable comments on an earlier draft of this chapter.

References

Abrahamse, W. and M. Keall. 2012. Effectiveness of a web-based intervention to encourage carpooling to work: A case study of Wellington, New Zealand. *Transport Policy*, 21, 45–51. https://doi.org/10.1016/j.tranpol.2012.01.005.

Associated Press. 2015. *AP Stylebook*. Retrieved December 12, 2016, from https://twitter.com/apstylebook/status/565515953430364163.

Auchincloss, A. H., R. Weinberger, S. Aytur, A. Namba, and A. Ricchezza. 2014. Public Parking Fees and Fines: A Survey of U.S. Cities. *Public Works Management & Policy*, 1087724X13514380-. https://doi.org/10.1177/1087724X13514380.

Batheja, A. 2014. Uber, Lyft Rolling Forward, but Uncertainty Lingers. Retrieved December 5, 2016, from https://www.texastribune.org/2014/06/10/uber-lyft-target-texas-cities-despite-unfriendly-r/

Bijker, W. E. 1995. *Of Bicycles, Bakelites, and Bulbs: Toward a Theory of Sociotechnical Change*. Boston, MA: MIT Press.

Blumenberg, E. and G. Pierce. 2014. A Driving Factor in Mobility? Transportation's Role in Connecting Subsidized Housing and Employment Outcomes in the Moving to Opportunity (MTO) Program. *Journal of the American Planning Association*, 80(February 2015), 52–66. https://doi.org/10.1080/01944363.2014.935267.

Casas, I. and E. C. Delmelle. 2017. Tweeting about public transit — Gleaning public perceptions from a social media microblog. *Case Studies on Transport Policy*, 5(4), 634–642. https://doi.org/10.1016/j.cstp.2017.08.004.

Castellanos, S. 2016. Delivering modal-shift incentives by using gamification and smartphones: A field study example in Bogota, Colombia. *Case Studies on Transport Policy*, 4(4), 269–278. https://doi.org/10.1016/j.cstp.2016.08.008.

Central Texas Regional Mobility Authority. 2015. *Setting Central Texas in Motion: CTRMA 2014 Annual Report*. Austin, TX.

Chan, N. D. and S. A. Shaheen. 2012. Ridesharing in North America: Past, Present, and Future. *Transport Reviews*, 32(1), 93–112. https://doi.org/10.1080/01441647.2011.621557.

Chen, L.-H., S. P. Baker, E. R. Braver, and G. Li. 2000. Carrying passengers as a risk factor for crashes fatal to 16-17 year old drivers. *JAMA*, 283(12), 1578–1582. https://doi.org/10.1001/jama.283.12.1578.

Christiansen, P., Ø. Engebretsen, N. Fearnley, and J. Usterud Hanssen. 2017. Parking facilities and the built environment: Impacts on travel behaviour. *Transportation Research Part A: Policy and Practice*, 95, 198–206. https://doi.org/10.1016/j.tra.2016.10.025.

Clark, B. Y., J. L. Brudney, M. Jakobsen, and S. C. Andersen. 2013. Coproduction of Government Services and the New Information Technology: Investigating the Distributional Biases. *Public Administration Review*, 73(5), 704–713. https://doi.org/10.1111/puar.12092.Coproduction.

Creswell, J. W. 2003. *Research design: Qualitative, quantitative, and mixed methods approaches*. Thousand Oaks, CA: SAGE Publications. https://doi.org/10.3109/08941939.2012.723954.

Creswell, J. W. 2010. Mapping the Developing Landscape of Mixed Methods Research. In *SAGE Handbook of Mixed Methods in Social & Behavioral Research* (pp. 45–68). Thousand Oaks, CA: SAGE Publications, Inc. https://doi.org/10.4135/9781506335193.n2.

Currie, G., A. Jones, and J. Woolley. 2014. Travel Demand Management and the Big Scare. *Transportation Research Record: Journal of the Transportation Research Board*, 2469, 11–22. https://doi.org/10.3141/2469-02.

Evans-Cowley, J. and G. Griffin. 2012. Microparticipation with Social Media for Community Engagement in Transportation Planning. *Transportation Research Record: Journal of the Transportation Research Board*, 2307, 90–98. https://doi.org/10.3141/2307-10.

Faraj, S. and B. Azad. 2012. The materiality of technology: an affordance perspective. In P. M. Leonardi, B. A. Nardi, & J. Kallinikos (Eds.), *Materiality and Organizing: social interaction in a technological world* (pp. 237–258). Oxford: Oxford University Press.

Gärling, T., et al. Vilhelmson. 2002. A conceptual analysis of the impact of travel demand management on private car use. *Transport Policy*, 9(1), 59–70. https://doi.org/10.1016/S0967-070X(01)00035-X.

Griffin, G. 2014, August. Real-Time Ridesharing Texas Experiments with Toll Roads and Carpools. *TrafficInfraTech Magazine*, June–July, 64–66.

Griffin, G. P. and J. Jiao. 2018. Crowdsourcing Bike Share Station Locations: Evaluating Participation and Placement. *Journal of the American Planning Association*, 84. https://doi.org/10.1080/01944363.2018.1476174.

Hall, J. and A. Krueger. 2015. *An Analysis of the Labor Market for Uber's Driver-Partners in the United States*. Princeton, NJ.

Hamre, A. and R. Buehler. 2014. Commuter Mode Choice and Free Car Parking, Public Transportation Benefits, Showers/Lockers, and Bike Parking at Work: Evidence from the Washington, D.C. Region. *Journal of Public Transportation*, 17(2), 67–91.

Harding, S., M. Kandlikar, and S. Gulati. 2016. Taxi apps, regulation, and the market for taxi journeys. *Transportation Research Part A: Policy and Practice*, 88(December 2014), 15–25. https://doi.org/10.1016/j.tra.2016.03.009.

Lee, A. and M. Savelsbergh. 2015. Dynamic ridesharing: Is there a role for dedicated drivers? *Transportation Research Part B: Methodological*, *81*, 483–497. https://doi.org/10.1016/j.trb.2015.02.013.

Leung, L. and R. Wei. 1999. Who are the Mobile Phone Have-Nots?: Influences and Consequences. *New Media & Society*, *1*(2), 209–226. https://doi.org/10.1177/1461444899001002003.

Li, J., P. Embry, S. P. Mattingly, K. F. Sadabadi, I. Rasmidatta, and M. W. Burris. 2007. Who Chooses to Carpool and Why? Examination of Texas Carpoolers. *Transportation Research Record: Journal of the Transportation Research Board*, *2021*, 110. https://doi.org/10.3141/2021-13

Markus, M. L. 1987. Toward a "Critical Mass" Theory of Interactive Media: Universal Access, Interdependence and Diffusion. *Communication Research*, *14*(5), 491–511. https://doi.org/10.1177/009365087014005003.

Martens, K., A. Golub, and G. Robinson. 2012. A justice-theoretic approach to the distribution of transportation benefits: Implications for transportation planning practice in the United States. *Transportation Research Part A: Policy and Practice*, *46*(4), 684–695. https://doi.org/10.1016/j.tra.2012.01.004.

Maternini, G., F. Ferrari, and A. Guga. 2017. Application of variable parking pricing techniques to innovate parking strategies. The case study of Brescia. *Case Studies on Transport Policy*, *5*(2), 425–437. https://doi.org/10.1016/j.cstp.2017.03.010

McKenzie, B. 2015. *Who Drives to Work? Commuting by Automobile in the United States: 2013. American Community Survey Reports*. Washington, D.C.

McLaren, D. and J. Agyeman. 2015. *Sharing Cities: A case for truly smart and sustainable cities*. Boston: Massachusetts Institute of Technology.

Meyer, M. D. 1999. Demand management as an element of transportation policy: Using carrots and sticks to influence travel behavior. *Transportation Research Part A: Policy and Practice*, *33*(7–8), 575–599. https://doi.org/10.1016/S0965-8564(99)00008-7.

Mitlin, D. 2008. With and beyond the state – co-production as a route to political influence, power and transformation for grassroots organizations. *Environment and Urbanization*, *20*(2), 339–360. https://doi.org/10.1177/0956247808096117.

Neoh, J. G., M. Chipulu, and A. Marshall. (2015). What encourages people to carpool? An evaluation of factors with meta-analysis. *Transportation*. https://doi.org/10.1007/s11116-015-9661-7.

Nielsen, J. R., H. Hovmøller, P.-L. Blyth, and B. K. Sovacool. 2015. Of "white crows" and "f savers:" A qualitative study of travel behavior and perceptions of ridesharing in Denmark. *Transportation Research Part A: Policy and Practice*, *78*, 113–123. https://doi.org/10.1016/j.tra.2015.04.033.

O'Brien, S. A. and J. Wattles. 2016. Austin Drivers in the lurch after Uber, Lyft exit. Retrieved December 5, 2016, from http://money.cnn.com/2016/05/09/technology/austin-uber-lyft-drivers/.

Oliver, P., G. Marwell, and R. Teixeria. 1985. A Theory of the Critical Mass. I. Interdependence, Group Heterogeneity, and the Production of Collective Action. *American Journal of Sociology*, *91*(3), 522–556.

Olson, M. 1965. *The Logic of Collective Action*. Cambridge, MA: Harvard University Press.

One Hundred Twelfth Congress of the United States of America. Moving Ahead for Progress in the 21st Century Act (MAP-21), Pub. L. No. 112–141 (2012). United States of America: U.S. Congress.

Patterson, S. J. and A. L. Kavanaugh. 2001. Building a Sustainable Community Network: an application of critical mass theory. *The Electronic Journal of Communication*, *11*(2). http://www.cios.org/EJCPUBLIC/011/2/01122.HTML.

Pearce, K. E. and R. E. Rice. 2013. Digital Divides From Access to Activities: Comparing Mobile and Personal Computer Internet Users. *Journal of Communication*, 63(4), 721–744. https://doi.org/10.1111/jcom.12045.

Perrin, A. and M. Duggan. 2015. Americans Internet Access: Percent of Adults 2000-2015. Retrieved November 28, 2015, from http://www.pewinternet.org/2015/06/26/americans-internet-access-2000-2015/.

Pew Research Center. 2016. *Shared, Collaborative and On Demand: The New Digital Economy*. Washington, D.C.

Resnick, P. 2001. Beyond Bowling Together: SocioTechnical Capital. *Human-Computer Interaction in the New Millenium*, 77(March), 247–272. https://doi.org/Can't find.

Riggs, W. 2014. Dealing with parking issues on an urban campus: The case of UC Berkeley. *Case Studies on Transport Policy*, 2(3), 168–176. https://doi.org/10.1016/j.cstp.2014.07.009.

Riggs, W. 2015. Testing personalized outreach as an effective TDM measure. *Transportation Research Part A: Policy and Practice*, 78, 178–186. https://doi.org/10.1016/j.tra.2015.05.012.

Riggs, W. 2017. Painting the fence: Social norms as economic incentives to non-automotive travel behavior. *Travel Behaviour and Society*, 7, 26–33. https://doi.org/10.1016/j.tbs.2016.11.004.

Rogers, E. M. 1995. *Diffusion of innovations*. Macmillian Publishing Co. New York: The Free Press. https://doi.org/citeulike-article-id:126680.

Ross, R. 2014, June 27. Getting off the Road. *Austin Chronicle*, pp. 22–25. Austin.

Schrock, A. R. 2015. Communicative Affordances of Mobile Media: Portability, Availability, Locatability, and Multimediality. *International Journal of Communication*, 9, 1229–1246. https://doi.org/10.1177/0094306111425016k.

Schwanen, T., K. Lucas, N. Akyelken, D. Cisternas Solsona, J. A. Carrasco, and T. Neutens. 2015. Rethinking the links between social exclusion and transport disadvantage through the lens of social capital. *Transportation Research Part A: Policy and Practice*, 74, 123–135. https://doi.org/10.1016/j.tra.2015.02.012.

Shaheen, S. A., N. D. Chan, and T. Gaynor. 2016. Casual carpooling in the San Francisco Bay Area: Understanding user characteristics, behaviors, and motivations. *Transport Policy*, 1–9. https://doi.org/10.1016/j.tranpol.2016.01.003.

Shirole, A. M. 2017. Case Studies on Transport Policy US-India bilateral collaboration to enhance transportation — A decade of experience. *Case Studies on Transport Policy*, 5(1), 22–30. https://doi.org/10.1016/j.cstp.2016.09.004.

Shoup, D. C. 2005. *The High Cost of Free Parking*. Chicago: Planners Press, American Planning Association.

Siddiqi, Z. and R. Buliung. 2013. Transportation Planning and Technology Dynamic ridesharing and information and communications technology: past, present and future prospects. *Transportation Planning and Technology*, 36(6), 479–498. https://doi.org/10.1080/03081060.2013.830895.

Samuels, A. 2017. Uber, Lyft return to Austin as Texas Gov. Abbott signs ride-hailing measure into law. Retrieved July 5, 2018, from https://www.texastribune.org/2017/05/29/texas-gov-greg-abbott-signs-measure-creating-statewide-regulations-rid/.

Stake, R. E. 1995. *The Art of Case Study Research*. Thousand Oaks, CA: SAGE Publications.

Stephens, K. K. 2007. The successive use of information and communication technologies at work. *Communication Theory*, 17(4), 486–507. https://doi.org/10.1111/j.1468-2885.2007.00308.x.

Stephens, K. K. and D. M. Mandhana. 2017. Media Choice/Use in Organizations. In C. R. Scott& L. K. Lewis (Eds.), *The International Encyclopedia of Organizational Communication* (pp. 1–14). Chichester, NY: Wiley Blackwell.

Stephens, K. K. and A. S. Sætre. 2008. Media Choice and ICT Use. In L. D. Browning, A. S. Sætre, K. K. Stephens, & J.-O. Sørnes (Eds.), *Information and Communication Technologies in Action* (revised, pp. 27–34). New York: Routledge.

Stephens, K. K., J. O. Sornes, R. E. Rice, L. D. Browning, and A. S. Saetre. 2008. Discrete, Sequential, and Follow-Up Use of Information and Communication Technology by Experienced ICT Users. *Management Communication Quarterly*, 22(2), 197–231. https://doi.org/10.1177/0893318908323149.

The Downtown Austin Alliance. 2016. Parking. Retrieved November 12, 2016, from http://www.downtownaustin.com/experience/parking.

Treem, J. W. and P. M. Leonardi. 2012. Social Media use in organizations. *Communication Yearbook*, 143–189. https://doi.org/10.2139/ssrn.2129853.

U.S. Energy Information Administration. 2015. Gulf Coast Gasoline and Diesel Retail Prices. Retrieved May 6, 2015, from http://www.eia.gov/dnav/pet/pet_pri_gnd_dcus_r30_w.htm.

Wall, G., B. Olaniyan, L. Woods, and C. Musselwhite. 2017. Encouraging sustainable modal shift—An evaluation of the Portsmouth Big Green Commuter Challenge. *Case Studies on Transport Policy*, 5(1), 105–111. https://doi.org/10.1016/j.cstp.2016.11.006.

Wang, Y., S. Winter, and N. Ronald. 2017. How much is trust: The cost and benefit of ridesharing with friends. *Computers, Environment and Urban Systems*, 65, 103–112. https://doi.org/10.1016/j.compenvurbsys.2017.06.002.

Wear, B. 2015, October 16. 'Friction' at heart of Austin's dispute with Uber and Lyft. *Austin American-Statesman*.

Whitfield, G. P., A. M. Wendel, and A. H. Auchincloss. 2016. Ecological Analysis of Parking Prices and Active Commuting in US Cities, 2009. *Preventing Chronic Disease*, 13, 160097. https://doi.org/10.5888/pcd13.160097.

Wood, N. S. and S. N. Jones-Meyer. 2016. Integrating Automated Toll Discounts into a Real-Time Ridesharing Program. *Transportation Research Record: Journal of the Transportation Research Board*, 2597, 20–27. https://doi.org/10.3141/2597-03.

Xia, J., K. M. Curtin, W. Li, and Y. Zhao. 2015. A New Model for a Carpool Matching Service. *Plos One*, 10(6), e0129257. https://doi.org/10.1371/journal.pone.0129257

Zhu, C., J. S. Yue, C. V. Mandayam, D. Merugu, H. K. Abadi, and B. Prabhakar. 2015. Reducing Road Congestion through Incentives: a case study. In *Transportation Research Board 94th Annual Meeting*. Washington, D.C.: Transportation Research Board of the National Academies.

11 Accessibility and equity

Can a shared and electric future be socially just?

Stephen Zoepf and William Riggs

Introduction

Merriam-Webster Dictionary defines the word mobility as, "the quality or state of being mobile or movable," yet if you ask an audience at conference to define "mobility" today, the responses will be mixed. They will contain a blend of concepts, products, and services, some of which exist today (e.g., ride-hailing and scooters) and others envisioned as just around the corner (e.g., driverless cars and deliver drones). Remarkably, after decades of different business models, and in a market where ride-hailing companies deliver billions of rides per year, we have not yet developed a stable, consistent vocabulary to describe how we get around. Business models in a specific country become synonymous with the largest local service provider ("I Ubered to work this morning"), and we may expect some of these terms to outlast the service providers that spawn them.

Part of this is attributable to a market which is in rapid flux. In his 1994 work *Mastering the Dynamics of Innovation* MIT Professor James Utterback characterizes periods of rapid innovation as going through two distinct phases: a first phase of product innovation, followed by a phase of process innovation. Between these phases emerges a dominant design, or a single basic concept which comes to dominate the market, with few variations and few competitors. During the phase of product innovation, hundreds of companies may compete to develop concepts that resound with customers.

In the early late-nineteenth and early-twentieth century, cars went through such an evolution. Little-to-no standardization existed around automotive controls. Hundreds of small manufacturers produced cars in which steering, gears, throttle, spark advance, and brakes were controlled with a myriad of different styles of levers, pedals, tillers, and wheels. By the 1930s, a dominant design emerged: steering wheel to control direction, pedals to control the brakes and throttle, and a few levers to control gears and ancillary controls.

In the mobility services market such a dominant design has yet to emerge, so our vocabulary and notions of what a mobility system are continuing to change. Current efforts are underway at standards organizations (SAE) to develop a taxonomy for shared mobility systems (J3163: Taxonomy and Definitions for Terms Related to Shared Mobility and Enabling Technologies), and we hope these will add clarity. In the near-term, there are six questions that engineers and policymakers ask to ensure that they have a common concept in mind when they discuss "mobility":

1 Who owns the vehicles?

   a Passengers (peer-to-peer rentals)
   b Paid drivers
   c Company (platform operator or other)

2 What is the trip type?

   a Round-trip (traditional carsharing)
   b One-way/Station-based (Car2Go)
   c Floating (vehicles can be used anywhere within a perimeter)

3 Who operates the vehicle?

   a Passengers
   b Paid driver
   c AI/Remote pilot

4 How long are trips?

   a Days
   b Hours
   c Minutes

5 Are trips combined with others?

   a Dedicated (direct route, no other passengers in the vehicle)
   b Shared

6 How far in advance are trips planned?

   a Days
   b Hours
   c Minutes

Until a dominant design emerges for mobility systems, researchers and policymakers will need to consider the impacts of policy and regulatory choices to a variety of mobility providers. Small differences in business models, incentive structures and operational characteristics may have enormous impact on the effectiveness or efficiency of policies.

Moves toward sustainability

Asking a group about sustainability or sustainable transportation will bring an even larger range of definitions, including electric cars, any transportation system with a managed life cycle, to exclusively human-powered modes like walking and biking. Hall and Sussman (2006) provide a concrete definition, elaborating a concept of sustainable transportation that is composed of three elements: environmental sustainability, economic sustainability, and equity or social sustainability.

> "Sustainability /sə‚stānə'bilədē/ noun 1: the ability to be maintained at a certain rate or level."

Of these three elements, perhaps environmental sustainability is the most widely understood concept: a truly sustainable transportation system cannot do ongoing damage to the environment. As issues of traditional criteria pollutants and local emissions are increasingly addressed through conventional regulations, environmental sustainability concerns around transportation largely focus on energy consumption and CO_2 emissions. In the United States the transportation sector is the largest source of energy consumption, and transportation-sector energy consumption has approximately tripled since 1950 in the United States. Later in this chapter, we propose a structure for thinking about this issue based on the Kaya identity proposed a quarter-century ago and adopted by the Intergovernmental Panel on Climate Change (IPCC).

Economic sustainability is a less-commonly recognized element of sustainable transportation, incorporating both the perspectives of corporations (the need for economic growth, well-being and effective use of innovation) as well as the needs of individuals through affordability. Today's mobility landscape is composed of a shifting array of startups and new business models. Many of these are not presently profitable (e.g., ride-hailing companies and electric car manufacturers) and are supported by funds from investors or social subsidies (e.g., taxes avoided). Later in this chapter we raise a number questions about the economic sustainability of future mobility systems.

The final element of sustainable transportation, equity, embodies the idea that transportation should be accessible to all without imposing undue burden on specific demographic groups. Hall and Sussman specifically note that a sustainable transportation system "promotes equity within and between successive generations." Truly sustainability future mobility systems will promote not just access but choice, allowing system participants to choose between more than one alternative. With transportation increasingly recognized as an important tool to escape poverty (Chetty & Hendren 2016), sustainable mobility systems should offer participants a means to economic improvement.

What does new mobility mean for access to transportation resources?

While modes of transportation such as cars, buses, and taxis have been the norm for decades, issues such as congestion and emissions have caused alternative forms of transportation to gain popularity. Social equity is also an issue for many riders and drivers. As such it is important that equity and social justice be considered when developing new policies and technologies.

Many of these issues are present in the new mobility movement which works to improve people's' mobility while simultaneously reducing emissions, congestion, and other negative factors that have recently become targets of social movements. The methods in question include autonomous vehicles, carpooling, ride sharing services such as Uber and Lyft, and increasing availability of other transportation methods like bikes and roller skates. These are in turn used to further goals related to social justice such as compensating for rural and urban differences as well as social, environmental, and economic ones.

One early study from Los Angeles offers evidence that new forms of mobility mean that more people, especially those of lower socio-economic status, can access transportation resources more easily (Brown 2018). Whether these results are indicative of results in other regions remains to be seen.

Due to the increasing popularity of these options, policy changes in planning for both urban and rural settings are needed. Examples of existing issues are driver income, conflict with the established industries, emissions, congestion, and policy and regulation difficulties.

Wages and other economic concerns

While ride-hailing companies like Uber and Lyft are increasing in popularity the taxi industry is suffering. Taxi usage has dramatically declined, and taxi drivers' wages have been cut (Brown 2018). The potential disruptions caused by the ride-hailing companies have resulted in public outcries and led to investigations such as one by Berger et al. in 2018. Also, due to a lack of available data, it is unclear exactly how much Uber and Lyft drivers make and if this qualifies as a livable wage. While various studies and surveys have been conducted, the results and methods of analyses have been criticized by both academics and those in the private sector, particularly executives in the ride-hailing companies (Zoepf et al. 2018).

This has led to calls for the regulation of ride-hailing companies in a manner similar to existing taxi companies. In turn, ride-hailing companies have decided to cease providing services in certain cities until the environment becomes more favorable to them. An example of this is Austin, Texas, where Uber was not allowed to use their own systems to check drivers' backgrounds (Hampshire et al. 2017). These issues can have adverse effects on those wishing to utilize ride-hailing services. If the services cease to run, then transportation options become more limited and the available options may be more expensive. On the other hand, without policies in place to ensure drivers are adequately compensated, equity will continue to be a problem within the industry and could lead to fewer drivers.

A study in 2018 by Brown showed that, as ride-hailing companies have become more popular, access to transportation has increased for those living in low-income communities. This is attributed to using Uber or Lyft as a cheaper alternative to owning a car. The data in this study also shows that Uber and Lyft drivers are less likely to racially discriminate against users than taxi drivers. For example, ride cancellations and wait times for black riders are reduced. Brown's study also shows that, compared to the taxi industry, if a rider experiences a cancellation they are often only delayed in reaching their destination rather than being completely robbed of transportation.

Some policy suggestions to further reduce discrimination involve keener observation of drivers who make cancellations, allowing drivers and riders to use pseudonyms, or changing the point at which drivers learn names or races of their riders and vice-versa. Introduction of congestion pricing for owners of private cars is also suggested in response to accusations that ride-hailing services are causing the aforementioned issues in taxi industry. Finally, it is noted that in lower-income areas there is less smartphone usage and thus less use of ride-hailing services. Future policy changes at both the corporate and city-wide level would do well to address these issues.

Thinking about emissions from mobility

How should we think about impact of new mobility systems on CO_2 emissions? In 1993, Yoichi Kaya proposed a framework for thinking about carbon output as a function of human activity, GDP and global population. The framework has become known as the Kaya identity (Kaya et al. 1997). In a similar manner, carbon emissions from each mode of the transportation sector can be thought of as the product of four terms: (1) the intensity of human transportation, in passenger-kilometers, (2) the efficiency of a transportation system in combining travel of passengers into vehicles, (3) the rate of energy consumption of vehicles, and (4) the carbon intensity of the fuel source.

$$CO_{2_{MODE}} = km_{pass} * \frac{km_{veh}}{km_{pass}} * \frac{kJ}{km_{veh}} * \frac{CO_2}{kJ}$$

Separating out these terms is useful to understand the different pathways by which the transportation system can be made more efficient, or to help understand the ways in which transportation regulations impact emissions. Within light-duty modes, traditional transportation regulations have focused on the rightmost terms, through technology-forcing requirements like the zero emissions vehicle (ZEV) mandate in the United States, or through efficiency standards such as the corporate average fuel economy (CAFE) standard that sets minimum efficiency standards for new passenger cars and light trucks in the United States.

Other, softer incentives such as carpool lane access, or policy choices such as prioritizing urban space for bike lanes and sidewalks can motivate citizens to choose transportation modes such as walking or biking that may offer lower rates of CO_2 emissions.

Perhaps the term of this equation where we have the least public information is the ratio of vehicle distance to passenger distance. Ride-hailing companies are sometimes referred to as ride-*sharing* companies. Sharing implies that two passengers are generally going the same direction and therefore by getting into a vehicle together they provide some environmental benefit. However, this is not true of all ride-hailing trip: only of trips where multiple passengers getting into the same vehicle result in a net reduction in total vehicle miles traveled.

Distance traveled: vehicles versus people

Specific ride-hailing services that combine passenger trips (typically at a lower price) are now available through services such as Lyft Line and UberPool. In an ideal world, combining passengers together in vehicles results in immediate, substantial benefits. This notion is consistent with our intuitive understanding of casually carpooling with a friend or co-worker: if we live and work near the same locations, we're more likely to meet and share a ride. If our start and end locations are the same, by traveling together and sharing a single car we reduce the vehicle distance traveled by 50 percent, as shown in Figure 11.1. Similarly, adding a third passenger and giving up a third car would mean that total vehicle distance traveled is a now a third of what it originally was.

But we cannot take this mental model of casual carpooling and apply it directly to the world of future mobility for a number of important reasons. As customers of a mobility system enter their origins and destinations into an app or platform, a dispatch algorithm attempts to combine their trips together. In today's ride-hailing systems, passengers are matched with drivers and other passengers in a matter of seconds or minutes. These dispatch algorithms are attempting to balance a number of different objectives including:

1 Driver satisfaction: drivers want to see a continuing stream of revenue-generating trips with limited deadhead (empty) travel.
2 Passenger satisfaction: Passengers have come to expect that they will have a driver assigned to them quickly, and preferably with short pickup times. They may also have preferences against riding with other passengers, despite having ordered a shared ride.
3 Vehicle types: Passengers should be transported in vehicles that are consistent with the service they choose or better.
4 System impact: The needs of current passengers must be balanced against the potential needs of future passengers.

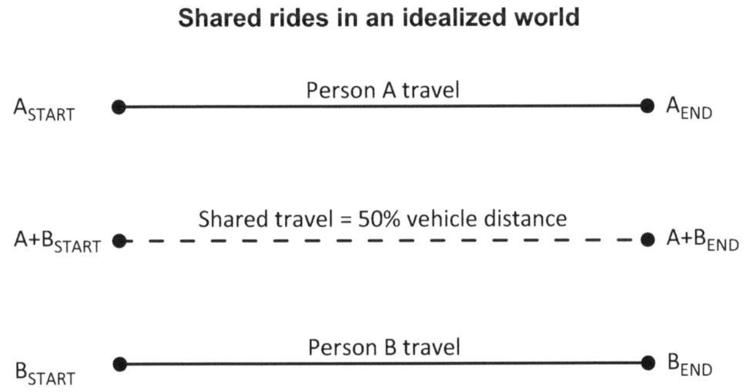

Shared rides in an idealized world

Figure 11.1 A simple shared ride diagram

Source: Zoepf.

Shared rides in a real world

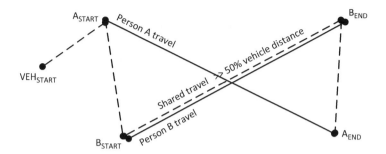

Figure 11.2 A mobility network of shared rides

Source: Zoepf.

Similarly, when not on a trip, drivers are given information about where future passengers are likely to be. While drivers may be more likely to find passengers, they will incur costs (fuel, wear and tear) without revenue as they drive with an empty vehicle. From a social perspective, these empty miles generate wear on infrastructure and externalities including emissions and road congestion.

Thus the reality of shared rides in a mobility system looks more like Figure 11.2: a vehicle travels empty to passenger A, takes a detour to pick up passenger B, and then drops off each passenger in sequence. In this illustrative example, we can see that while combining passengers may reduce vehicle miles traveled, it is highly dependent on the route that the vehicle takes, and when/where passengers embark and disembark.

The critical measure of interest in mobility system efficiency is the ratio of vehicle miles to passenger miles, where passenger miles are calculated as the sum of total miles each passenger would travel if optimally routed individually, and vehicle miles are the total miles traveled by the vehicle, including empty miles at the start of the trip chain. Other metrics such as (A) passengers that choose shared-ride services over solo rides, (B) match rates between passengers in a shared service, or (C) average-occupancy rates should be avoided, since they fail to capture the additional distance that a vehicle may travel to add new passengers to a trip chain.

If passenger trips can be combined with minimal deadheading and re-routing, mobility systems have the potential to deliver passengers to destinations at a lower environmental impact. But if vehicles need to take long detours to add passengers to a trip chain, the environmental impact of combining trips may not be substantially different from individual trips.

Opportunities and challenges of electric mobility

One way to reduce the emissions impact of mobility systems is to shift kilometers traveled from petroleum to electricity generated from renewable sources. Most highly-motorized countries have now implemented policies to push consumers to purchase electric vehicles (EVs), but despite these policies, adoption rates in most countries remain at just a few percent of new vehicles sales.

There are several basic reasons why mainstream consumers may not be ready to purchase EVs. (1) With only a few models on the market, consumers may not find an electric vehicle that has the basic features they want. (2) Despite advances in charging technology and standardization, recharging an electric vehicle still takes longer than refueling a vehicle, and charging stations are fewer in number than gas stations. (3) The range and cost of electric vehicles are also not yet on par with gasoline vehicles. Electric vehicles are improving rapidly. While this rapid improvement gives reason for optimism about future EV adoption, it creates an additional challenge for the present: the early adopter penalty.

Consumers are familiar with the concept that the first people to purchase a new technology are saddled with a product that is quickly outdated. Figure 11.3 illustrates this concept. In a disrupted market, a new technology is initially inferior to the original technology, but quickly catches up. During this period, the disruptive product (an electric vehicle) is rapid improving, while the original product (gasoline vehicle) is changing more slowly.

Consumers have shown their willingness to ignore the early adopter penalties for small consumer electronics such as smartphones, but these devices cost only a few hundred dollars. For a car that costs tens of thousands of dollars, a perfectly rational consumer might not want to buy a first- or second-generation product. Simply put, if consumers know that EVs are rapidly improving, why should they buy one now?

Using electric vehicles in mobility systems offer a solution to this early adopter problem. Because vehicles are not owned by a single driver, the early adopter penalty isn't borne by a single buyer, but by a group of collective users. And since vehicles in shared mobility systems are generally driven far more than privately owned vehicles, EVs used in these services will be scrapped or recycled before the early adopter penalty becomes acute.

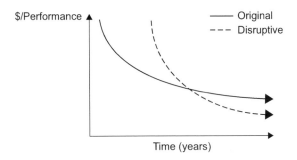

Figure 11.3 The early adopter penalty for disruptive technology/EVs/AVs

Source: Zoepf.

Integrating EVs into mobility systems also presents some real-world challenges, but the specific challenges differ based on the type of mobility system (as discussed previously). For example, for centrally organized mobility systems profitable operations depend on efficient use of vehicles. Under ideal circumstances, vehicles would be active and earning revenue at all times. Electric vehicles, however, require time between reservations to allow for recharging. Jacquillat and Zoepf (2017) explored this tradeoff in round-trip carsharing systems and found that while a substantial fraction (nearly 50 percent) of vehicles could be converted from gasoline to EVs profitably, a fleet composed of 100 percent EVs would be unable to adequately serve demand. Also noteworthy in this paper is the concept that centrally-organized mobility systems can solve the chicken-and-egg problem of charger-vehicle coordination, since a single entity invests in infrastructure up front and benefits from lower cost of vehicle operation.

Ride-hailing systems face a different set of challenges in using electric vehicles. For Uber and Lyft drivers, their vehicle is not just a mode of transportation, it's a tool with which to earn revenue. An electric vehicle with a flat battery is inconvenient for anyone, but for a ride-hailing driver it stops their stream of revenue cold. So, Uber and Lyft drivers might reasonably feel conflicted about electric vehicles. On one hand, the lower cost of operation of EVs could squeeze out a few extra pennies per mile of much-needed profit. But on the other hand, they might also worry more than a private driver about running out of energy.

Put yourself in the shoes of an Uber or Lyft driver. Now, imagine yourself getting into the car to start delivering rides. What does your travel day look like? You have absolutely no idea! So how can you have confidence to driver an EV? Ideally, EV ride-hailing drivers would be assigned only trips that are feasible for them. At present, this is impossible, because drivers know very little about what trips they will be assigned, and ride-hailing dispatch algorithms know nothing about the state of a driver's vehicle.

In order to overcome these challenges, vehicles and mobility systems will need to become more tightly integrated. Drivers will need to know they can complete their travel day, or have adequate access to charging infrastructure when needed. And ride-hailing companies will need to be able to guarantee drivers and passengers that trips won't be assigned to vehicles with insufficient range to reach the destination.

Mobility and the use of public space

As mobility systems become everyday transportation in metropolitan areas, questions of the use of public space become increasingly important. As former mayor of Bogotá, Enrique Peñalosa, has said,

> "Public space is for living, doing business, kissing, and playing. Its value can't be measured with economics or mathematics; it must be felt with the soul." (*Project for Public Spaces, 2008*)

Over the last century, in developed countries streets have evolved from chaotic, multimodal environments to highly structured zones in which space is allocated by mode: streets for cars and buses, sidewalks for pedestrians, bike lanes for cyclists, tunnels for subways, and elevated tracks for trains or trams.

However, highly structured and stratified streetscapes leave little room for adaptation. As new types of mobility devices and services enter the marketplace, we should expect increased friction around how space is allocated and used. Should electric bicycles be allowed to use bike lanes or share space with cars? Should small electric devices (Segways, hoverboards, electric scooters) be allowed on the sidewalk? And how fast should they be allowed to drive? And where should passengers be allowed to park idle vehicles? Fundamentally, since urban space is limited, we're faced with a choice: we can (A) carve up the street into even more dedicated parcels, (B) restrict new vehicle or service types, or (C) force different travel modes to share space.

Beyond allocation of space, questions are beginning to arise around the level of usage of existing infrastructure. Researchers and policymakers (Clewlow and Mishra 2017; Schaller 2017) are providing evidence pointing to increased congestion caused by ride-hailing services. However, it's important to remember that travel behavior isn't inherently a bad thing: travel enables us to socialize, care for family members, and access employment. As Chetty and Hendren (2018) discovered, it is also provides a crucial tool to escape poverty. Critically, it is the *externalities* associated with travel: emissions, congestion, noise, and risk that must be addressed.

Within existing constraints of space assignment, usage is also changing. Greater numbers of travelers rely on automated routing tools embedded in vehicles, mobile devices and servers. Some drivers face positive reinforcement for use of these tools (perceived reductions in travel time), while other drivers may face negative reinforcement—financial penalties for non-adherence to recommended routes, for instance.

Either type of reinforcement leads to greater dependence on automated routing tools. These routing tools are leading to encounters, both positive and negative, between local communities and companies that develop routing algorithms. In one highly-publicized case, a Los Angeles City Councilman complained that automated routing tools were sending drivers onto a dangerous 32 percent grade (Farivar 2018). However, routing tool developers assert that their platforms permit first respond to locate and respond to accidents more quickly.

The use of automated routing tools leads to important questions that researchers need to answer:

- What factors should be taken into account in choosing a route? Should all drivers act selfishly, merely attempting to minimize their own travel time?
- Who should be involved in choosing routes?
- What is the impact of automated routing on equity?
- Are there uncaptured social costs associated with automated routing?

Conclusions: other open questions and future directions

The transportation system is changing faster than ever before. Ride-hailing services alone now account for tens of millions of trips per day and make up more than 20 percent of peak traffic in mature markets (SFCTA 2017). Yet at least some of these trips are offsetting use of personal vehicles, and presumably leading to greater utilization of vehicles and fewer parked cars. As transportation planners and policymakers, how should we think about these tradeoffs—are fewer parked cars worth more moving cars? How can we capture the best that new forms of mobility have to offer, while simultaneously being conscious of the negative effects that they may also bring?

At present, mobility-service providers wield enormous power to encourage desired behavior primarily using soft incentives: pay drivers more to work during peak hours, offer bonuses for long-term commitment to the platform, and charge passengers more for desirable rides. However, they also use more aggressive measures: both drivers and passengers can be booted from mobility platforms at the sole discretion of the platform operator.

In a similar manner, mobility providers engage with metropolitan transportation organizations in ways that span the spectrum from friendly to hostile. Friendly collaborations have sparked creative solutions such on-demand paratransit that offers wheelchair users improved services at a reduced price (Urban 2017). In a less amicable manner, transportation providers have leveraged their platforms to generate AstroTurfed public backlash against regulations that they view as unfavorable, such as Uber's "De Blasio Mode" launched in New York City in 2015. Ultimately, transportation providers can invoke a "nuclear option" if they reach an impasse with cities: deactivate service for an entire region. Uber and Lyft elected to use this option in Austin, Texas, after the city passed a measure requiring background checks for ride-hailing drivers, suspending service to the city with a few days' notice.

Policymaking on a region-by-region basis may offer the opportunity to locally optimize for the needs specific populations or geography. It also offers the opportunity to experiment with new transportation concepts quickly and to test what works and what doesn't. However, local transportation policy experimentation also runs the risk of a "race to the bottom" for lenient regulation, and at present transportation policymakers have few tools at their disposal to ensure they learn from each other.

In the longer term, the transportation community expects mobility systems to migrate from human-driven vehicles to autonomous vehicles—such systems are already deployed in experimental phases in Boston, San Francisco, Phoenix, and numerous other cities worldwide. As these systems mature from prototype phases to commercial use, operators will no longer be reliant on soft incentives: rather than encourage drivers to operate at specific times and places using pricing, mobility system providers will be able to explicitly dictate when and where service is available, how trips are combined, which roads are used, and what types of vehicles are in operation.

One aspect that is becoming clear is that researchers must increase the rate at which we strive to understand the impact of these services. They have a bearing on the future of our cities and our citizens. And at present, innovation is outpacing both the ability of researchers to evaluate these impacts, and the ability of policymakers to guide them.

References

Berger, T., C. Chen, and C. B. Frey. 2018. "Drivers of Disruption? Estimating the Uber Effect." *European Economic Review*, 2018. doi:10.1016/j.euroecorev.2018.05.006.

Brown, A. E. (2018). Ridehail Revolution: Ridehail Travel and Equity in Los Angeles. *UCLA*. ProQuest ID: Brown_ucla_0031D_16839. Merritt ID: ark:/13030/m5d847t1. Retrieved from https://escholarship.org/uc/item/4r22m57k.

Chetty, R. and N. Hendren (2018). The Impacts of Neighborhoods on Intergenerational Mobility I: Childhood Exposure Effects. *The Quarterly Journal of Economics*, 133(3), 1107–1162. https://doi.org/10.1093/qje/qjy007.

Clewlow, R. R., and G.S. Mishra. 2017. Disruptive transportation: the adoption, utilization, and impacts of ride-hailng in the United States. Research Report–UCD-ITS-RR-17.

Farivar, C. 2018, April 14. Google refuses to fix Waze so it won't route people on 32%-grade road. Retrieved April 17, 2018, from https://arstechnica.com/tech-policy/2018/04/waze-seems-to-suggest-route-over-32-grade-road-is-fine/.

Hall, R. P. and J. M. Sussman. 2006. Promoting the Concept of Sustainable Transportation within the Federal System—The Need to Reinvent the U.S. DOT (Working Paper). Massachusetts Institute of Technology. Engineering Systems Division. Retrieved from http://dspace.mit.edu/handle/1721.1/102801.

Hampshire, R. C., C. Simek, T. Fabusuyi, and X. Chen. 2017. "Measuring the Impact of an Unanticipated Suspension of Ride-Sourcing in Austin, Texas." *SSRN Electronic Journal*. doi:10.2139/ssrn.2977969.

Jacquillat, A. and S. Zoepf. 2017. Deployment and utilization of plug-in electric vehicles in round-trip carsharing systems. *International Journal of Sustainable Transportation*. Retrieved from http://www.tandfonline.com/doi/abs/10.1080/15568318.2017.1328624.

Kaya, Y. and K. Yokobori (eds.). 1997. Environment, Energy, and Economy: Strategies for Sustainability. New York: United Nations University Press.

Project for Public Spaces. (2008). Enrique Peñalosa. Retrieved September 29, 2018, from https://www.pps.org/article/epenalosa-2.

SFCTA. 2017. EMERGING MOBILITY | TNCS TODAY REPORT | San Francisco County Transportation Authority. Retrieved from https://www.sfcta.org/tncstoday.

Schaller, B. 2017. UNSUSTAINABLE? The Growth of App-Based Ride Services and Traffic, Travel and the Future of New York City. Retrieved from http://schallerconsult.com/rideservices/unsustainable.htm.

Zoepf, S., S. Chen, P. Adu, and G. Pozo. 2018. "The Economics of Ride Hailing: Driver Revenue, Expenses and Taxes." *Working Paper Series*, February 1, 2018. Accessed July 8, 2018. https://orfe.princeton.edu/~alaink/SmartDrivingCars/PDFs/Zoepf_The%20Economics%20of%20RideHialing_OriginalPdfFeb2018.pdf.

12 Exploring the environmental ramifications of future transport

Frank Petrilli

Introduction

With the advent of disruptive technologies such as AVs and ride-sharing companies, cities have significant opportunities to get ahead of the curve and shape new urban spaces. But their ability to do so is influenced by a number of both practical and legal constraints. This chapter explores some of the challenges facing progressive urban and transportation planning from a legal and regulatory perspective, with a particular focus on examples in California and an emphasis on how local government operates in practice. In part, the questions I'm interested in exploring are diagnostic, but they are also focused on the critical question of how to facilitate change—and specifically, what are some of the constraints that affect how well cities tolerate and are able to implement potentially beneficial change?

After providing some initial caveats and observations, I begin by briefly outlining some of the bigger picture principles and features that characterize "business as usual" approaches to planning and development within the land use arena, including items such as the high degree of local control and lack of centralized or regional planning, relatively slow planning and processing timeframes, and the influence of deliberative democracy (and demagoguery) on local politics. The focus here is on planning at the local level, although of course federal and state agency rulemaking is also critical.

As a California lawyer, I also spend some time addressing some of the constraints arising from California's environmental review requirements under the California Environmental Quality Act (or CEQA, pronounced "See-Qwah"). While not as directly relevant for new development in other parts of the world, some of the concerns we have seen over the last few years, and foresee on the horizon, associated with CEQA are indicative of some of the same trends we see in other domains. Analogous issues also arise under the National Environmental Policy Act (NEPA) which is a similar environmental review statute that applies to federal projects or projects that are funded with federal dollars, and several other states also have similar statutes on the books as well. A separate reason why the CEQA discussion may be worth reading for those uninterested in the development process in California is that it dovetails with many of the broader historical trends in transportation planning (e.g., a focus on congestion and "level of service" as the primary metric in analyzing traffic impacts and conducting long-term transportation planning).

In the next section, I provide a brief summary of how approaches to transportation analysis and planning have evolved over time (and how that process has interacted with the specific rules under CEQA), and then turn to some of the legislative changes within that domain. Specifically, I address the history of SB 743, the landmark legislation adopted in 2013 to shift the focus of transportation impact analysis away from level-of-service and toward measuring vehicle miles traveled. (As we explain, implementing SB 743 has not been easy and final regulations have still not been adopted as of July 2018 when this chapter was written.) The discussion of SB 743 is intended to illustrate the challenges arising from paradigm-shifting approaches when you factor in the force of inertia, and the desire for inclusivity and outreach which can sometimes result in poor, rather than improved, outcomes. I also try to provide examples about why the current uncertainty around AVs and TNCs poses unique challenges for cities and the planning process in general.

Finally, I suggest a few prescriptive measures that may help local government be more proactive and deliberative about responding to new technologies and promoting better planning and development outcomes – with the common thread focused on how change occurs over time. While many of the other chapters focus on substantive policy recommendations, the intent of this chapter is to focus more on the procedural constraints that prevent the development and implementation of good policy. In other words, this chapter focuses more on the "how" than the why and what, which is addressed in other chapters.

Initial observations

As a land-use and zoning attorney in the San Francisco Bay Area, my observations are unique to the regulatory environment in which I practice. So, at the outset, I'd like to offer a few observations that may help provide context for the discussion that follows.

First, land use is inherently interdisciplinary, political, and "foggy." Land use is not about the neutral application of "law to facts," except in the relatively rare instances where litigation is involved; and even then, court decisions in CEQA and land use cases are often subtly colored by political factors as well. So, while land-use lawyers often wish that cities were more rigorous in applying the law to the facts in a given situation, that just isn't how it works. For that reason, and although I am a practicing attorney, much of the following discussion bleeds between what is strictly "legal" and what occurs as a matter of practice. (It also means that land use can be quite fun and challenging, insofar as there can sometimes be greater room for creative interpretations and solutions to complex problems.)

Second, land use and planning decisions generally involve a lot of discretion and subjectivity. As a consequence, land use and zoning regulations often invoke legal "standards" as opposed to legal rules.[1] The distinction is subtle, but "rules" essentially "offer precision and transparency." Some zoning standards, like strict height limits, for example, are clear examples of rules. "Standards" by contrast, are understood as directives that "incorporate thick, substantive terms"—normative or policy considerations—that make it more difficult to predict what a given outcome will be, since those subjective standards can sometimes create room for "pretextual" decision making. Examples of standards include the kind of subjective determinations or "findings" about neighborhood compatibility that decision-makers are often required to make in approving projects. Standards are inherently flexible and subject to interpretation. And because land use and environmental law operate primarily in the domain of standards, that means that creative interpretation and application of normative policy considerations is a critical part of how decisions are made.

Land use is also highly context-dependent. How projects are approved and planning decisions are made in the Bay Area is different from how projects are approved in Los Angeles. That makes it difficult to provide "one-size-fits-all" recommendations, and also means that many of the observations below may not hold true in different jurisdictions. Context matters a lot, and so the following is not intended to be comprehensive or scientific. The hope is only to make a few tentative observations, and then suggest that cities may be more empowered then they may think.

Some characteristics of business-as-usual planning

At its heart, much of the urban-planning process in California is predicated on local control. There are scant incentives really for regional collaboration or "top down," that is state or regional "command and control-style" planning. State planning and zoning laws give cities and counties a lot of discretion, and efforts to reduce or limit that discretion are generally met with hostility. A good example of this is the defeat of Scott Weiner's housing bill, SB 827, which would have required cities to allow four to eight story multi-family projects adjacent to transit as a matter of right; the California League of Cities, joined by many others, mounted a well-organized campaign against the measure, which ultimately led to the measure being voted down in early 2018.

And because local government is run by elected officials, short term thinking sometimes tends to dominate. Politically expedient tradeoffs are often made in the interest of appeasing the most vocal stakeholders (even if those stakeholders are not representative of the majority). City officials often make decisions with their next election in mind, rather than focusing on what's in the best interest of the communities they were elected to serve. In other instances, cities make decisions in order to solve immediate short-term problems, without appropriately considering longer-term implications.[2] This is also not a uniquely Californian problem. As one ULI Europe report succinctly puts it:

> "At the heart of this discussion lies a major cultural challenge: our democracy is sometimes at odds with our long term interests. Planning and investment decisions made by democratic local governments far too often prioritize the preferences of current residents, who seek to protect what they have, over the needs and interests of citizens who have not yet arrived, or have not yet been born."[3]

"Enlightened" governance is unfortunately the exception rather than the rule. Elected officials are often most responsive to whomever is most vocal in the arenas in which they're encountered (i.e., the folks who show up and actually speak at planning commission and city council meetings). Planning processes are also usually driven by extensive outreach campaigns in which elected officials are tasked with pleasing a large number of very diverse stakeholders. So, while planning processes often start with very ambitious goals, those goals can be watered down over time as different stakeholders voice opposition to those measures that impact them directly (even where those measures may provide broader benefits for the community or region at large). Perhaps more importantly, making tough decisions is difficult and it is frequently easier to seek cover than making unpopular decisions—even if they are the right ones.

Another characteristic of typical planning processes is that they are slow. Painfully slow. A typical process in California is driven by a cadre of consultants and include extensive community outreach meetings, study sessions, online surveys, citizens' advisory committees, special committee meetings, etc. Planning processes, whether focused on a specific geographic area or the long-term future of a city, frequently take years, with dozens upon dozens of different meetings and an extensive environmental review process prior to adoption. These processes are also largely dominated by relatively few stakeholders and special interests, each of whom are able to influence the process in highly impactful ways just by showing up and being vocal. And while that kind of special interest advocacy can result in positive changes being included, that is often not the case.

A final constraint is that cities are very risk averse and highly sensitive to setting "precedent." Specifically, where a given outcome may make sense for a single project within a given context, planners and city officials may not be willing to endorse that concept for fear of the precedent it may set for future developments in different contexts. And this is just one example of perhaps a non-obvious concern that we hear again and again from cities that can sometimes compromise optimal outcomes in the interest of conservatism and risk avoidance.

In sum, the land-use and planning process exhibits the following features:

- Highly political processes
- Takes a long time/subject to high uncertainty
- Not particularly friendly to non-insiders (i.e., hard to penetrate)
- Risk averse
- Subject to the "tyranny of the minority" phenomenon

You can see where I'm going with this already. The bottom line is that cities are often poorly equipped to rapidly and proactively respond to major paradigm shifts. And they are not always well equipped to deal with complicated and non-linear processes, which include many of the technical regulatory hurdles that apply to local development and planning decisions in a number of different jurisdictions, including California.

Constraints Arising under CEQA

Apart from the practical considerations outlined above, there are a number of legal constraints and challenges that also affect good planning and development outcomes. Providing a comprehensive and technical inventory of all of these constraints is, again, far beyond the scope of this chapter. But because CEQA is often cited as a major obstacle (at least in California), I focus on providing a brief history and explanation of the CEQA process and why the current uncertainty surrounding how current technologies like TNCs, and the pending transition to autonomous vehicles, poses particular challenges that CEQA has been ill-suited to account for.

A brief overview of CEQA

CEQA was adopted in the 1970s and has given rise to a cottage industry of professional consultants. Those consultants include air quality experts, traffic engineers, geotechnical engineers, water and energy modelers, archaeologists, biologists, and so forth, as well as the document preparers themselves who function more as CEQA "generalists." Environmental Impact Reports (or EIRs) are generally prepared for large projects, and those reports must be certified by the "lead agency" (e.g., city councils, state agencies, etc.) before a project can be approved. EIRs can run hundreds, and in some cases thousands, of pages long, with a myriad of appendices, and they are not user or layperson friendly. To provide a visual example of how complicated the process can be, take some time to Google the CEQA process. A very convoluted flowchart can be found on Wikipedia.[4]

While the process is convoluted and technical, at its core, CEQA is concerned with ensuring that governmental decision-makers are informed about the environmental impacts associated with the projects they approve (and "projects" are defined broadly), and that mitigation measures to reduce those impacts are implemented where feasible.

Environmental impacts are evaluated against "thresholds of significance," which may be set individually by lead agencies if supported by substantial evidence but are generally standardized for many impact categories. Often, these thresholds rely upon standardized assumptions set by regulatory agencies, such as regional air quality districts, for example. While cities have the discretion to depart from those assumptions, that rarely occurs or occurs very gradually over time.

Analysis of traffic and transportation impacts under CEQA

A clear example of where cities have been slow to embrace change occurs in the analysis of transportation and traffic impacts under CEQA. Historically, traffic impact assessments have been a focal point for planners, developers, and local officials because of the political importance of traffic congestion. For the last few decades, traditional approaches to evaluating traffic and transportation impacts have focused primarily on vehicle trips and traffic congestion, using a "level of service" or LOS-based threshold of significance in which a projects impacts are gauged based on whether associated trips will cause additional delay at specific intersections or roadway segments. Meanwhile, assumptions about trip generation have largely been based on standardized assumptions drawn from historic data about specific uses and driver patterns. And while the modeling has grown significantly more sophisticated over time, it is still largely predicated on assumptions about private car ownership and mobility that predominated in the late-twentieth and early-twenty-first centuries.

Because of CEQA's emphasis on mitigating impacts that are considered "significant," this LOS-centric approach to analyzing transportation impacts resulted in new development being tasked with funding or constructing new infrastructure to add new capacity. Widening roads, adding lanes, providing new interchanges, and contributing impact fees to fund capital improvements focused on adding capacity has historically been the norm. Meanwhile, not much attention was paid to other travel modes including transit, pedestrians, and bicyclists, unless their presence would cause potential delays for cars. And that pattern has largely held constant without much interrogation or critique, at least until relatively recently, in part due to two important developments.

First, urban planning began to focus on density – and particularly density near transit – as the solution to a number of social problems, especially the housing crisis, but also other problems including health and well-being. As population growth continues and more and more people have moved into cities, density by definition has emerged as a highly desirable priority, if not a necessity for urban planning and development. As a 2015 ULI report puts it:

> "[D]densifying cities can accommodate population growth within a contained environmental footprint, they can enjoy better connectivity, amenities, open spaces, and social interaction, and they become more productive and spawn innovation. Density is a way to have better cities and to provide for all the extra people."[5]

But because density can cause increased congestion, even accounting for allowing density adjacent to transit, a shift in values has occurred such that congestion—rather than being the primary value for urban planners—can now be considered an acceptable cost or tradeoff of "smart growth." (That is not to say that this idea is embraced by everyone—and particularly by many city officials who are beholden to constituents understandably upset by traffic conditions.)

A second major development has been the increased attention and importance given to climate change. Surface transportation is a major contributor of greenhouse gas emissions, and roughly a third of the United States' emissions come from moving people and goods (80% of those are from cars and trucks). Policymakers have primarily paid attention to addressing this critical problem by focusing on more efficient vehicles and alternative fuels, but less attention has historically been paid to moving people out of their cars and into higher-occupancy vehicles and mass transit.

As a consequence of these developments, renewed attention in CEQA documents has been rightly given to prioritizing multimodal forms of transportation, looking at traffic calming as a mitigation to mitigate impacts on pedestrians and bicyclists, and so forth. Attention has also been paid to the costs and perils of LOS-centric approaches to evaluating transportation impacts under CEQA. The unintended consequences of that approach have included longer commutes, more reliance on cars as opposed to transit, more congestion, increased emissions, discouraging infill development and infrastructure for transit, pedestrians and bicyclists, and higher housing and transportation costs.

While incremental changes have occurred around the edges, we still see the vast majority of California cities employing LOS-centric approaches, which we all know—and almost every planner I know would agree—are seriously flawed. And that is in spite of the fact that as of 2013, important legislation was passed that authorized (and ultimately will mandate) the use of an alternative transportation metric, namely vehicle miles traveled or VMT. Unfortunately, the history of how that legislation has been implemented dovetails with some of the observations earlier about why change is slow to come.

SB 743

In 2013, Governor Jerry Brown signed SB 743 into law. Among other things, the bill was intended to change the way transportation analysis under CEQA was conducted in order to replace a LOS-centric approach to transportation analysis with VMT. As opposed to LOS, which is exclusively considered with delay times, VMT is a measure of many vehicle miles travelled will be associated with new development. In the case of an infill project adjacent to transit and employment centers, a VMT analysis would provide a more favorable treatment than an LOS analysis because it would account for reduced trip lengths associated with the project. VMT would therefore be reduced because fewer people would be driving long distances. Greenfield projects, by contrast, would fare worse under a VMT analysis because the trip lengths would be inherently longer.

With respect to thresholds of significance, the technical advisory prepared by the Governor's Office of Planning and Research for SB 743 (which has not yet been finalized—more on which later) suggests that a project's estimated VMT be measured against either regional average VMT on either a per capita or per employee basis. Projects which would result in a per capita or per employee VMT that is less than 85 percent of the respective regional averages would be considered as having a "less than significant impact," and therefore not trigger the need for mitigation.

A comprehensive recent treatment of SB 743 and the shift away from LOS-centric approaches to traffic analysis is provided by an article written by Amy Lee and Susan Handy, entitled "Leaving level-of-service behind: The implications of a shift to VMT impact metrics" (2018)[6] and I would encourage readers to review that text for a much more thorough treatment of the subject. For the purposes of this chapter, however, attention should be drawn to what was alluded to previously – namely how slow agencies have been in adopting VMT, and the current status of the regulations intended to implement VMT.

As of 2018, only a handful of jurisdictions have affirmatively embraced a VMT-oriented approach. Those cities include Pasadena, San Francisco, Oakland, and most recently San Jose. The vast majority of California's other cities have not been nearly as bold.

Part of the problem is also reflected in how slow the rulemaking process for SB 743 has been. Although SB 743 became law in September 2013, it took over four years (and nearly 200 stakeholder meetings and events) to develop the proposed CEQA Guidelines that help implement the law. The Guidelines are now undergoing the formal rulemaking process (providing an additional opportunity for feedback and discussion), and assuming that process remains on track, the Guidelines are scheduled to take effect later this year. But they still will not be binding statewide until January 1, 2020. This seven-year process required many individual steps just to develop the proposed changes, including a first draft of the Guidelines that was released in August 2014. After further engagement with the public, public agencies, environmental organizations, development advocates, industry experts, and others, a second draft of the Guidelines was released in January 2016. Multiple draft technical advisories have subsequently been released, with the latest version released in July 2018, but OPR has still not adopted a final version.

In stark contrast, there is much more uncertainty about the long-term impacts of new development and technology created by the private sector, such as TNCs and AVs, which are generally being deployed without any environmental review under CEQA whatsoever, despite having the potential to create profound impacts on the environment and how our cities operate.

Impact of disruptive technologies on CEQA analysis and ongoing uncertainty

The recent advent of disruptive transportation technologies from shared ride companies like Uber and Lyft to AVs and electric scooters further complicate planning and development outcomes. The speed at which these technologies have been adopted does not comport well with the slow and deliberative public process that guides urban planning and land use decision-making. And ironically, these companies and technologies have flourished in part because they appeared out of the blue, didn't ask for permission or seek public input, weren't risk averse (and indeed proceeded in the face of tremendous uncertainty about whether they would succeed and what their impacts would be) and took advantage of a lack of specific regulations targeting their industries.

Meanwhile, we still have scant information about how these disruptive technologies will ultimately impact both the environment and how our cities function. As a survey of the literature indicates, there is currently no good way to gauge the trip and emission implications of transportation network companies (TNCs) (Schneider et al. 2015). Some studies have established common ways to conduct "trip degeneration" and estimate the impacts of smart growth on ITE Trip Generation Rates; however, no work has estimated the effect TNCs have on project related trips or come up with a model that environmental professionals can use to evaluate impacts. This uncertainty is reflected in a report from 2018 compiled by Caltrans' Division of Research, Innovation and System Information (DRISI), that surveys a range of studies on the potential impacts of AVs.[7] The report concludes that while AVs can provide significant benefits, their deployment may also lead to congestion and more emissions depending on a wide variety of factors. Other studies suggest that VMT will rise in general, although these impacts have not yet been connected to specific projects and behaviors.

In light of the discussion about the relatively conservative and reactive nature of cities in responding to change, this uncertainty about outcomes is not especially helpful. As practitioners, we really do not yet understand how to factor in these new technological and social shifts into the environmental review process.

But all is not lost, and much work remains to be done. If TNCs are contributing to an increase in total auto trips for urban development accounted for in trip generation models and environmental documents, including car-free or car-light development. then additional policy steps may need to be taken as we move toward less auto-intensive development. It will remain an uncertain, evolving and iterative process for the foreseeable future, and new techniques and methodologies for evaluating projects will need to be developed in order to account for a range of possible future scenarios.

Conclusions

As discussed previously, cities face a variety of challenges that can make it difficult to experiment, innovate, move quickly, and ultimately navigate change in a complex, fast-paced world that is subject to ever-accelerating disruption. While no clear solutions are immediately apparent, I offer the following as possible considerations for those interested in addressing the challenge.

First, those looking to implement radical shifts in policy need to be sensitive to the political process and how local government works in practice. Educating city officials and staff on the benefits and risks associated with disruptive technologies and the need to embrace alternative ways of thinking is critical. As is the need to mobilize advocates, generate community support, and work from within the process to ensure that city officials feel empowered to explore new territory, experiment and take risks. Open lines of communication are, of course, essential. While the topic of effective communication is way beyond the scope of this chapter, it is important to be mindful that conversations around urban planning, development, and growth are—fundamentally— conversations, and subject to all of the usual traps that interfere with effective open dialogue in other aspects of life.[8]

Second, transformative leadership matters. And we need to see much more of it from all quarters and at all levels of government. Leadership does not require status or even authority, but it does require vision, empathy, courage, and the ability to inspire others to take action. Transformative leaders inspire others and help to guide fundamental and radical transitions. Leaders therefore need to be attentive to a broad array of perspectives, including those who do not frequently have a seat at the table or the tools or capacity to participate. Good leadership requires asking whose voices are not being heard, and then taking corrective action to make sure that collective input is truly collective. And that means listening not only to local constituents, but also thinking regionally and taking into account those who do not have a voice in the political process (including future generations). Governmental officials need to be prepared to make politically unpopular moves. Otherwise, the private sector will move faster, and cities will lose important opportunities to get ahead of the curve on important issues.

I would also suggest that more listening needs to occur from experts and innovators to determine how to implement changes that are consistent with those values. All too often, innovative solutions never see the light of day because they are too complicated to explain. So brilliant ideas coming out of modern transportation and urban planners may fall on deaf ears, become diluted or watered down, and are often discarded as "politically infeasible." The truth is that the most progressive and ingenious solutions to the challenges we face, whether with regard to the housing crisis, traffic congestion, etc., are almost all politically infeasible. But that should not be sufficient reason to discard them.

Working within existing constraints also means allowing greater flexibility within the regulatory and environmental review processes. Greater experimentation and creativity will be necessary in order to accommodate an increasingly uncertain world and defaulting to conventional ways of doing business will not yield the best outcomes. We therefore need to expand our horizons and look more holistically and regionally at how new development will impact our environment. Forecasting future scenarios with precision will remain difficult for the foreseeable future but that cannot get in the way of decision-making.

A final recommendation is to look to the private sector and embrace opportunities to partner together. Although real estate developers are often portrayed as solely interested in profit, most developers are genuinely interested in building great places and shaping the future landscape of our cities for the better. They are willing to take risks, invest in new sustainable technologies, and cities should let them (within reason). And part of that means creating frameworks that allow for greater flexibility without rigid standards and guidelines. The world is moving faster than it ever has before, and cities need to be highly adaptive in order to be resilient and responsive to change. We are all in this together and as meaningful opportunities for collaboration between public and private sectors present themselves, cities should embrace them. Trust is vital, as is the need to listen and compromise in order to move forward responsibly and leverage the ever-increasing pace of technological change for the long-term benefit of our communities.

Notes

1. For an interesting perspective on the difference between these two concepts in the context of moral deliberation, see Seana Shiffrin, "Inducing Moral Deliberation: On the Occasional Virtues of Fog," 123 *Harvard Law Review* 1214-46 (2010). Available here: https://harvardlawreview.org/wp-content/uploads/pdfs/123_shiffrin.pdf
2. For a good example, see https://www.wired.com/story/sidewalk-labs-toronto-google-risks/ which examines the instance of Chicago handing over control of its parking meters to the private sector as part of a seventy-five-year lease in exchange for an upfront, lump sum payment. That payment, apparently, was valued at about $1 billion less than the value of the lease.
3. http://europe.uli.org/wp-content/uploads/sites/3/ULI-Documents/Density-Drivers-Dividends-Debates.pdf
4. See: https://upload.wikimedia.org/wikipedia/commons/e/ec/CEQA_Process_Flow_Chart.gif
5. http://europe.uli.org/wp-content/uploads/sites/3/ULI-Documents/Density-Drivers-Dividends-Debates.pdf
6. Lee, A.E., Research in Transportation Business & Management (2018), https://doi.org/10.1016/j.rtbm.2018.02.003
7. http://www.dot.ca.gov/newtech/researchreports/preliminary_investigations/docs/environmental_impacts_of_connected_and_automated_vehicles_preliminary_investigation_2-2-18.pdf
8. For that reason, I would highly suggest that anyone involved in the planning and development world read works such as *Difficult Conversations: How to Discuss What Matters Most* by Douglas Stone, Bruce Patton, and Sheila Heen (1999).

Reference

Schneider, R. J., K. Shafizadeh, and S. L. Handy. 2015. "Method to Adjust Institute of Transportation Engineers Vehicle Trip-Generation Estimates in Smart-Growth Areas." Journal of Transport and Land Use 8(1), 69–83. https://doi.org/10.5198/jtlu.v0i0.416.

13 Climate change and automation

Do we have an emissions problem?

William Riggs, Michael R. Boswell,
Louis Yudowitz, and Matthew Kawashima

Introduction

New mobility provides a variety of environmental benefits compared to existing transportation options and various sources have begun analyzing the environmental impacts associated with new mobility—the question remains in the new mobility future is there an emissions issue. Studies have looked at a wide variety of environmental concerns and have attempted to quantify the level of impact compared to existing transportation modes. Slowik and Kamakaté (2017) have summarized some of the key findings from existing literature from laboratories, universities, and independent research and found that research suggests that new mobility will provide significant environmental benefits. However, they also noted that further research is required in many cases due to the rapidly changing nature of the technology and the unknown implications of its use in some instances.

And if you think this sounds uncertain, you are right. Very little existing literature has analyzed the environmental benefits of particular elements of new mobility (Slowik and Kamakaté 2017). A handful of studies have attempted to model the potential environmental ramifications of fully autonomous or semi-autonomous vehicles, and they indicate quite significant potential impacts. In one study, various metrics were analyzed including driving efficiency, efficient routing, travel by the underserved, time spent looking for parking, speed of travel, and overall travel, among other factors to identify the amount of energy that would be required (Brown et al. 2015). This study concluded that autonomous vehicles, regardless of automation levels, would lead to dramatic energy outcomes. While the study identified positive environmental outcomes related to electrification of vehicles, higher occupancy vehicles, less hunting for parking, more efficient routing and driving, and platooning many potential negative environmental outcomes were identified. These related to two things: more travel and faster travel. Brown's study in particular found autonomous vehicle use could lead to a 50 percent increase in energy use.

That statistic alone warrants scrutiny and concern on the behalf of planners and engineers, and it has been echoed by others. In a June 2016 article in the *Wall Street Journal*, journalist Christopher Mimms predicts changes in urban growth patterns, with more cities sprawling beyond their bounds, will result in a "new class of exurbs (Mims 2016)." Esteemed author Rebecca Solnit has argued that AVs will poach from transit and kill the walkable city (Solnit 2016).

We believe that longer "super-commutes" are unlikely outcomes of AVs for two key reasons: (1) the presence of existing land use, transportation, and infrastructure controls and growth management plans; (2) trends in housing consumption and residential preferences.[1] Yet we believe that government leaders and citizens should also consider them deeply and put them in the context of the aforementioned environmental costs. It may be that we will see an increase in energy consumption either way.

In considering the danger that energy use may continue to increase beyond our capacity to meet demand, we (Boswell and Riggs) have had many long talks about the important of "dark-side theorists" Flyvbjerg (2001), Hillier (2005), and Yiftachel (1998). These individuals think about the bounds of rationality and believe that we have reached the limits of rational planning. If this is the case, then it may be important for citizens as well as planners and policymakers to not look through the world through "rose colored glasses" and be overly optimistic about outcomes. There has been much work on the concept of human bias and tendencies to be overly optimistic in the face of extreme (certain) uncertainty, and we should all be skeptics. Our world has a dramatic need to address climate-related missions from driving yesterday. In this situation, we all may have a tendency to overestimate the impacts of models, programs, and their impact on travel.

So, what is to be done to mitigate these? Three policies will likely address the greenhouse gas emissions issues associated with new disruptive automobility. First, we can look at electrification. Yet this is only the first step. In near term, consistent to what our colleagues at UC Davis, 3 Revolutions suggest we must increase the number of shared vehicles (Fulton et al. 2017). Yet in a departure from our Davis colleagues we do not think that the future of transport is simply electrified, shared and automated—we believe it is about transformed behavior in that we need to change the way we travel altogether. This change will not only impact our environmental future but help address the many social disparities our systems currently experience, and we discuss these over the following pages.

Electrification

It is often said that all new vehicles, and particularly those that are automated should be electric. Authors like Dan Sperling make the case aggressively that electrification is a critical part of the future transportation revolution (Sperling 2018), and vehicles are becoming more commonplace and competitive with conventional vehicles. This is despite some concerns about the fuel type.

In 2011, Michalek et al. found that, after performing a lifecycle analysis of the potential environmental benefits, electric vehicles generate about $1,100 more in environmental harm than vehicles using gasoline. This analysis took environmental impacts due to using the vehicle and the manufacturing process into consideration.

More recently, in 2015, Holland et al. performed a study looking at how environmental impacts varied between regions in the United States. Their study showed that there are issues with providing subsidies for buying electric cars when the money is issued uniformly. They found that in western areas of the United States, where the electric grid is cleaner because of using a mixture of hydro, nuclear, and natural gas methods, the benefit of electric vehicles is quite pronounced and beneficial relative to the provided subsidies. The opposite was seen further east where the electric grids rely more heavily on coal and natural gas. They also found that the environmental damages caused by driving electric cars are easily exported to other states.

At the same time, over the long run (just like Sperling argues), electric vehicles will result in fewer GHG emissions and result in environmental benefits compared to gasoline-powered vehicles but there are barriers including cost, equity of access and quality of electrical power. Additionally, studies suggest that new mobility is "unlikely to result in electric vehicle adoption by design" (Slowik and Kamakaté 2017). In California, the City of Los Angeles was awarded $1.6 million by the California Air Resources Board (CARB) to test the potential of an electric vehicle car sharing program in disadvantaged communities (California State Senate 2015). It is expected that the program would reduce approximately 2,150 tons of emissions each year (Slowik and Kamakaté 2017).

Sharing

Clearly, electrification will not solve all of the issues of new mobility, which may have some detrimental environmental impacts, but what about sharing. Some research has pointed to the possibility of transportation network companies (TNCs) such as Uber and Lyft increasing GHG emissions congestion and ultimately harming the environment. Limited studies evaluating the impact of TNCs on the environment have been conducted but one study based on data from New York City's Taxi and Limousine Commission found that TNCs led to a 7 percent increase in VMT from 2013-2016 (Schaler Consulting 2017). However, due to the limited body of research in this arena, additional research is needed to fully understand the environmental impacts of the TNCs.

Sharing is another component of new mobility that will reduce GHG emissions, congestion, and fossil-fuel usage by encouraging mode shifting (Slowik and Kamakaté 2017). As was seen in some of the early chapters of this book, if a shared future can be achieved the impacts and potential for "peril" in the built environment is dramatically reduced. And while some have argued that ridesharing may serve as a substitute for public transportation and increase overall travel, researchers (and most of the authors of this book) believe that there is a future role for both transit and ridesharing / shared mobility and that the environmental impacts will be better than without them. Filling empty seats in any vehicle is an effective strategy in reducing GHG emissions, congestion, and fossil fuel usage. Yet on a similar note, bike-sharing programs are also increasing in popularity and many help reduce environmental impacts by reducing the number of people using cars (and emitting carbon) altogether.

Transformed behavior

Remember that discussion that we said Boswell and Riggs had about "dark-side theorists"? Well, they had it while riding a bike, and this illustrates what we think the single-biggest contribution to reducing GHG emissions might be in our future—changing behavior to facilitate cycling, scooting, walking, and getting on any kind of personal transportation device.

And these devises are becoming more prevalent. Communally shared bikes and scooters have been steadily introduced worldwide to improve transit, particularly in urban areas. This has the obvious benefits of reducing congestion and emissions. However, various issues such as tracking, distribution, and installation do exist (DeMaio 2009).

Multiple studies have been conducted to investigate these issues, as well as other factors affecting sharing programs. Guo et al. (2017) conducted a study to analyze these factors in Ningbo, China. They found that household income, gender, travel time, bike-sharing station location, and many others affect bike usage. Additionally, they found that installing sharing stations closer to residential areas, as well as having more along less traveled roads, could improve usage. Also, they state that the smart technology used in fourth generation sharing plans is an effective addition. Finally, they found that usage was hindered by Ningbo residents being unfamiliar with the sharing program. They therefore suggested that more public awareness programs should be present in areas where bike sharing is newer or not as prevalent.

A second study involving Chinese users by Zhang et al. (2016) looked at the changes in users, system usage, and the impact of system expansion over a span of years. They found that there was variation among the usage of the bike sharing system after a system expansion. In general, however, it was shown that the expansion extended the range that users could travel and attracted new users. They also made suggestions for future expansions: investigate spatial patterns of user demands and available bike supply and build new stations in areas with higher demand relative to the available supply rather than expand to new areas unless there is a pressing need to expand.

Other sharing programs, such as those in London and Paris have also proved successful. However, some programs such as those in San Francisco have encountered difficulties due to lack of social awareness and responsibility, as well as design flaws. This could be resolved by having better tracking technology present in the communal bikes and scooters, as well as the awareness mentioned above. Bike and scooter friendly environments should also be a considered by companies and governments implementing these programs. Some work has been done on this by Ghanem et al. (2017), specifically looking at bike-sharing in San Francisco. They focused on finding optimal routes for bike users, possible routes that could be developed to aid the sharing program, and ways that traffic congestion could be reduced.

Moving forward it seems that bike and scooter sharing programs have many potential benefits. Emissions are lessened, people living in poorer neighborhoods can use them, congestion due to cars can certainly be decreased, and rural areas can have more mobility without having to rely on cars or public transport that may run infrequently.

Conclusion

At the end of the day, to get to this end state of transformed behavior, planners and policymakers must think about consumer preferences. A few years ago, one of our Master's students, Charlie Coles, interviewed former United States Department of Transportation Assistant Secretary for Research and Technology Dr. Robert Bertini on the topic of AVs and social connectedness (Coles 2016). Dr. Bertini had a comparable perspective. He argued that people are unlikely to value spending enough time in a vehicle to become super-commuters. He was quoted as follows:

> Some people gravitate more towards those types of long driving experiences, but it removes the human component… The idea of home is still something that people seem to value… It seems to me that people would still assign value to the interaction with the people they care about… In terms of quality of life, I think to a lot of people that means spending time and interacting with people. Even with the developments in electronics, I'm not sure that people have changed so much that they won't value human-to-human interactions. One of the advantages, when I think about Millennials living in the city center and maybe not wanting to own a vehicle, is that … they're not wasting time in commuting so they can substitute that with more fun things that they value… Overall, I still think humans are social creatures. While there may be outliers that support the 'pod-lifestyle'… most people would not. 32"

And within that social construct we must reinforce the power of behavioral economics and decisions, and nudge people to make better and more informed choices. This necessitates better, and sometimes not more, information.

Renowned behavioral economist Dan Ariely argues that people make "predictably irrational" decisions based on lifestyle and cultural factors (emotions, limited information, cultural biases, etc.) that are not in their best interest (Ariely 2008). When there is not appropriate information, people can rely on cognitive illusions, and do things that are not totally rational or in their best interest. For example, driving three blocks to the grocery for milk when it is healthier and cheaper to walk, or having a third slice of pizza when you are on a diet.

Better information can improve predictably irrational decision making, improving the information available about the environmental costs of choosing a car verses walking or biking AV. That is one of the promises of new and disruptive mobility. New mobility can potentially provide a more robust and informed set of travel choices and information. It could allow transportation planners to make better use of both market and social incentives (Riggs 2017) and to take into account factors like health, the environment, and remind travelers of the human connection they have with their friends, neighbors, and fellow citizens.

Note

1. **Land use, transportation, and infrastructure controls:** Throughout the United States (and for that matter most of the world), land-use policies exist that would not be eliminated (or subordinated) for the sake of an emerging technology. Though there is currently very little land use policy focusing on AVs, the emergence of this technology is not happening in a policy vacuum. Land use plans, for instance, still control development in cities and regions. Housing and transportation plans and, in some cases, greenbelt policies still guide regional development in many parts it the country.

   Yes, in a world of AVs, adjustments to greenbelts and exurban growth controls might need adjustment to disincentivize long-haul commuting, but the policy groundwork and regional thinking for such changes are already in place. Many communities have already developed sophisticated ways of controlling sustainable (and climate-conscious) growth. Furthermore, some locations have devised strategies to incentivize smart growth by providing funding. For example, the grants stemming from creative programs like California's Affordable Housing for Sustainable Communities program, funded from the AB32-established carbon market, can be applied to affordable and transit connected housing units in the urban core.

   Existing water and utility policies could also limit extreme commutes. In many communities these policies limit suburban development—especially in an era of extreme weather heat events. Likewise, moves by transportation engineers and planners to begin quantifying the environmental impacts of development projects based on vehicle miles traveled (VMT) rather than intersection level of service (LOS) provides an additional regulatory tool to slow the rise of a cadre of super-commuters, traveling ever-increasing distances as AVs become more widely adopted.

   And while there may be counter-arguments that traditional land use policy has not countered sprawl—we agree—we need to break tradition. Planning literature has shown that we have effective policy for mitigating exurban growth relating to these issues. They include but are not limited to: greenbelt policy; infrastructure and public service limitations; VMT impact fees and mitigations; even parking controls. More to the point on VMT: emerging policy to focus on VMT as an environmental impact (regardless of fuel type or efficiency standard) and shift away from LOS traffic analysis, underscore these efforts. In sum, these emerging policies illustrate a way that land use may continue to develop in a more (or equally) compactly manner as AV technology becomes widely adopted.

   Housing Preference: Another reason doom-and-gloom claims about AVs may be overstated is that housing preferences have not changed. While those such as Kotkin continue to claim that all Americans really want are single-family homes, peer reviewed work by others suggest that is not the case and that many Americans want more urban lifestyles and smaller, more urban homes (Kotkin 2014). Pitkin and Myers suggest that these housing preferences (small and urban) are most common in some of the largest cohorts of the U.S. population—namely the Baby Boomers and Millennials (Myers and Pitkin 2009; Myers 2016). Regardless of housing preference, research also suggests that while post-recession demand for suburban housing might increase, preferences toward walkability and urban accessibility will still be prevalent. Given this data, it is likely that a significant number of people will not choose to endure longer commutes, or want to change where they live because they change how they travel.

   Furthermore, it should be noted that transportation is not the only factor in housing choice. On the contrary, housing choice is very complex. Many times, housing choice is dictated by factors other than transportation. Classic housing choice literature by experts like John Quigley suggests that there many factors that make up "residential services," and that travel mode may not be a primary choice, be it biking, walking, transit, driving, or being driven by an AV (Kain and Quigley 1970).

For many individuals housing choice relates less to travel needs, and more to buyer preferences for things like affordability, school quality, neighborhood quality-of-life, accessibility to goods and services, social connectivity, etc. While these kinds of studies do not dismiss the importance of the built environment and "residential sorting" (Pinjari et al. 2011), they reinforce that these housing decisions are complex and that there are other factors than transportation that influence housing decisions. These factors will likely not change in an AV future—undermining claims that AVs will dramatically reshape living patterns in the short term.

References

Ariely, D. 2008. *Predictably Irrational: The Hidden Forces That Shape Our Decisions*. New York: Harper.

Brown, A., C. Gearhart, J. Gonder, and A. Schroeder, A. 2015. Possible Energy Impacts of Vehicle Automation. Retrieved from: https://cedmcenter.org/wp-content/uploads/2015/02/Energy-Impacts-of-CAVs.pdf.

California State Senate. 2015. *L.A. selected to debut electric vehicle carsharing project*. Retrieved from: http://sd24.senate.ca.gov/news/2015-07-24-la-selected-debut-electricvehicle-car-sharing-project.

Coles, C. 2016. "Automated Vehicles: A Guide for Planners and Policymakers." Graduate Thesis: Cal Poly San Luis Obispo. Retrieved from: https://digitalcommons.calpoly.edu/cgi/viewcontent.cgi?referer=https://www.google.com/&httpsredir=1&article=2700&context=theses.

DeMaio, P. "Bike-sharing: History, Impacts, Models of Provision, and Future." *Journal of Public Transportation* 12, no. 4 (2009): 41–56. doi:10.5038/2375-0901.12.4.3.

Flyvbjerg, B. 2001. "Beyond the Limits of Planning Theory: Response to My Critics."

Fulton, L., J. Mason, and D. Meroux. 2017. "Three Revolutions in Urban Transportation." Davis, CA: Institute for Transportation & Development Policy. https://www.itdp.org/publication/3rs-in-urban-transport/.

Ghanem, A., M. Elhenawy, M. Almannaa, H. I. Ashqar, and H. A. Rakha, "Bike share travel time modeling: San Francisco bay area case study," *2017 5th IEEE International Conference on Models and Technologies for Intelligent Transportation Systems (MT-ITS)*, Naples, 2017, pp. 586–591. doi: 10.1109/MTITS.2017.8005582.

Guo, Y., J. Zhou, Y. Wu, and Z. Li. "Identifying the Factors Affecting Bike-sharing Usage and Degree of Satisfaction in Ningbo, China." *Plos One* 12, no. 9 (2017). doi:10.1371/journal.pone.0185100.

Hillier, J. 2005. "Straddling the Post-Structuralist Abyss: Between Transcendence and Immanence?" *Planning Theory* 4(3): 271–299.

Holland, S., E. Mansur, N. Muller, and A. Yates. "Environmental Benefits from Driving Electric Vehicles?" 2015. doi:10.3386/w21291.

Kain, J. F. and J. M. Quigley. 1970. "Measuring the Value of Housing Quality." *Journal of the American Statistical Association* 65(330): 532–548.

Kotkin, J. 2014. "The People Designing Your Cities Don't Care What You Want. They're Planning for Hipsters." *The Washington Post*. 2014. https://www.washingtonpost.com/posteverything/wp/2014/08/15/the-people-designing-your-cities-have-no-idea-what-you-or-the-rest-of-the-middle-class-want/.

Michalek, J., M. Chester, P. Jaramillo, C. Samaras, C. Shiau, and L. Lave. 2011. "Valuation of plug-in vehicle life-cycle air emissions and oil displacement benefits," *Proceedings of the National Academy of Sciences*, 108: 16554–16558.

Mims, C. 2016. "Driverless Cars to Fuel Suburban Sprawl." *Wall Street Journal*. https:// www.wsj.com/articles/driverless-cars-to-fuel-suburban-sprawl-1466395201.

Myers, D. 2016. "Peak Millennials: Three Reinforcing Cycles That Amplify the Rise and Fall of Urban Concentration by Millennials." *Housing Policy Debate* 26 (6): 928–947. https://doi.org/10.1080/10511482.2016.1165722.

Myers, D. and J. Pitkin. 2009. "Demographic Forces and Turning Points in the American City, 1950-2040." *The ANNALS of the American Academy of Political and Social Science* 626 (1): 91–111. https://doi.org/10.1177/0002716209344838.

Pinjari, R. A., R. M. Pendyala, C. R. Bhat, and P. A. Waddell. 2011. "Modeling the Choice Continuum: An Integrated Model of Residential Location, Auto Ownership, Bicycle Ownership, and Commute Tour Mode Choice Decisions." *Transportation* 38(6): 933–958. http://dx.doi.org.ezproxy.lib.calpoly.edu/10.1007/s11116-011-9360-y.

Riggs, W. 2017. "Painting the Fence: Social Norms as Economic Incentives to Non-Automotive Travel Behavior." *Travel Behaviour and Society* 7 (April): 26–33. https://doi.org/10.1016/j.tbs.2016.11.004.

Schaler Consulting. 2017. *The Growth of App-Based Ride Services and Traffic, Travel and the Future of New York City*. Retrieved from http://www.schallerconsult.com/rideservices/unsustainable.pdf.

Slowik, P. and K. Fanta 2017. *New Mobility: Today's Technology and Policy Landscape*. The International Council on Clean Transportation. Retrieved from: https:// www.theicct.org/sites/default/files/publications/New-mobility-landscape_ICCT-white-paper_27072017_vF.pdf.

Solnit, R. 2016. "We Don't Need Self-Driving Cars–We Need to Ditch Our Vehicles Entirely | Opinion | The Guardian." The Guardian. 2016. https://www.theguardian.com/commentisfree/2016/apr/06/self-driving-cars-public-transportation.

Sperling, D. 2018. *Three Revolutions: Steering Automated, Shared, and Electric Vehicles to a Better Future*. Island Press.

Yiftachel, O. 1998. "Planning and Social Control: Exploring the Dark Side." *CPL Bibliography* 12(4): 395–406.

Zhang, Y., T. Thomas, M. J. G. Brussel, and M. F. A. M. Van Maarseveen. "Expanding Bicycle-Sharing Systems: Lessons Learnt from an Analysis of Usage." *Plos One* 11, no. 12 (2016). doi:10.1371/journal.pone.0168604.

Part IV

Conclusive directions

14 A vision for livability

Bruce Appleyard and William Riggs

Introduction

What is the best outcome for health and humanity in a disruptive and autonomous transportation future? How can we balance transportation efficiency with effective land use and a desire for livable cities? For planners, the best outcome is one that does not allow cars to dominate humans (pedestrians, bicyclists, and residents), likely achieved through a stronger, integrated, and balanced transportation-land use connection (Moore et al. 2007) At the very least, the future of transport should not degrade livability—leading to sprawl and/or lengthy trips, thereby paradoxically consuming any new capacity created by the technological advances of autonomous vehicles (AVs).

Yet this is not a vision that departs from some of the most prominent ideas from city planners and engineers over the past century—from Howard's town-and-country magnets and Garden City model, to Clarence Perry's Neighborhood Unit, and Calthorpe's model for Transit Oriented Development (Howard 1902; Perry 1929; Calthorpe 2002). Such tools help guide the planning and development of cities and engineering practice. At the same time, new mobility and driverless cars or autonomous vehicles presents a potential unprecedented (and upending) technological shift (Lipson and Kurman 2016). New potential frameworks are needed to explore and refine thinking about these new forms of networked transportation, how they affect land use, and vice versa. Such conceptual models are necessary to help frame our thinking, our approaches, and measuring our success and shortcomings toward goals and objectives (Jabareen 2006).

A need for a model is important to better measure and guide our future with autonomous vehicles to ensure equitably livable for all. A growing body of literature suggests that creation of a model for land-use and transportation planning is as an important next step in planning for the best possible future for driverless cars (Anderson et al. 2014). Given the implications for increased accessibility and supply of rides anticipated with such technology, such a model will need to manage demand for travel by using more comprehensive land-use planning—framing allocation of origins and destinations through more coordinated transportation, and land-use integration (Moore et al. 2007).

This chapter provides a conceptual model for evaluating performance of various policy scenarios and understanding the framework for how planners and engineers should treat these new mobility futures before us. Such a model should place a premium on service effectiveness (prioritizing the movement of people, over the movement of vehicles) and overall street livability, which can be achieved most sustainably through fewer cars, traveling at slower speeds, and over shorter trip distances (Appleyard 1981a; Dumbaugh and Gattis 2005; D. Appleyard 1981b; Wheeler 2013). A key approach to achieve this is to employ a comprehensive regional land use-planning program to shorten distances between important origins and destinations that ultimately supports walking and bicycling.

In this chapter, we first discuss the emergence of autonomous vehicles and other conceptual models. We then discuss how these conceptual models can build through a new autonomous-livability framework. We then outline how this model might apply to certain street transects and what that means for specific urban policy. This chapter then outlines key indicators that need to be assessed as autonomous vehicle platforms become more widely adopted. We then detail the importance of specific policies around right-of-way that support and underpin this framework for street livability. The goal of all of this is to help guide the future of autonomous vehicles toward an integrated transportation land-use planning approach to achieve sustainability, livability, and equity for streets and communities throughout an entire region.

Background

While there has been ample discussion over the anticipated pros and cons of autonomous driving technology (Fagnant and Kockelman 2014; Litman 2014; Thrun 2010), very little work has been given to decision-making and planning for this "revolution" in this highly uncertain environment—especially given that land use and transportation actions have long inertial properties (Riggs and Boswell 2016; Riggs and Boswell 2016). There is ample speculation about the implications of cars that drive themselves (Lipson and Kurman 2016). Most believe that the transition from a human to computerized driver is likely to be an indicator that points toward quicker adoption based on the risks posed by potential collisions in mixed driverless and traditional autonomous flow (Litman 2014). Some studies have suggested that the delay in driver response poses a significant collision risk as drivers transition between semi-autonomous to manual driving (Lipson and Kurman 2016; Llaneras et al. 2013). Others have predicted sprawl and speculated on the potentially dramatic implications of adopting land use patterns and travel behavior (Isaacs 2016; Anderson et al. 2014).

Some reports go as far as predicting the eminent collapse of the fossil fuel industry due to electrified autonomous vehicles (Airbib and Seba 2017) – with Brown, Gonder, and Repac estimating as much as 80 percent reduction in fuel consumption in a shared an high-proliferation environment (Brown et al. 2014). Indeed, there are other social benefits that could be realized, even with modest increases in vehicle automation, such as data connectivity, communication with the built infrastructure, and the potential to influence driver/vehicle behavior and routing choices in real time.

Of the many things that shape our cities and regions, none of these reports deal with how this new transportation technology will affect the design, operation, and equally important, the sensory quality and feel of streets and communities for people traveling outside the protective confines of automobiles. According to Vasconcellos' (Alcântara De Vasconcellos 2004), the general theory of street livability, developed in 1970s by Donald Appleyard, establishes that streets should be designed for people, over cars and vehicle travel (Appleyard 1980; Appleyard 1981a).

Kevin Lynch, in *Managing the Sense of a Region* (Lynch 1976: 3), concludes that "plans that ignore [sensory qualities] make disheartening cities." Failing to properly value street livability in light of autonomous vehicle could risk our losing of (a) important gains by planners and engineers who have worked years to design and cultivate street livability (Jacobs 1993; Donald Appleyard 1980), (b) an understanding of how things could affect the experience of vulnerable street users (Appleyard 1981a; Dumbaugh and Gattis 2005; Appleyard 1981b; Wheeler 2013), and (c) the effects on people's cognitive/physical health (B. Appleyard 2017). Meeting the livability needs of people in an exposed, vulnerable state outside-of-vehicles, as sustainably and equitably as possible is in alignment with *Livability Ethics* principles to mediate between livability pursuits in conflict to protect the rights of the less powerful and more vulnerable, including human modes of travel (Appleyard et al. 2014), and is a central focus of the framework presented in this chapter.

Of course, many potential benefits of autonomous vehicles that can contribute to the livability experiences of our urban streets and communities. A major one is the ability to lower vehicle casualty rates, with some studies estimating reductions of 90 percent (Litman 2014; Fagnant and Kockelman 2014). And there are potentially other advantages that could make our streets and downtowns more livable. For example:

1 There could be greater street right-of-way recapture, as autonomous vehicles can travel, closer together in platoons, with tighter vehicle tracking (side to side), and possibly via smaller vehicles.

2 Even with modest increases in vehicle automation, there is the potential to influence driver/vehicle behavior in real-time to travel at slower speeds, and routed to avoid sensitive areas, such as residential neighborhoods.

3 There could be opportunities to convert parking spaces and lots into other uses. Further reductions could be realized with greater vehicle sharing, potentially freeing up valuable land for redevelopment and the provision of things such as much needed affordable housing.

4 Autonomous vehicles could present benefits for longer, intercity trips by requiring fewer per person resources (sustainability), presenting fewer neighborhood impacts (livability), and are accessible to all (equity), but our focus is on daily commute patterns of a region, that could be dramatically expanded in their distance and frequency through the significant lowering of personal travel costs.

But these benefits hinge on the assumption that there will not be dramatic increases in the number of vehicles in need of accommodation, whereas most studies show that there will be significant increases in vehicle travel and demands on already burdened capacity. According to UC Davis 3 Revolutions report, without vehicle sharing we could see a 15 to 20 percent increase in overall vehicle travel, assuming a modest 50 percent reduction in the personal cost of travel (Fulton et al. 2017). Even in optimistic vehicle-sharing scenarios, which could lead to a 90 percent drop in vehicles overall, could still lead to a 10 percent increase in travel (Mekuria et al. 2017).

In response, the following overarching policy objectives could lower the amount of vehicle miles travelled, and thus street capacity demand, which in turn could lower the chances of potentially benefiting vulnerable road users as well as undermining sustainability and equity objectives.

1 More vehicle sharing, which can be achieved through transportation demand management (TDM) policies and pricing incentives, while achieving sustainability objectives by encouraging lower resource consumption.
2 Slower, human scale vehicles, that are guided to travel on appropriate streets and away from sensitive districts (e.g., commercial districts, and away from residential neighborhoods). This helps achieve livability and equity objectives, especially when low-income, minority neighborhoods are protected from cruising autonomous or driven TNC vehicles.
3 Shorter trip distances, which can be achieved through land-use planning strategies that a) accommodate infill development, and b) work to curtail the forces of sprawl that often come with reducing the personal cost of travel (Cervero 2002, 2003), again helping achieve sustainability objectives through lower consumption of energy and land resources.

Greater vehicle sharing and smaller vehicles are both possibilities, but not certain for automakers (Firnkorn and Müller 2012). Transportation network companies like Uber and Lyft are certainly making headway in developing transportation as a shared service, but to the degree which this takes hold in any place is still unknown. Considering the sheer magnitude of this potential market, we should expect the competition between a shared or privately-owned autonomous vehicle futures to be fierce and uncertain. This speaks to the need for a concerted effort on behalf of planners and engineers to employ performance measurement frameworks that prioritize travel demand management (through transportation, as well as land use policies) as we build up to this disruptive new mobility and autonomous future.

However, counting on shortening overall trip distances through land-use planning policy implementation, is proving to be an uncertain strategy at this point, as, virtually no peer-reviewed work has gone into proactive land use planning for autonomous vehicles. We appear to be falling short on the transportation planning side as well, as work by Guerra clearly articulates this, finding that only two of the twenty-five largest metropolitan areas mention autonomous or connected vehicles in their planning documents (Guerra 2015). Despite some wide level policy suggestions (Bahamonde Birke et al. 2016), any planning policy appears to be lagging these technological transformations before us.

In sum, there is no clear roadmap for how such a dramatic disruption to the status quo should be handled. Therefore, it is important to provide clear performance measuring frameworks to guide local and regional planning policy responses to autonomous vehicle technology in an environment where the pace of technology appears to be exceeding the pace of empirical planning. Herein lies an opportunity for a conceptual model and performance measurement framework to provide a roadmap with performance evaluation and indicators that provide a basis for decision-making going forward.

Conceptual frameworks, performance measures, and indicators

The concept of transport performance evaluation and the development of performance indicators is not new. Many of the measures and standards used to evaluate transit today date back to the comprehensive 1958 report by The National Committee on Urban Transportation (National Committee on Urban Transportation 1958), which specified service standards, objectives, and measurement techniques for transit. Tomazini defines the conceptual and methodological aspects of evaluating productivity, efficiency, and quality of urban transportation systems. He insists that measures of *efficiency* in the use of resources be separated from measures of *effectiveness* (quality) in achieving ridership (Tomazinis 1975). Allen and DiCesare discuss the need for evaluation of a transit service and provide an overview of the theory of evaluation methodology (Allen and DiCesare 1976). They conclude that transit service can indeed be measured and that the effort to develop a comprehensive evaluation scheme, while considerable, would be justified.

Gilbert and Dajani examine possible perspectives (federal, state, local, user, and operator), which an evaluation system might take and conclude that the interrelated nature of these perspectives is necessary for a conceptual performance evaluation framework to assist in selecting appropriate performance indicators (Gilbert and Dajani 1975). Their conceptual framework emphasizes three levels of evaluation: efficiency, effectiveness, and impact. First developed by Fielding et al., this is one of the more compelling conceptual performance evaluation frameworks that we can build upon (Fielding et al. 1977, 1978; Fielding et al. 1985). Fielding's Conceptual performance measurement framework for transit under the following categories; cost-efficiency, cost-effectiveness, and service effectiveness (Fielding, Brenner, and Faust 1985; Fielding et al. 1977, 1978; Fielding, Babitsky, and Brenner 1985).

The original organizing framework developed by Fielding et al. measures inputs and outputs to achieve efficiency (Fielding, Brenner, and Faust 1985; Fielding, Glauthier, and Lave 1977, 1978; Fielding, Babitsky, and Brenner 1985). *Cost-efficiency indicators* measure service inputs (labor, capital, fuel) to the amount of service produced (service outputs: vehicle hours, vehicle miles, capacity miles, service reliability). *Cost-effectiveness* indicators measure the level of service consumption (passengers, passenger miles, operating revenue) against service inputs. Finally, *service-effectiveness* indicators measure the extent to which service outputs are consumed.

Efficiency measures the rate by which service inputs (labor, capital, fuel) become translated into service outputs, in this case transit, or transport service. Fielding et al. characterize this approach as "Doing things right," hence the use of this phrase in this chapter's title (Fielding, Glauthier, and Lave 1978). An issue of concern with solely relying on this *cost-efficiency* performance dimension in the future, is that it is the only dimension that will not require human participation, especially as labor or even driving goes to almost nothing. By only dealing with non-human resources inputs and service outputs—a large fleet of zero occupancy vehicles covering long distances at fast speeds would actually perform well under the efficiency dimension—but this is potentially over-valuing the movement of vehicles and likely under-valuing the movement of people –posing obvious problems when trying to ensure our streets are for people (D. Appleyard 1981a). Furthermore, *efficiency* provides only a limited view of input and output interactions, isolated within the domain of transport services—an approach that is arguably too constrained for a problem requiring multi-disciplinary land use as well as transportation solutions. Therefore, placing priority on a performance dimension that not only values, but places a priority on servicing human needs, including their movement, and which is captured in measuring *effectiveness*, makes sense when working towards sustainable, livable, and equitable future scenarios with new mobility and autonomous vehicles.

In contrast with *efficiency*, *effectiveness*, is a more expansive and comprehensive performance dimension as it deals with how well a transport system actually meets the access and mobility needs of the people, as well as a transportation systems "intended goals for ridership and service" (Fielding, Glauthier, and Lave 1978). *Effectiveness* indicators compare service actually provided to output or objectives, which were intended, examining the character and location of the demand for service, and how it matches and fits the service provided (Fielding, Glauthier, and Lave 1978). Arguably, this expands into the domain, and accounts for, land use and how well a city or region is planned and designed to lower the demand for travel (VMT, trips, and trip distances). According to Fielding et al. *effectiveness* can be characterized as "Doing the right things," (Fielding, Glauthier, and Lave 1978) hence the rationale for using this term in this chapter's title, which we expand to more explicitly that this is also about "Measuring" the right things, and placing a priority on the movement of people over vehicles.

Again, this provides a framework for cross-referencing measurable inputs and outputs along different dimensions that we could, and perhaps should, use for evaluating our transportation and land use approaches, simultaneously in our move toward a future of vehicular automation. While there will be many social and societal benefits of automation, particularly the promise of reduced collisions and greater vehicle throughput, even at lower levels of automation (Litman 2014), there will be an increasing need to improve land use planning methods to optimize the attainment of these benefits—which may include but are not limited to data connectivity, communication with the built infrastructure, and the potential to influence driver behavior and routing choices in real time.

The Fielding framework, first developed in 1979, may provide such a framework for us to build on. As a conceptual model, it was first created to help with the analysis needed to meet Section 15 of the Urban Mass Transportation Act of 1964. This analysis provided for the collection of a unique set of comparable transit statistics by requiring all transit systems applying for operating assistance to provide a uniform set of information about their transit systems. Fielding originally developed this conceptual model to compare performance across transit systems, and perhaps more critical to our discussion, in both suburban and urban contexts.

This comparison of urban transit systems with suburban transit systems in vastly different contexts, and vastly different outcomes along different dimensions, presents clear challenges to adopting this model without modification. For example, a suburban transit system could perform well regarding *cost-efficiency* (transit vehicle miles per operating cost and labor), but actually carry few passengers (number of passengers per vehicle hours of operation)—underperforming in terms of *service effectiveness* and prioritizing the movement of people over vehicles. Conversely, an urban transit system could carry more passengers (*service effectiveness*), but perhaps less *efficiently* move vehicles because of slower speeds in more urban pedestrian- and bicycle-friendly (and livable) environments (Mekuria et al. 2017).

One reason for this equivocation within the Fielding framework might lie in a political desire to have transit systems perform well in both suburban as well as urban contexts. But how is this not unlike asking students to grade themselves, leading to grade inflation but no clear signal regarding desired goals for performance? Thus, equivocating suburban and urban contexts is problematic in that it will fail to send clear signals for how transport or land use, in either context, should change to better manage transport demand, and for evaluating performance in terms of sustainability, livability, and equity objectives.

Therefore, we recommend modifying this framework to more clearly value and promote policies that place a higher value on effectively moving people over efficiently moving vehicles by: (a) promote greater sharing, (b) value slower speeds, and (c) value land use planning and urban design that lowers the demand for vehicle travel, irrespective of whether this is happening in either an urban or suburban context. While Fielding's model was designed for different transport service types in different urban contexts to evaluate themselves in their most advantageous performance dimension of their choosing, it can be modified to more intentionally compare alternative approaches for how we plan our transportation and land use so that varying degrees of autonomous vehicles can be deployed in ways that are sustainable, livable, and equitable.

Discussion

So, how can we adopt this model to best evaluate the range of future disruptive mobility? To lead to a more livable, sustainable and equitable future, we argue that policy should focus on the area of this diagram where cost-effectiveness and service effectiveness converge toward Service Consumption found in the lower right of Fielding et al.'s original diagram we propose to rotate and move this function (Figure 14.1). In this conceptual situation, the costs of the fleet, fuel, and operation (in time and distance) serve the greatest number of people for the lowest costs and service provided—worthy goals when considering any number of policy options relating to autonomous vehicle futures. Currently, no such conceptual guide exists for policy to date.

Even with this change of emphasis, however, the Fielding model is not fully adequate. Some limitations include:

- It does not yet emphasize the importance of lowering consumption of transportation services—a key goal we should consider in any autonomous vehicle future.
- It virtually ignores any land-use planning actions that can actually lower overall travel demand to achieve future outcomes at the convergence of both *service* and *cost effectiveness.*

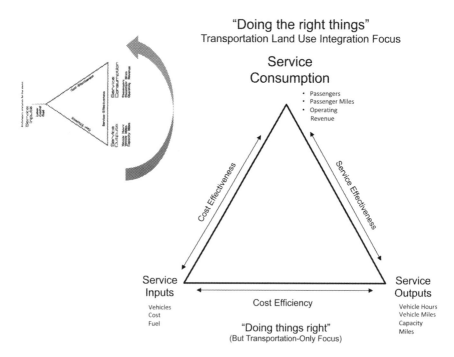

Figure 14.1 A rotated model better fits a focus on service consumption, and the effective movement of people, as opposed to the efficient movement of vehicles, yet is still incomplete as it not yet recognize key land use actions into the policy decision framework that can support this effectiveness of transportation operations

- It has an myopic focus on transit operations a the movement of vehicles (especially along the *cost-efficiency* dimension) and does not yet take into account: (a) how land use planning can benefit the transport system by lowering demand and (b) the impact or benefit to the experiences of *people* traveling in exposed conditions within the street environment (pedestrians and bicyclists)—both important considerations when making policy decisions about alternative autonomous car futures.

To address these limitations and to place a stronger emphasis on lowering consumption, especially as is pertains to vehicle travel, we recommend rotating the Fielding triangle to place *Service Consumption* at the top, as illustrated in Figure 14.1.

This concept model still does not bring in elements of land-use planning needed to readily achieve cost and service effectiveness dimensions that more clearly value the movement of people over the efficient movement of vehicles. Therefore, it can be further augmented to consider the dramatic implications and predictions that could transpire with autonomous vehicles. While we do not speculate on outcomes, a fully revised service model could provide direction to planning in advance of land use shifts—particularly if the Three Revolution strategies of electrification, automation, and sharing (Fulton et al. 2017) are overstated and if there are increases in driving and sprawl that result in exacerbated increases in vehicle capacity demands that take street space away from walking, cycling, and even automated transit service.

For this iteration of the conceptual model, the traditional transit performance measures and their components (Inputs, Outputs, Consumption) are now located inside the triangle. We then more fully illustrate the elements of transportation land-use integration needed to achieve a more sustainable, livable, and equitable driverless car future.

In this conceptual framework, the following elements have been added. First, "land use," with an emphasis on accessibility has been placed on the right as the major approach associated with service effectiveness, especially as it relates to the movement of people. As land use helps determine the demand for transportation services, it makes sense to have it situated and aligned with *service effectiveness*. One rationale for this is that comprehensive land-use planning and urban design can lead to better jobs/housing balances with shorter distance between origins and destinations, which can simultaneously result in lower vehicle miles traveled (VMT), and more walking, bicycling, and transit ridership (which can also be autonomous) (Cervero 1989; Zhou, Wang, and Schweitzer 2012; Giuliano 2009; Cervero, Rood, and Appleyard 1995, 1999; Ewing and Cervero 2010; Stevens 2017). In terms of our new performance dimensions, shorter vehicle trips can lead to a greater number of passengers served for transportation service miles provided (meeting *service effectiveness* dimension), and thus achieving greater sustainability performance through lower resource consumption per person effectively moved from one location to another.

Second, "transportation," with an emphasis on *multimodal effectiveness* has been placed on the left as a major approach aligned with *cost-effectiveness*. This

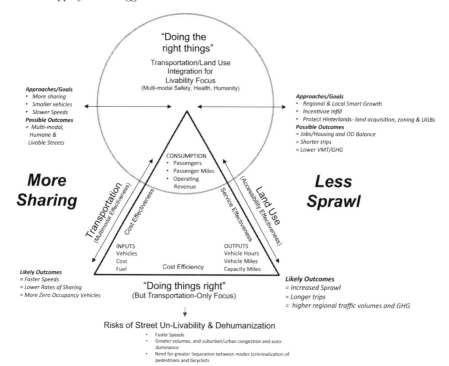

Figure 14.2 Beyond the service consumption framework to a transportation and land-use integration pyramid that supports livability, sustainability, and equity

makes sense as transportation is situated more on the supply-side of travel (land use on the demand-side). Some of the main objectives for greater regional livability and livable streets is to have greater sharing and be able to program cars to travel at slower speeds and to keep them from travelling in areas that need protection from being overwhelmed by volumes of vehicles, autonomous or otherwise (residential neighborhoods, pedestrian zones, and activity centers). Finally, at the top of the graphic are the overall goals for sustainability, livability, and equity that can be achieved through policy approaches that integrate transportation and land use planning (Appleyard, Ferrell, and Taecker 2017, 2016).

What happens if we disregard this framework and recommended approaches, and instead move toward (1) less sharing (private ownership model—the understandably favored approach of businesses selling cars), and (2) lack of public agency wherewithal to program vehicle traveling speeds and routing, or (3) more sprawl through unconstrained land use planning, resulting in longer commute (and other daily trip) distances? It is hard to know for sure, but these will likely to contribute in more vehicles, creating greater demand on the road system as more vehicles need to travel further distances on a daily basis. With this greater demand for vehicle travel, comes greater pressures to accommodate larger volumes of fast moving vehicles, which a number of studies have consistently shown lower levels of street livability for people experiencing the streets outside protective vehicle confines (Appleyard 1980; Appleyard 2017; McAndrews n.d.).

Furthermore, this increased need to meet vehicle travel demands could likely come at the expense of pedestrians, bicyclists, and other out-of-vehicle street users. If these users are viewed to disrupt vehicle operations, as documented in a recent piece by Millard-Ball (Millard-Ball 2016), there is a chance pedestrian re-criminalization campaigns could occur, as witnessed with the emergence of jay-walking laws with the rise of "motordom" in the early twentieth century (Norton n.d.). Finally, this increased need to accommodate vehicle travel could likely lessen the ability of local public agencies to have the authority or wherewithal to proactively respond to these threats to livability by programming vehicles to travel at lower speeds, and away from sensitive areas.

A term is needed to identify this potential undermining of street and neighborhood livability that could come with a predominate focus on cost *efficiency*, with primary emphasis on the movement of vehicles(along the bottom side of the triangle) that could lead to degradation of street livability. For guidance, we turn back to the general theory of street livability, developed in 1970s by Donald Appleyard, which establishes that streets should be designed for people, over cars and vehicle travel, (Donald Appleyard 1980; D. Appleyard 1981a). Therefore, when faced with a potential degradation of the quality of the street environment for people, discouraging their use and enjoyment of the public realm, then "dehumanization" appears to be an appropriate term. Further supporting the use of dehumanization is the fact that the *cost efficiency* performance dimension does not clearly value meeting human needs (persons served) in any of its measures. While labor inputs are a current factor, with the future of autonomous vehicles, even human inputs, in terms of labor or driving will further diminish.

Conversely, on the high point of this triangle, serving human needs (e.g., passengers served) is a central measure for high scores in both cost and service *effectiveness*. In planning for the future of vehicle autonomy, it appears wise to adopt a performance measurement framework that clearly values the movement of people (over vehicles), and their needs in our most accessible public spaces— our streets. Otherwise, it seems reasonable to clearly state how we run the risk of literally programming humans out of our streets; exposing them to dehumanizing conditions.

Next steps

This research asks the question: "What is the best outcome for our streets and communities to integrate with a future of new disruptive transport and autonomous vehicles?" The best outcome is balanced autonomy – one that does not dominate humans, land use, and pedestrian environments. Core to achieving this is to intentionally integrate our land use planning as a form of travel demand management (TDM) that both lowers the amount of travel (sustainability), the impact of that travel (livability), and making sure places and transport services are accessible without unduly harming vulnerable groups (equity). Based on this optimal scenario, the following policy recommendations/principles might help achieve the best outcomes for a future with autonomous vehicles:

1 All autonomous vehicles should be low emission emitters—electric or hybrid minimum.
2 In neighborhood rights-of-way and areas of high pedestrian activity, pedestrians, cyclists, and vulnerable road users should be prioritized and protected by (a) reduced auto right-of-way, (b) routing traffic onto appropriate streets (commercial over residential) and recognizing road hierarchies, and (c) by limiting speed of autonomous vehicles to 20 kilometers (12 miles) per hour to improve safety and livability in urban areas.
3 Comprehensive regional land use planning and growth management practices should also be mandatory in cities allowing the use of autonomous vehicles so to reduce the potential for urban sprawl. For example, land use planning that seeks to achieve better jobs/housing balance that can demonstrably lower the amount of vehicle travel (Cervero 1989; Cervero and Duncan 2006).
4 Autonomous vehicles need to be implemented on a leased or shared-ownership basis to encourage carpooling and to incentivize longevity of product life.
5 Pedestrian and cycling-based infrastructure need to be given similar or equal investment in comparison to autonomous vehicle infrastructure and street re-design.

To help bring about these changes, we should seek to leverage new technology to smartly determine pricing, use incentives, and principles of behavioral economics, for both transportation and land use. In the emerging field of human dynamics, handheld computers (iPhones, Androids, etc.) are recognized to dramatically improve "urban access"—an individual's technology enhanced capacity to discover, navigate, and participate in the exchange and management of goods and services in urban environments, central to the sharing economy phenomenon" (Appleyard 2016). And we should leverage these technologies as much as possible to facilitate exchanges around transportation (Lyft, Uber, parking), and land use to help properly incentivize consumption and behavior. For example, handhelds can now transmit what modes people are using, and therefore, regional transportation agencies might be able engage in real-time transportation demand management strategies to provide price and reward incentives for people willing to engage in sustainable and active travel behavior—e.g., bicycling, walking, taking transit, and sharing vehicles. Cities should embrace this as soon as possible to encourage and reinforce a future of vehicle sharing.

If these principles can be addressed, we can likely minimize the growth in vehicle travel that is predicted to come with the rise of autonomous vehicles (Fagnant and Kockelman 2014; Fulton, Mason, and Meroux 2017), therefore lowering the need to accommodate vehicle demand capacity at the expense of street and neighborhood livability. This, in turn can achieve a higher amount of vehicle right-of-way recapture in both cities and suburban areas, further improving prospects for street livability. Our traditional policies of roadway widening to support

20m ROW (~65')

20m ROW (~65')

30m Lot Face
(~100')

Potential for 600m² (6,500 square feet)
of additional real estate for civic or private
use for every lot / block face.

Existing Single-Family Housing Stock / Lot

Recaptured Right-of-Way (Civic or Private Benefit)

New Multifamily Recaptured Right-of-Way

Figure 14.3 Street transect indicating potential for right-of-way recapture

auto mobility may even become irrelevant. There may be no need for larger public right-of-way and multiple lanes of auto travel. There may be an opportunity to reduce the width of travel lanes to less than the normal twelve feet of space and to allocate this to other modes, use bikes lanes, or parklets. Furthermore, these right of way reductions offer an opportunity to recapture municipal land on these streets and repurpose it for other things.

As illustrated in the transects in Figure 14.3, this could be a valued proposition for cities and residents. Cities could conduct "right-of-way recapture" and then choose to repurpose that for bicycle or pedestrian infrastructure, or for things like gardens and play areas. They could also consider deeding this real estate back to private owners for them to do what they please—an action that would not only increase property value for owners but municipal property tax revenue on an annual basis.

Conclusions and policy guidance

In their book *Driverless* Lipson and Kurman state:

> "In an ideal future, our streets and highways will glisten with schools of tightly packed driverless cars. Like fish, swarms of driverless cars will demonstrate extraordinary anti-collision abilities, navigating intelligently and instinctively through urban streets full of pedestrians, and falling gracefully into fuel-efficient formations on long, empty stretches of highway. Some cars will carry a passenger or two. Others will be empty, on their way to drop off a pizza or to pick up a child from daycare." *(p. 4)*

If this is the ideal scenario, why would streets be full of pedestrians? People would not need to purchase food themselves and instead utilize automated delivery and benefit from costs through streamlined efficiencies. It seems like efficiency is the ultimate goal in this scenario with convenience for the sake of convenience. And this is consistent with what we are seeing in private industry. For example, Ford's website for autonomous vehicles headlines goals for efficiency alongside safety. But as we have discussed in this chapter, *efficiency* before *effectiveness* risks undervaluing the role of people, and possibly pushing people out of our city streets—our most accessible public spaces. Therefore, we recommend placing *effectiveness*, "Doing the Right Things," before *efficiency*, and "Doing Things Right"—nevertheless, we wholeheartedly suggest pursuing both, but *effectiveness* should clearly lead.

Concepts for livability in the disruptive and autonomous transport future

See more at: https://www.planetizen.com/features/96769

The Vehicles: Leverage for Sustainable Urbanism

1 **Leverage new technology to determine pricing, use incentives, and utilize principles of behavioral economics, for both transportation and land-use exchanges, and to facilitate a digital and just future mobility**
2 **Sustainable and human scale vehicle design.**

The Streets and Users: Design and Program for Livability and Humanity

3 **Prioritize the needs of people before vehicles.**
4 **Proactively design and program streets and driving for livability, safety, and humanity.**

Land Use Planning and Design: "Refilling" (with urban reinvestment) Before "Spilling" (sprawl)

5 **Encourage urban reinvestment to "refill" urban core areas before "spilling" onto sprawl.**
6 **A good regional land use plan is a good regional transportation plan: Manage land use patterns to lower trip distance and get ahead of the AV-driven "spilling" forces of sprawl.**
7 **Available parking spaces coming soon: strategically leverage newly available space to further offset the forces of sprawl.**
8 **"Refill" and prioritize the vitality of urban transit corridors and TODs through land use planning and urban design (place-making).**
9 **Proactively change zoning and parking requirements in order to prioritize the "refilling" of urban areas before "spilling" onto sprawl.**
10 **Value planning: create a vision, a performance-measurement framework, and scenario-testing process that can serve to guide subsequent planning decisions.**

As an antipode to this, we envision a a more sustainable future shaped around equitable livability. This would mean creating the type of places that we want to live in, work in, and play in by allowing vehicular technology to serve us. In that light, it is important to emphasize that there is more research needed in this area. We provide a measurement framework and potential indicators for transportation/land use integration strategies that can achieve higher service and cost-effective performance that clearly values the movement of people over the movement of vehicles, that can actually encourage greater transport and land efficiency. These could be tested for various planning scenarios.

The next step would be to test these proposed measures and models by particularly looking at street layouts or designs that need to be explored in order to pro-actively plan for places we desire to live in protecting the public realm from deactivation and dehumanization—perhaps some of the same street concepts that we have explored in this book.

There is much work to be done. As Handy suggests in her response to Stevens' findings that compact development does not always significantly lower driving (Stevens 2017), "it must work, and we must get on with doing the hard work of planning these kind of communities" (Handy 2017). So, channeling Handy (2017), "let's get on with it."

References

Airbib, J. and T. Seba. 2017. "Rethinking Transportation 2020-2030: The Disruption of Transportation and the Collapse of the Internal-Combustion Vehicle and Oil Industries." RethinkTransportation. RethinkX.

Alcântara De Vasconcellos, E. 2004. "The Use of Streets: A Reassessment and Tribute to Donald Appleyard." *Journal of Urban Design* 9 (1): 3–22. https://doi.org/10.1080/1357480042000187686.

Allen, G. and F. DiCesare. 1976. "Transit Service Evaluation: An Introduction and Preliminary Identification of Variables Characterizing Level of Service." *Transportation Research Record: Journal of the Transportation Research Board*. 606. pp 41–47. https://trid.trb.org/view/52872.

Anderson, J. M., K. Nidhi, K. D. Stanley, P. Sorensen, C. Samaras, and O. A. Oluwatola. 2014. *Autonomous Vehicle Technology: A Guide for Policymakers*. Rand Corporation. https://books.google.com/books?hl=en&lr=&id=y0WrAgAAQBAJ&oi=fnd&pg=PP1&dq=Autonomous+17+Vehicle+Technology:+A+Guide+for+Policymakers.&ots=-6K7e4NENQ&sig=ZeCAbm066Tpr_gG3A7q1CueUmb4.

Appleyard, B. 2016. "Urban Planning: Human Dynamics." In *International Encyclopedia of Geography: People, the Earth, Environment and Technology*. John Wiley & Sons, Ltd. https://doi.org/10.1002/9781118786352.wbieg1061.

———. 2017. "The Meaning of Livable Streets to Schoolchildren: An Image Mapping Study of the Effects of Traffic on Children's Cognitive Development of Spatial Knowledge." *Journal of Transport & Health*, Walking and Walkability: A review of the evidence on health, 5 (Supplement C): 27–41. https://doi.org/10.1016/j.jth.2016.08.002.

Appleyard, B., C. E. Ferrell, and M. Taecker. 2016. "Toward a Typology of Transit Corridor Livability." *Transportation Research Record: Journal of the Transportation Research Board*, no 2543. https://trid.trb.org/view.aspx?id=1392701.

———. 2017. "Transit Corridor Livability: Realizing the Potential of Transportation and Land Use Integration." http://docs.trb.org/prp/17-03490.pdf.

Appleyard, B., C. Ferrell, M. Carroll, and M. Taecker. 2014. "Toward Livability Ethics: A Framework to Guide Planning, Design, and Engineering Decisions." *Transportation Research Record: Journal of the Transportation Research Board*. 2403: 62–71.

Appleyard, D. 1981a. *Livable Streets*. Berkeley: University of California Press.

———. 1981b. "Three Streets in San Francisco." In *Livable Streets*, edited by D. Appleyard, 15–28. Berkeley: University of California Press.

Appleyard, D. 1980. "Livable Streets: Protected Neighborhoods?" *The ANNALS of the American Academy of Political and Social Science* 451 (1): 106–17. https://doi.org/10.1177/000271628045100111.

Bahamonde B., F. Jose, B. Kickhöfer, D. Heinrichs, and T. Kuhnimhof. 2016. "A Systemic View on Autonomous Vehicles: Policy Aspects for a Sustainable Transportation Planning." http://elib.dlr.de/108647/.

Brown, A., J. Gonder, and B. Repac. 2014. "An Analysis of Possible Energy Impacts of Automated Vehicle." In *Road Vehicle Automation*, 137–153. Springer.

Calthorpe, P. 2002. "The Urban Network: A Radical Proposal—Peter Calthorpe Makes the Case for a New Suburban Transportation Network." *Planning* 68(5): 6.

Cervero, R., and M. Duncan. "Which Reduces Vehicle Travel More: Jobs-Housing Balance or Retail-Housing Mixing?" *Journal of the American Planning Association* 72, no. 4 (December 31, 2006): 475–90. https://doi.org/10.1080/01944360608976767.

Cervero, R., T. Rood, and B. Appleyard. 1995. "Job Accessibility as a Performance Indicator: An Analysis of Trends and Their Social Policy Implications in the San Francisco Bay Area."

———. 1999. "Tracking Accessibility: Employment and Housing Opportunities in the San Francisco Bay Area." *Environment and Planning A* 31(7): 1259–1278.

Cervero, Robert. 1989. "Jobs-Housing Balancing and Regional Mobility." *Journal of the American Planning Association* 55(2): 136–50. https://doi.org/10.1080/01944368908976014.

———. 2002. "Induced Travel Demand: Research Design, Empirical Evidence, and Normative Policies." *Journal of Planning Literature* 17(1): 3–20. https://doi.org/10.1177/088122017001001.

———. 2003. "Road Expansion, Urban Growth, and Induced Travel: A Path Analysis." *Journal of the American Planning Association* 69(2): 145–63. https://doi.org/10.1080/01944360308976303.

Dumbaugh, E. and J. L. Gattis. 2005. "Safe Streets, Livable Streets." *Journal of the American Planning Association* 71(3): 283–300.

Ewing, R. and R. Cervero. 2010. "Travel and the Built Environment." *Journal of the American Planning Association* 76(3): 265–94. https://doi.org/10.1080/01944361003766766.

Fagnant, D. J. and K. M. Kockelman. 2014. "The Travel and Environmental Implications of Shared Autonomous Vehicles, Using Agent-Based Model Scenarios." *Transportation Research Part C: Emerging Technologies* 40: 1–13.

Fielding, G. J., T. T. Babitsky, and M. E. Brenner. 1985. "Performance Evaluation for Bus Transit." *Transportation Research Part A: General* 19(1): 73–82.

Fielding, G. J., M. E. Brenner, and K. Faust. 1985. "Typology for Bus Transit." *Transportation Research Part A: General* 19(3): 269–278.

Fielding, G. J., R. E. Glauthier, and C. A. Lave. 1977. "Development of Performance Indicators for Transit." https://trid.trb.org/view.aspx?id=70054.

———. 1978. "Performance Indicators for Transit Management." *Transportation* 7 (4): 365–79. https://doi.org/10.1007/BF00168037.

Firnkorn, J., and M. Müller. 2012. "Selling Mobility Instead of Cars: New Business Strategies of Automakers and the Impact on Private Vehicle Holding." *Business Strategy and the Environment* 21(4): 264–280.

Fulton, L., J. Mason, and D. Meroux. 2017. "Three Revolutions in Urban Transportation." Davis, CA: Institute for Transportation & Development Policy. https://www.itdp.org/publication/3rs-in-urban-transport/.

Gilbert, G. and J. Dajani. 1975. "Measuring the Performance of Transit Service." Chapel Hill, North Carolina: University of North Carolina Press. https://scholar.google.com/scholar_lookup?title=Measuring%20the.%20Performance%20of%20Transit%20Service&author=G..%20Gilbert&author=J..%20Dajani&publication_year=1975.

Giuliano, G. 2009. "Is Jobs-Housing Balance a Transportation Issue?" *ANALYSIS* 4: 46AM.

Guerra, E. 2015. "Planning for Cars That Drive Themselves Metropolitan Planning Organizations, Regional Transportation Plans, and Autonomous Vehicles." *Journal of Planning Education and Research*, November, 0739456X15613591. https://doi.org/10.1177/0739456X15613591.

Handy, S. 2017. "Thoughts on the Meaning of Mark Stevens's Meta-Analysis." *Journal of the American Planning Association* 83(1): 26–28. https://doi.org/10.1080/01944363.2016.1246379.

Howard, S. E. 1902. *Garden Cities of To-Morrow:(To-Morrow: A Peaceful Path to Real Reform)*. London, S. Sonnenschein & co., ltd.

Isaacs, L. 2016. "Driving Toward Driverless." New York: WSP | Parsons Brinckerhoff. http://www.wsp-pb.com/Globaln/USA/Transportation%20and%20Infrastructure/driving-towards-driverless-WBP-Fellow-monograph-lauren-isaac-feb-24-2016.pdf.

Jabareen, Y. R. 2006. "Sustainable Urban Forms: Their Typologies, Models, and Concepts." *Journal of Planning Education and Research* 26(1): 38.

Jacobs, A. B. 1993. *Great Streets*. MIT Press.

Lipson, H. and M. Kurman. 2016. *Driverless: Intelligent Cars and the Road Ahead*. MIT Press.

Litman, T. 2014. "Autonomous Vehicle Implementation Predictions." *Victoria Transport Policy Institute* 28. http://sh.st/st/787f28ed3e745c14417e4aec27303038/http://www.vtpi.org/avip.pdf.

Llaneras, R. E., J. Salinger, and C. A. Green. 2013. "Human Factors Issues Associated with Limited Ability Autonomous Driving Systems: Drivers' Allocation of Visual Attention to the Forward Roadway." In *Proceedings of the 7th International Driving Symposium on Human Factors in Driver Assessment, Training and Vehicle Design*, 92–98. Public Policy Center, University of Iowa Iowa City. https://pdfs.semanticscholar.org/344d/7759e45e059b9b73a0de25e7d8b4af52f5bb.pdf.

Lynch, K. 1976. "Managing the Sense of a Region." http://www.bcin.ca/Interface/openbcin.cgi?submit=submit&Chinkey=16794.

McAndrews, C. n.d. "Understanding and Improving Arterial Roads to Support Public Health and Transportation Goals | AJPH | Vol. 107 Issue 8." Accessed November 4, 2017. http://ajph.aphapublications.org/doi/abs/10.2105/AJPH.2017.303898.

Mekuria, M. C., B. Appleyard, and H. Nixon. 2017. "Improving Livability Using Green and Active Modes: A Traffic Stress Level Analysis of Transit, Bicycle, and Pedestrian Access and Mobility," Mineta Transportation Institute Publications. http://scholar-works.sjsu.edu/mti_publications/228.

Millard-Ball, A. 2016. "Pedestrians, Autonomous Vehicles, and Cities." *Journal of Planning Education and Research*, October, 0739456X16675674. https://doi.org/10.1177/0739456X16675674.

Moeder, London. n.d. "A Train Without Tracks: Talking Points on the Impact of AV on Land Use." *London Moeder Advisors* (blog). Accessed November 5, 2017. http://londonmoeder.com/2017/10/04/a-train-without-tracks-talking-points-on-the-impact-of-av-on-land-use/.

Moore, T., P. Thorsnes, and B. Appleyard. 2007. "The Transportation/Land Use Connection (PAS 546/547)." Washington, D.C.: American Planning Association. https://www.planning.org/publications/report/9026872/.

National Committee on Urban Transportation. 1958. "Recommended Standards, Warrants, and Objectives for Transit Services and Facilities." Chicago, Illinois: Public Administration Service. https://scholar.google.com/scholar_lookup?title=Recommended%20Standards%2C%20Warrants%2C%20and%20Objectives%20for%20Transit%20Services%20and%20Facilities&publication_year=1958.

Norton, P. n.d. *Fighting Traffic*. Accessed November 5, 2017. https://books.google.com/books/about/Fighting_Traffic.html?id=RxfqJoqhtpUC.

Perry, C. A. 1929. *The Neighbourhood Unit*. Routledge/Thoemmes.

Riggs, W. and M. R. Boswell. 2016. "Thinking Beyond the (Autonomous) Vehicle: The Promise of Saved Lives." https://works.bepress.com/williamriggs/71/.

Riggs, W. and M. R. Boswell. 2016. "No Business as Usual in an Autonomous Vehicle Future." https://works.bepress.com/williamriggs/53/.

Stevens, M. R. 2017. "Does Compact Development Make People Drive Less?" *Journal of the American Planning Association* 83(1): 7–18. https://doi.org/10.1080/01944363.2016.1240044.

Thrun, S. 2010. "Toward Robotic Cars." *Communications of the ACM* 53(4): 99–106.

Tomazinis, A. R. 1975. "Productivity, Efficiency, and Quality in Urban Transportation Systems." https://trid.trb.org/view.aspx?id=141842.

"Toward Livability Ethics: A Framework to Guide Planning, Design and Engineering Decisions - 14-4272.Pdf." n.d. Accessed September 30, 2016. http://docs.trb.org/prp/14-4272.pdf.

Wheeler, S. M. 2013. *Planning for Sustainability: Creating Livable, Equitable and Ecological Communities*. Routledge.

Zhou, J., Y. Wang, and L. Schweitzer. 2012. "Jobs/Housing Balance and Employer-Based Travel Demand Management Program Returns to Scale: Evidence from Los Angeles." *Transport Policy* 20: 22–35.

15 Learning from the past and avoiding future mistakes

Andrea Broaddus

Introduction

Today's urban mobility system would be recognizable to a time traveler from one hundred years ago. Cutting-edge technologies from the early twentieth century are in widespread use today, including automobiles and buses, rail transit and subways, and traffic signs and signals. New communications, robotics, and artificial intelligence technologies that will shape the next century's urban mobility are just gaining a foothold. We have the potential to transform the mobility system for better or for worse. As we enter a new era where autonomous on-demand modes are integrated into urban mobility, we have an opportunity to correct past mistakes and improve outcomes and efficiencies, and a challenge to not make things worse.

Learning from the past

Looking back, there are two previous technological revolutions that we can learn from. The first was the rise of motorized mass transportation in the Victorian era, and the second the rise of personalized motor transport, post-World War II. Both of these were spurred by innovations in transportation technology which re-shaped travel behavior and the physical structure of cities. Yet they had opposite outcomes—subways and electric railways drove the centralization of cities and densification of economic activity, while private automobile ownership drove de-centralization and urban sprawl. Denser settlements translate to more environmentally sustainable outcomes. If we assume that human behavior has remained constant, in terms of the preferences and constraints that determine the number and type of trips we make, the time we spend traveling, and our mode choice, then other factors must explain these divergent outcomes.

Consider the view from the turn of the twentieth century when the automobile was on the rise. In the first three decades, cars were the emerging technology, challenging norms in cities. In this early stage, motorized vehicles represented potential, much as autonomous vehicles do today, to utterly disrupt the existing mobility ecosystem, or to develop a complementary niche within it. It was not a foregone conclusion that cars would come to dominate cities, or that cities would be ripped apart and re-engineered to accommodate them. The pre-automobile city as imagined by a historian included a wide range of affordable travel options,

> "Despite its peculiar status in modern society...the rise of the gasoline automobile was by no means inevitable. An almost limitless number of transit options existed for Americans at the beginning of the 20th century. A resident of New York City could leave her apartment in 1899 and take an electric taxi to the subway, where she could catch an underground light train to the Grand Central Terminal, ride a comfortable locomotive to San Francisco, disembark and transit on a cable car or trolley, and then hail a taxi, take a horse, or walk to her final destination." (Sovacool 2009, page 412)

The same journey could be made today, only substituting the locomotive with an airplane and the horse with an Uber. The main differences between the pre- and post-automobile city are the travel speeds and the spatial allocation of the streets. The historic film, "A Journey Down Market Street," offers a window into this world through the lens of a front-mounted camera on a trolley rolling through downtown San Francisco in 1906 (Miles Brothers 1906). Here we see the street as a multimodal, shared space. Pedestrians, bicycles, horse-drawn wagons and early automobiles move across the path of the slow-moving trolley. No vehicle is moving faster than about 10 miles per hour. There are no lanes on the road, no traffic signals or stop signs. It is a self-organized urban mobility ecosystem operating by subtle interactions and negotiations between the users, all of whom had equal rights to occupy the road space.

The rise of the automobile

In 1912 there were 944,000 registered vehicles in the United States, .01 cars per capita, and only 10 states had driver's license laws (FHWA 1996). New York City introduced the first comprehensive traffic code in 1903, and Connecticut passed the first speed limit law in 1903, setting the legal speed of motor vehicles to 12 miles per hour in cities and 15 miles per hour on country roads (Brown 2006). With all of the vehicles moving relatively slowly, collisions could only do so much damage, but as cars became faster and more numerous, roads became more dangerous, especially for pedestrians. Historic data from Australia shows that typical mode shares for major cities up to 1920 were 30 to 40 percent for walking and biking, 50 to 60 percent for public transit (horse-drawn omnibus, electric trolley, etc.), and 10 percent for private transport (horse-drawn carriages and passenger cars) (Cosgrove 2011).

The mode split changed after cars became more affordable. In 1913, Ford introduced moving assembly line production and the low-cost mass-produced Model T, and cars began selling at high volumes. From 2010 to 2020 the number of registered vehicles increased by a factor of 10, to 9.2 million, or 0.09 cars per capita, yet only five more states had passed driver licensing laws by 2020 (FHWA 1996). With their greater speed and inexperienced drivers, cars created an unprecedented surge in collisions, injuries and death on the roadways as they became more numerous on the roads. During the 1920s, car registrations tripled again, to 26.7 million in 2030 (FHWA 1996). By 1926, just over a decade after they became affordable to the masses, 16% of the population owned a private automobile, moving cars from "early adopter" stage to "early mainstream" on the Rogers innovation diffusion curve (Rogers 2003). The same year was an inflection point for urban public transit ridership, which peaked at a patronage of 17.2 billion before declining until the war years (Schrag 2002).

With their greater speed and inexperienced drivers, cars created an unprecedented surge in collisions, injuries and death on the roadways as they became more numerous. Over the 1920s, motor vehicle crashes killed more than 200,000 people in the United States, the great majority of them pedestrians and children (Norton 2008). Public pressure at this stage made safety the primary rationale for regulatory and design interventions. By 1930, automobiles had become significant enough to warrant standardization of engineering and signage approaches, and to require driver education and licensing (McShane 1999). The transportation engineering profession came into being to respond to the road safety crisis, and invented traffic lanes, signals, and segregation of slow moving traffic to the sidewalk. Yet cars were still a minority of traffic. At that point about one in four people had a car (.22 cars per capita), a level that remained stable until after World War II (FHWA 1996).

Engineers introduced solutions like traffic lanes and signals to improve road safety and alleviate traffic congestion as flows of private motor vehicles on city streets increased. Segregated lanes helped improve the performance of streetcars stuck in mixed traffic. However, these interventions ultimately had the effect of privileging road space for cars, contributing to their attractiveness. "The great paradox of early traffic engineering...was that improving mobility only attracted more traffic, by either moving from another road or, if the improvements were more general, encouraging car owners to abandon transit riding." (McShane 1999, page 397) The "traffic engineering" approach prioritizing motor vehicle flows was replicated by cities around the world.

Streetcars lost ridership and revenues along with the ability to offer swift and reliable service during the 1920s. Some were cutting back on capital investment and employees due to inflation, high wages, and contracts with regulators limiting their ability to raise fares (Schrag 2000). Yet streetcar operators found no sympathy from the public. They were unpopular, viewed as corrupt monopolists who cared more for profits than customers. People perceived the transit industry as a private business, not a public asset deserving government investment when private capital dried up (Young 2015). Throughout this period, while the public invested heavily in motor vehicle infrastructure, streetcar infrastructure deteriorated. By the 1940s, after decades of deferred maintenance and service cuts, streetcars were slow and unreliable in comparison to cars. With political will and public capital lacking, most cities either let them go bankrupt or replaced them with buses.

As cities lost control of financing urban transport, they had to compromise on what got built. Traditional local financing sources like property taxes and bonds broke down during the Depression, and state and federal motor fuel taxes came to dominate transport finance, representing a shift of power and priorities away from cities (Brown, Morris, and Taylor 2009). High-capacity thoroughfares designed to speed streetcar and motor vehicle traffic were ultimately built for cars only, with an emphasis on suburban and intercity travel. Cities lacked the financial resources to take over broken-down streetcar systems and subway expansion plans had to be abandoned (Schrag 2002). In Europe, greater city autonomy and positive perceptions of public transit contributed to the preservation of historic trams and light rail systems as car ownership rose.

As cars became dominant, urban transportation was increasingly designed around them such that public transportation, bicycling and walking became increasingly inconvenient and unsafe, further reinforcing the dominance of cars. Twentieth-century transportation planning was largely concerned with enabling cars to travel faster. As noted by Banister, "the conventional transport paradigm is heavily embedded in the belief that travel time needs to be minimized and consequently speeds need to be increased" (Banister 2011, page 955). The overarching goal of reducing travel times led to an over-emphasis on engineering for faster vehicle flows, such as "level of service" measures for urban streets which prioritize higher traffic speeds and volumes to detriment of walkability. Pedestrians and bicyclists were viewed as impediments to vehicular flows and so banished from the street.

Unintended consequences

Looking back, history offers a couple of lessons learned. In the early 1900s, the public sector took an early and proactive role regulating vehicle speeds and traffic flows. Yet early efforts to control and rationalize flows of vehicles through signals and engineering resulted in a transformation of urban streets from public spaces shared by a range of transport modes into spaces dominated by cars and hostile to transit, pedestrians and bikes—an unintended consequence. This utter transformation of urban space occurred in a relatively short timeframe. The demise of streetcars was arguably another unintended consequence. Streetcars, taken for granted as profitable monopolies, were undervalued for their efficient use of road space and role in the spatial organization of the city. Perceptions of motor vehicles as "modern progress" and streetcars as old-fashioned contributed to a lack of concern for protecting streetcar lines as assets with public value. Excitement about shiny new high-tech things may cause valuable "old" things to be overlooked.

How will autonomous vehicles influence travel behavior?

The confluence of automation, electrification, and communications technologies allow for new ways of matching riders for sharing trips. Some predict that emerging on-demand services—including ride-hailing, car-sharing, bike-sharing, and micro-mobility sharing—will displace car ownership as the most affordable and convenient mobility solution in urban areas. Travel has traditionally been treated as a derived demand. Transport planners begin with the assumption that travel is not consumed as an end in itself, but as a means to accomplish other ends, such as access to employment, education, and retail goods. Previously suppressed trips in low-density areas could be "unlocked" by low-cost on-demand ride-hailing services. For example, the number of trips people make per day depends in part upon their level of access. The number of trips made per day tends to increase with age, along with income and starting a family, up to a peak at about age forty-five. Truong et al. have identified gaps in this travel needs curve where people aged twelve to thirty and older than seventy who are dependent upon public transit would likely take more trips if they had access to affordably priced AV taxis (Truong et al. 2017).

Constraints to travel

There are likely to be limits to how much people's behavior will change in response to emerging technologies. Some behavioral patterns are deeply consistent over time, regardless of technological change. The twenty-four hour day and circadian rhythm govern human behavior to a large extent. According to the American Time Use Survey (ATUS), we dedicate approximately 42 percent of our time each day to primary activities like eating (1.17 hours) and sleeping (8.79 hours), on average (BLS, 2016). Employed people spend another 32 percent of each day working (7.63 hours), and parents spend 6 percent caring for children (1.42 hours), on average. For working parents, that leaves only 20 percent of the day (4.8 hours) for all other activities, including travel. These patterns are consistent across cultures, as shown in Figure 15.1. On average, across 14 OECD countries, people spend nearly half of the day on personal care (46 percent), and the other half split between paid work or study (16 percent), unpaid work, care work and unspecified activities (17 percent) and leisure (21 percent) (OECD 2018).

When it comes to travel, some behavioral patterns have proven resistant to technological change. The amount of time people are willing to spend commuting to work is remarkably stable at about an hour per day across cultures (Zahavi 1979). Marchetti, an anthropologist, attributed this to a Neolithic need to reduce exposure to danger, which still influences modern behavior. He noted that ancient Greek and medieval villages were defined by a radius of 2.5 kilometers, correlating with the distance that a person can walk in a round-trip, in one hour (at a speed of 5 kilometers per hour), and argued that the size of cities ever since has expanded *in proportion* to the top speed that humans can travel in thirty minutes. (Marchetti 1994). Thus during the twentieth century, as personal vehicles became faster, people reallocated commute trip time savings to travel longer distances, rather than to other time uses. Rather than enjoying a shorter commute and more leisure time, people moved further away from their jobs to maintain a thirty minute commute. Evidence of the "Marchetti constant" has been found in a global study by Schaefer, illustrates that the travel budget, or the amount of time people are willing to spend travelling each day, is highly

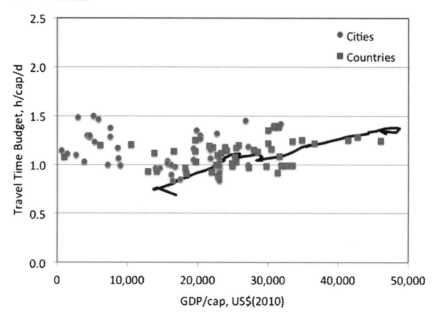

Figure 15.1 Time spent traveling per day, by income level

Source: Figure 2f, Determinants of aggregate passenger travel by per person gross domestic product (GDP): daily amount of travel time per person for countries (59 data points) and African villages and cities (48 data points), and the use of time dedicated to motorized travel within the domestic US from 1946 to 2010 (black line). (Schäfer 2017, page 296) (Reprinted with permission of the author)

independent of income or urban versus rural setting. (Schäfer 2017). However, the average of one hour travel time obscures important differences in the disaggregate data (Mokhtarian & Chen 2004).

Another constraint to how much people are able to travel is the traditional work day. Modern society is organized around a work day of approximately 9:00 to 5:00, because the economy requires human interaction during simultaneous work times; school hours are aligned so that parents may participate in the workforce. Workers who must be in a workplace for a set number of hours are more constrained in the number, length, and duration of trips they make. There is some evidence that the traditional work day is eroding as jobs with non-traditional hours form a larger share of employment, such as service jobs (health care, hospitality, food service, retail, nightlife (entertainment) and gig economy jobs. In New York, nearly 60 percent of job growth has been in these industries over the past decade; from 2010 to 2016 the number of subway riders travelling between 5:00 to 7:00 a.m. and 7:00 to 11:00 p.m. grew by 14 and 13 percent, respectively (Nir 2018). During off-peak hours, public transit is less frequent and traffic congestion is not an issue, while personal security may be a concern, so these workers could be expected to switch to an affordable AV taxi if it were available. There is also a growing share of workers doing some or all of their work at home, from

19 percent in 2000 to 22 percent in 2016, which reduces the number of work trips, but also frees up time spent commuting for leisure trips (BLS 2016).

Avoiding future mistakes

Today's technological revolution has a different character, as travel speeds are not expected to increase. Where past technological innovation resulted in *faster vehicles* that reduced the amount of time required to travel a given distance, automation and connectivity promise only modest travel time savings via system efficiencies such as traveling more closely together and removing parking search and walking time. The main benefit of current technological innovations is the removal of the driving task, resulting in qualitatively different *multifunctional vehicles*. We can conclude that there is only so much time available in the day for travel time, even given the ability to delegate driving to when using an autonomous vehicles. Work/school hours and related travel times are not likely to change for the majority of the population. Drivers of travel choice are likely to remain the classics: cost, travel time, vehicle availability, and individual preference.

The crossroads before us

Several studies considering impacts of AVs have converged upon two future scenarios: utopian and dystopian (BCG 2016; ITF, 2015; Sperling et al. 2018; WEF 2018; Zmud et al. 2013). These studies posit that we are at a crossroads between potential futures where today's problems have either been solved or have become much worse.

The utopian scenario is characterized by more travel choices, better access for non-drivers, less traffic congestion and environmental impacts, safer streets and repurposed parking, and more efficient public transit, while the dystopian scenario is characterized by more vehicle use and empty vehicle circulation, more urban sprawl, cyber attacks and privacy violations, and declining transit use and social equity (Sperling et al. 2018).

Two of these studies modeled what could happen if all private vehicle trips in a city were replaced by shared autonomous vehicles (SAVs) and public transit. This hypothetical "utopia" scenario was modeled for Lisbon, Portugal, and Boston, Massachusetts[1] (central area only) (ITF 2015) (BCG 2017). Both studies concluded that the availability of on-demand shared AVs would reduce the use of private cars and demand for parking. In Lisbon, SAVs paired with high-capacity public transit delivered nearly the same mobility as today with only 10 percent of the cars. In Boston, the number of vehicles on the road was reduced by 28 percent, and the number of parking spaces needed by 48 percent. Higher rates of sharing meant less traffic congestion and shorter travel times— 30 percent fewer vehicles on the roads in Boston and 65 percent fewer in Lisbon. However, both studies also found that overall vehicle miles travelled would increase by 6 percent for both cities, due to empty repositioning trips and shifts from transit, biking or walking. If the SAVs were electric, there would not be any associated increase in CO_2 emissions.

Another study modeled four scenarios for a generic city in 2030 testing the impacts of policy actions: (1) do nothing, (2) encourage AVs and electrification, (3) same as 2, plus discourage private AVs, and (4) same as 3, plus encourage sharing (WEF 2018). In the "do nothing" base case scenario, personal AVs gradually replace traditional cars but mode split remains similar to today, with 46 percent of trips by personal vehicle, 10 percent by traditional or AV taxi, 39 percent by public transit, and 5 percent by walking. Traffic volumes and congestion levels are unchanged from the base case, but there is a nearly 20 percent reduction in traffic crashes. In scenario 2, the city acts to encourage AVs and electrification (but not sharing), and the mode split remains very similar, but with a higher percentage of AVs. Crashes are reduced by half, but reductions in traffic volumes and parking space demand are modest (–8 percent and –5 percent). In scenario 3, when the city actively discourages private vehicle trips through measures like taxes or bans, the effect is transformative. Only 6 percent of trips are made by private vehicle, nearly half by AV taxi, 36 percent by public transit, and 9 percent by biking and walking. Car crashes plummet (–86 percent), along with car ownership (–46 percent) and demand for parking (–39 percent). In scenario 4, incentives encouraging ride sharing are added (e.g., discounted fares, dedicated lanes), increasing the share of trips by AV taxi to 53 percent while car ownerships falls even further (–59 percent), as does parking demand (–54 percent). In all scenarios, electrification reduces emissions by –9 percent to –85 percent.

From this study we can conclude an active city role makes the difference between business as usual and progress towards utopia. Even in the least controversial scenario, encouragement of AV electric vehicle uptake through measures like infrastructure provision and incentives, resulted in significant emissions and safety benefits. We can also conclude that and that boldness and sequencing of measures also matters. Only when such "carrot" measures were paired with "stick" measures discouraging private vehicle use were other benefits like reduced traffic congestion and travel times realized. Measures discouraging private car use are historically politically unpopular, but as people shift to shared modes, a policy window is opening. If we fail to act while the trend toward sharing is underway, and *before* widespread uptake of private AVs, as in scenario 2, measures like congestion charging will become impossible. Measures to encourage sharing are less controversial, and will encourage people to give up cars and settle into new mobility habits and lifestyles before AVs become affordable for private use.

Conclusion

Are we headed for utopia or dystopia? The question hinges on how proactive a role the public sector—at the city, state, and federal levels—takes in steering the current transportation revolution towards socially beneficial outcomes. As demonstrated by history and by future models, sequencing new technologies matters. What that means is governmental action which strikes a balance between allowing new technologies to innovate and disrupt traditional markets and regulating proactively to protect public assets and prevent externalities. This could be achieved by:

- Setting public policy goals and design street space to maximize flows of people, rather than vehicles.
  - High-occupancy vehicle (HOV) lanes
  - Compact walkable development pattern
- Setting user fees to price externalities, rather than consumption, getting the prices right for desired levels of demand.
  - Pricing by occupancy
  - Pricing by time of day (congestion charging)
- Regulate to ensure that on-demand SAV services serve a markets equitably rather than "cream skimming" the most profitable areas and ignoring the rest.
  - Performance contracting to meet service targets
  - Subsidize travel cards for vulnerable populations
- Aim to develop a mature SAV market before AVs are in widespread private use
  - Integrate SAVs with existing transit system

Note

1. The Lisbon study was for the whole city and included rail transit, shared taxis and shuttles, and private cars. The Boston study was for the central business district only and included rail and bus transit, shared taxis and shuttles, and single-occupancy autonomous taxis.

References

Banister, D. 2011. The trilogy of distance, speed and time. *Journal of Transport Geography,* 19(4), 950–959. https://doi.org/10.1016/j.jtrangeo.2010.12.004.

BCG. 2016. *Self-Driving Vehicles, Robo-Taxis, and the Urban Mobility Revolution.* Boston, MA: Boston Consulting Group. Retrieved from http://image-src.bcg.com/Images/BCG-Self-Driving-Vehicles-Robo-Taxis-and-the-Urban-Mobility-Revolution_tcm30-59714.pdf.

BCG. 2017. *Making Autonomous Vehicles a Reality: Lessons from Boston and Beyond.* Boston, MA: Boston Consulting Group. Retrieved from http://image-src.bcg.com/Images/BCG-Making-Autonomous-Vehicles-a-Reality-Oct-2017_tcm9-173687.pdf.

BLS. 2016. *American Time Use Survey.* Washington, D.C.: Bureau of Labor Statistics. Retrieved from https://www.bls.gov/tus/.

Brown, J. 2006. From Traffic Regulation to Limited Ways: The Effort to Build a Science of Transportation Planning. *Journal of Planning History,* 5(1), 3–34. https://doi.org/10.1177/1538513205284628.

Brown, J. R., E. A. Morris, and B. D. Taylor, 2009. Planning for Cars in Cities: Planners, Engineers, and Freeways in the 20th Century. *Journal of the American Planning Association*, 75(2), 161–177. https://doi.org/10.1080/01944360802640016.

Cosgrove, D. 2011. Long-term patterns of Australian public transport use. In *Proceedings*. Adelaide, Australia: ATRF. Retrieved from http://atrf.info/papers/2011/2011_Cosgrove.pdf.

FHWA. 1996. *Highway Statistics, Summary to 1995*. Washington, D.C.: Federal Highway Administration. Retrieved from https://www.fhwa.dot.gov/ohim/summary95/.

ITF. 2015. *Urban Mobility System Upgrade: How shared self-driving cars could change city traffic* (International Transport Forum Policy Paper No. 6). Paris: OECD Publishing. Retrieved from https://www.itf-oecd.org/sites/default/files/docs/15cpb_self-drivingcars.pdf.

Marchetti, C. 1994. "Anthropological invariants in travel behavior." *Technological Forecasting and Social Change*, 47(1), 75–88. https://doi.org/10.1016/0040-1625(94)90041-8.

McShane, C. 1994. The uses and abuses of streets. In *Down the Asphalt Path*. New York: University of Columbia Press. Retrieved from https://cup.columbia.edu/book/down-the-asphalt-path/9780231083911.

McShane, C. 1999. The Origins and Globalization of Traffic Control Signals. *Journal of Urban History*, 25(3), 379–404. https://doi.org/10.1177/009614429902500304.

Miles Brothers. 1906. *A Trip Down Market Street Before the Fire*. Library of Congress. Retrieved from https://www.loc.gov/item/00694408/.

Mokhtarian, P. L. and C. Chen 2004. TTB or not TTB, that is the question: a review and analysis of the empirical literature on travel time (and money) budgets. *Transportation Research Part A: Policy and Practice*, 38(9), 643–675. https://doi.org/10.1016/j.tra.2003.12.004.

Nir, S. M. 2018. "City Never Sleeps, Yet Number of Trains at Off-Peak Hours Decline." *The New York Times*. Retrieved from https://www.nytimes.com/2018/03/23/nyregion/city-never-sleeps-yet-number-of-trains-at-off-peak-hours-decline.html.

Norton, Peter D. 2008. "Blood, Grief, and Anger." In *Fighting Traffic: The Dawn of the Motor Age in the American City*, 21–46. Cambridge, MA: MIT Press.

OECD. 2018. *OECD Family Database*. Paris, France: Organization for Economic Co-operation and Development. Retrieved from http://www.oecd.org/els/family/database.htm.

Rogers, E. 2003. *The Diffusion of Innovations*. Fifth. New York: Free Press.

Schäfer, A. W. 2017. Long-term trends in domestic US passenger travel: the past 110 years and the next 90. *Transportation*, 44(2), 293–310. https://doi.org/10.1007/s11116-015-9638-6.

Schrag, Z. 2002. "Urban Mass Transit In The United States." *EH.Net Encyclopedia*. Economic History Association. http://eh.net/encyclopedia/urban-mass-transit-in-the-united-states/.

Schrag, Z. M. 2000. "'The Bus Is Young and Honest': Transportation Politics, Technical Choice, and the Motorization of Manhattan Surface Transit, 1919-1936." *Technology and Culture* 41 (1): 51–79.

Sovacool, B. K. 2009. Early modes of transport in the United States: Lessons for modern energy policymakers. *Policy and Society*, 27(4), 411–427. https://doi.org/10.1016/j.polsoc.2009.01.006.

Sperling, D., S. Pike, and R. Chase. 2018. Will the transportation revolutions improve our lives–or make them worse? In *Three Revolutions: Steering Automated, Shared, and Electric Vehicles to a Better Future*, 1–20. Washington, D.C.: Island Press.

Truong, L. T., C. D. Gruyter, G. Currie, and A. Delbosc, 2017. Estimating the trip generation impacts of autonomous vehicles on car travel in Victoria, Australia. *Transportation*,
44(6), 1279–1292. https://doi.org/10.1007/s11116-017-9802-2.

WEF. 2018. *Reshaping Urban Mobility with Autonomous Vehicles: Lessons from the City of Boston*
(System Initiative on Shaping the Future of Mobility). Geneva, Switzerland: World
Economic Forum. Retrieved from http://www3.weforum.org/docs/WEF_Reshaping_
Urban_Mobility_with_Autonomous_Vehicles_2018.pdf.

Young, J. 2015. "Infrastructure: Mass Transit in 19th- and 20th-Century Urban America."
Oxford Research Encyclopedia of American History. Oxford Research Encyclopedias.
http://americanhistory.oxfordre.com/view/10.1093/acrefore/9780199329175.001.0001/
acrefore-9780199329175-e-28.

Zahavi, Y. 1979. *The Unified Mechanisms of Travel (UMOT) Project* (Research and Special
Programs Administration No. DOT-RSPA-DPB-20-79-3). Washington, D.C.: US
Department of Transportation. Retrieved from http://www.surveyarchive.org/zahavi.
html.

Zmud, J., L. Ecola, P. Phleps, and I. Feige. (2013). *The Future of Mobility: Scenarios for the
United States in 2030*. Santa Monica, CA: RAND Corporation. Retrieved from https://
www.rand.org/pubs/research_reports/RR246.html.

16 Conclusions

Time for action in the era of disruptive transport

William Riggs

Introduction

As you have likely seen throughout this book, this is an exciting time in the world of mobility—where transportation can be like turning on the lights or pouring a glass of water. This will lead to new levels of access to space and place, but as you have seen in this book it also has the potential to generate many secondary impacts on cities. These impacts include things like whether new mobility will encourage people to live further away from their place or work, and whether they will travel more in cars. This will lead to new development in suburban areas and related environment impacts. New and disruptive transport will impact parking and economic development, and jobs. Disruptive transport may negatively impact health and wellness—particularly if people end up walking, biking, or taking transit less.

Yet much of this disruption is facilitated by data—something that has brought promise and prosperity to our society. Data drives some the most innovative transportation technology in development—including mobility on demand, geo-spatially enable bikes and scooters, and emerging autonomous vehicles. Autonomous vehicles particularly offer some of the most groundbreaking and revolutionary changes in the way to rethink the way cities are built and function.

As we have discussed in this book, AVs present new opportunities to connect individuals to jobs and change the way cities organize space and optimize trips (Fagnant & Kockelman 2014; Guerra 2015). While much of this is predicated on how much car manufactures are able to transition, or perhaps wean, customers from the idea of owning a car (a shared/subscription-based assumption that embedded throughout this text), many car companies are working on this and to challenge the centrality of the automobile in our public realm. They are welcoming the need for appropriate street design (i.e., pedestrians and active transportation will have at least equality, if not priority) in denser urban street systems. I particularly am exciting about the possibilities that this presents. What an exciting time to be in the field of transportation!

But despite these opportunities to improve the public realm, and improvements to our lives by doing things like providing better access to jobs and healthcare, there are undeniable risks. In this book you have heard a lot about the potential risks to design and land use and the policies need to mitigate them. We have also talk about some financial and economic risks, and some of the environmental limitations of disruptive travel. At the same time, most of us in this book are talking about things we hardly understand—things that are not yet developed. I sometimes joked with my wife in editing and writing this book, I should include a warning. The warning would read something like, "Warning. This book will be out-of-date by the time of publication."

But the funny part, is that the warning would not be accurate. This book will not be irrelevant. Shaping the built environment is an ongoing action that evolves with time. And while there are challenges and things change, these developments are never as unique as we make them out to be. Many of the questions put forth in this book are the same questions that civilization has faced for hundreds, if not thousands, of years. These include things like: How can we lead more peaceful, happy and harmonious lives? Can our cities be beautiful livable and equitable? Can we enrich our bodies and spirits in a place close to where we live?

My colleague Mike Boswell and I have said that active planning, and collaborative discussion is needed to deal with these issues in an uncertain environment (Riggs & Boswell 2016). Yet, I believe it also takes a degree of anticipation— where we "lean in" to the future, understand what changes are taking place, and respond by building the kind of places we want see and being the kind of cities we want to be. In light of this, let me offer three parting considerations that are important for all of us (citizens, students, parents, professionals, entrepreneurs, policymakers, etc.) to consider.

Consideration 1: The mobility of tomorrow may not be not the mobility of tomorrow

I used to read a lot of sci-fi as a child. It was stuff like Tom Swift from the 1950s, where the kids were living on a satellite and engaging in space travel. Likewise, you may remember the space-like towns (and driverless cars) of Disney's Tomorrowland, and think, "what happened?" This is exactly my point when I say, the future and disruptive mobility of tomorrow may not be the mobility of tomorrow. Our vision will change, and consistent with Moore's Law,[1] the current disruption will be disrupted even faster than we anticipate.

Take for example the Segway of the 1990s. With innovative gyroscope technology, it was hailed as an innovation that would change the face of urban travel. Some police departments and mall security guards were early adopters (remember Paul Blart in the movie *Mall Cop*), yet the technology fell flat and there was only limited adoption.

Fast forward to 2018, and we have seen a new revolution. The integration of e-bikes and e-scooters into cities has seemed almost instantaneous. Using some of the same technology as the Segway, companies such as Bird, Lime, and Spin are offer first- and last-mile solutions on e-bikes and have millions of dollars in funding to expand. According to *Wired* magazine the company "gave more than 95,000 rides to 32,000 different people in just its first 30 days of service in the city" (Aarian 2018). According to Bird their scooters provide an "unprecedented opportunity to reduce car trips… roughly 40 percent of trips under two miles—thereby reducing traffic, congestion, and greenhouse gas emissions" (Bird 2018). In my opinion, they are also quite fun, convenient, and have the potential to provide cheap and equitable mobility like no other disruptive transport that has emerged.

Yet where these new innovations have deployed, they have not been welcome. Recently these scooter companies have been going head to head with city officials in places like San Francisco, Austin, and Santa Monica. Concerns lie in things like rules around scootering on the sidewalk and helmets along with the notion of how they may create on the streets for pedestrians and cyclist. While some companies are requiring users to photograph where and how they left their scooter to mitigate these concerns, cities have now become the obstacle. Not until they begin to innovate and embrace disruption at the speed of these companies, will the benefits be realized to their full potential.

The same can be said for autonomous vehicles. Cities, states, and national governments are trying to regulate the vehicle based on their current idea of what a vehicle is. What happens when that is disrupted? While I could try to speculate and say that cars will look more like personal self-driving transportation pods that people dial up and do not own, the principle here is more important. Put simply, there is a high likelihood that the car of today is not the car of tomorrow, just likely the Segway of yesterday is not the e-scooter of today or the Hyperloop of today will be the train of tomorrow.

Consideration 2: Data are the new oil

My students will know that in my classes I talk a lot about how data are like the Force from the *Star Wars* movies. It's all around us, permeates us, etc., but it is really true. Data drive most of the things we do in the twenty-first century. In my opinion, it's like oil was one hundred years ago when they called it "black gold." And when you think about data-enable travel that brings up some an important thought—particularly that it is no longer the trip that you take that matters but everything else about it, including you.

Just envision the future of ad-based, on-demand travel. All you need to do is to call up an autonomous vehicle and look at some ads, and you get free mobility. Along your route your ads may change because your data have been sold instantaneously to local vendors who want to service you along your ride or want you to stop in. When you get to your destination all the details about your trip, including your mobile phone activities are then resold to marketers so that on your return trip it is even more difficult not to get out of the car to purchase that big juicy hamburger—or perhaps get it delivered to your vehicle.

Clearly this is just the tip of the iceberg because the really valuable data are the aggregate data about all of your habits. This information about where you are going and what you are doing can be sold to numerous companies looking to do targeted marketing and sales. And while that sounds like much like the vision depicted in movies like *Blade Runner*, it really is a reality. Data are an important part of how these companies do business.

But what happens when transit and shared rides become owned by a private company. Should that company have the right to deny you access to their platform? Should they have a right to deny cities data about the vehicles they are running on city roads? Should they have a right to leave a city, or a portion of a city without notice? This could yield a trouble reality of data-driven transportation, meaning that certain parts of the city, perhaps those that are less dense, less safe or less profitable, become less served by future mobility. Lyft CEO John Zimmer recently pledged transportation equity and to provide service to low-income communities as they roll out scooters (Zimmer 2018). Yet, absent policy, what is the long-term certainty of such a commitment. There may always the temptation to capitalize-on or profit-from (as opposed to serve) populations that are under-represented and have limited transportation access.

Consideration 3: What will the social costs really be?

This leads to a final consideration, what is and will be the social costs of What are the social and environmental issues and opportunities of autonomy? Who will reap the benefits of disruptive transport? Many experts recognize that the benefits new transportation technology will not be readily accessible to the general public and there may be dramatic social costs—and this becomes particularly acute with jobs and access in an AV future.

First with regard to jobs, the introduction of AVs poses a threat to thousands of individuals who currently rely on human drivers. With replacement of professional human drivers there is a need to address how these jobs will be replaced in a fair and equitable manner. Job loss and replacement will not be limited to ridesharing jobs but result in far reaching impacts that affect everyone from traditional taxi drivers, mail carriers, and freight and cargo drivers, to name a few.

The timeframe for this might be gradual and involve incremental changes. In some instances, the traditional jobs might be replaced with alternative jobs, but there will still be impacts. For example, ridesharing companies may need to retain workers to supervise vehicles while they are in use so while there may no longer be a need for a human driver, there is likely a need for individuals to troubleshoot vehicles and supervise cars while in use or helping those with a disability enter and exit the vehicle.

More acute may be access issues and impacts on low-income individuals and neighborhoods. With the ability to commute and live farther distances from urban cores and downtown districts, AVs may incentivize the wealthy to move farther away and commute into the inner city for work. With the movement of the wealthy to the suburbs, tax dollars and revenues may also move to the suburbs further decaying the inner cities. The loss of tax revenue in these neighborhoods could lead to decreased revenues for services such as social services and schools that the lower income individuals depend more heavily on than the wealthy—some of which you have heard about in this book.

These social costs underscore the importance of vehicle sharing in the future, since it mitigates many of the social and environmental costs. Ridesharing may provide the gateway to getting people comfortable with this—reducing skepticism through experiential marketing. While people may be hesitant to share at first, eventually, perhaps through word of mouth, they will become more and more comfortable with them. They to this may be to make shared vehicles as commonplace as a utility—to get users to view the trip as *unremarkable*. What we have referred to in this trip as transportation like indoor plumbing or running water.

A time for action

These thoughts bring us to a point of action. According to the U.S. CDC, each year there are more than 1.25 million vehicular deaths globally (U.S. CDC 2015). In the United States, more than 32,000 people are killed and 2 million are injured each year in motor vehicle collisions. How many are preventable? Some statistics from a report I did with colleagues from Florida State University, show that 94 percent are attributed to human error; 28 percent are traffic fatalities from alcohol impairment; and 9.2 percent of fatalities are caused by distracted drivers.

At the same time the new mobility market is increasing with some estimates that it will reach into the hundreds of billions. Yet too few cities are planning directly for a future of disruptive and new transport. For example a 2016 Bloomberg report lists approximately 30 cities with plans for autonomous vehicles (Bloomberg 2016, 2017). 17 of these are in the United States; less than 1 percent of major cities. This is clearly a technology that many cities might perceive as being too distance, too futuristic. Yet, if the time horizon is even 10 to 15 years away the time to plan and prepare is now.

It is clear that technology is swiftly evolving and our vision for our cities must also evolve. When I give talks, I like to say that city policies move "at the speed of decomposition." While this is clearly a joke, urban policy moves so much slower than innovation and disruption, that it is becoming a liability. What happens when we lose control of the things that bring us happiness in our cities? If corporations control transit and access, do we lose the experiences and encounters that cause us to consider opinions other than our own—to have compassion for the people around us.

While again, clearly it sounds like I'm painting a picture of *Brave New World* or *Blade Runner*, these are issues that we should be thinking about, and we should be looking for efficiency and agility in our city leaders and decision-makers, so we can keep up with the pace of change. At the same time, we can take action. As people like Jeff Speck have argued—we can make our streets safer now.

In 2015, Mike Boswell and I talked about a dialogue that was happening in Florida about road diets and argued that road-widening should stop. I repeat, projects auto mobility and increase the size of our roads and related policies should cease to exist. We felt that in the absence of many unknowns, and in an environment of uncertainly the best action to take was one of inaction—no new roads.

Why do I say this? Because it is counter to current federal funding practice, but also because there are some transportation officials at the state and local level that have started moving in this direction. Mike and I quoted Richard Biter, the assistant secretary of the Florida Department of Transportation, in the *The Washington Post* where he said that he could do lane narrowing without increasing the size of the roads. He suggested the state could, "get by with 9½- or 10-foot lanes… (and that) We can turn that four-lane express highway into a six-lane express highway with literally the same right-of-way footprint."

Stopping expansion and doing road diets are simple actions that cities, states and federal governments can take to facilitate the type of spaces and places they want to see, but they can also be open to experimentation. They can do things like adopting vision zero policies to reduce roadway deaths to zero and working to work with technology companies to iron out issues and pilot new technologies. They can develop clear policy, standards and funding strategies for maintaining up-to-date digital and physical street markings—things every transportation company needs—rather than focusing on smart roads and sensors that may be obsolete in years or even months.

Cities can stop building parking. They can consider a car-free downtown. Cities can implement local plans and regulations that support and prioritizes bicycles, pedestrians and transit without limiting the potential for the transportation marketplace to continue to innovate. They can consider appropriate locations for drop offs, to ensure lively downtown environments—locations that not only support convenience but interaction and vitality through exchange with between people and the environment. They can set up land use and growth controls that protect open spaces, habitat, or places each community values. They can build housing and provide opportunities for people to live local and experience the benefits.

Our cities are ecosystems that can evolve, and disruptive transportation is accelerating the need for that evolution. Yet calling it an evolution may be deceptive. We may need to undo much of what has been done for the past fifty to one hundred years. Many of the strategies to make our cities better are not new. Whether they are putting in a bench or planting a tree or striping the road for bike lanes, they are the strategies we have had for ages that make many of our cities and neighborhoods special. We should not wait to see for what kind type of technology that will be here in five years or fifteen years out. We will never know that. We should nudge our cities and our streets toward sustainability and equity now. It is time to act.

So onward. Let's embrace disruption and build the city of the future, today.

Note

1. Moore's Law is a principle popularized by George Moore one of the original founders of Intel. It hypothesized that chip speed would continue to double with every generation of technological advancement. This leads to exponential growth in speed and computing power. The same principle has been applied to most technological and computational devices that have emerged over the last thirty years, and the trend has generally held.

References

Aarian, M. 2018. "The Love of the People Isn't Enough to Keep Shared Electric Scooters Rolling." *Wired Magazine*. Retrieved from http://www.wired.com/story/shared-electric-scooters-rolling/.

Bird. 2018. Bird. Retrieved from http://www.bird.co/.

Bloomberg. 2016. Bloomberg Aspen Initiative on Cities and Autonomous Vehicles. Retrieved March 20, 2018, from https://avsincities.bloomberg.org/.

Bloomberg, M. 2017. *Taming the Autonomous Vehicle: A Primer for Cities*. New York: Bloomberg Philanthopies. Retrieved from https://www.bbhub.io/dotorg/sites/2/2017/05/TamingtheAutonomousVehicleSpreadsPDF.pdf.

Fagnant, D. J. and K. M. Kockelman. 2014. "The Travel and Environmental Implications Of Shared Autonomous Vehicles, Using Agent-Based Model Scenarios." *Transportation Research Part C: Emerging Technologies*, 40, 1–13.

Guerra, E. 2015. "When Autonomous Cars Take to the Road." *Planning*, 81(5). Retrieved from https://trid.trb.org/view.aspx?id=1358466.

Riggs, W. and M. R. Boswell. 2016. Thinking Beyond the (Autonomous) Vehicle: The Promise of Saved Lives. Retrieved from https://works.bepress.com/williamriggs/71/.

U.S. CDC. 2015. Motor Vehicle Safety. Retrieved July 18, 2018, from https://www.cdc.gov/vitalsigns/motor-vehicle-safety/.

Zimmer, J. 2018, July 16. "Lyft's Approach To Bikes & Scooters": Retrieved July 30, 2018, from https://medium.com/@johnzimmer/lyfts-approach-to-bikes-scooters-90ce505ff496.

Index